S0-DUV-163

Roger Laporte
The Orphic Text

THE EUROPEAN HUMANITIES
RESEARCH CENTRE

UNIVERSITY OF OXFORD

The European Humanities Research Centre of the University of Oxford organizes a range of academic activities, including conferences and workshops, and publishes scholarly works under its own imprint, LEGENDA. Within Oxford, the EHRC bridges, at the research level, the main humanities faculties: Modern Languages, English, Modern History, Literae Humaniores, Music and Theology. The Centre stimulates interdisciplinary research collaboration throughout these subject areas and provides an Oxford base for advanced researchers in the humanities.

The Centre's publications programme focuses on making available the results of advanced research in medieval and modern languages and related interdisciplinary areas. An Editorial Board, whose members are drawn from across the British university system, covers the principal European languages. Titles include works on French, German, Italian, Portuguese, Russian and Spanish literature. In addition, the EHRC co-publishes with the Society for French Studies, the British Comparative Literature Association and the Modern Humanities Research Association. The Centre also publishes *Oxford German Studies* and *Film Studies*, and has launched a Special Lecture Series under the LEGENDA imprint.

Enquiries about the Centre's publishing activities should be addressed to:
Professor Malcolm Bowie, Director

Further information:
Kareni Bannister, Senior Publications Officer
European Humanities Research Centre
University of Oxford
47 Wellington Square, Oxford OX1 2JF
enquiries@ehrc.ox.ac.uk
www.ehrc.ox.ac.uk

LEGENDA EDITORIAL BOARD

Chairman
Professor Malcolm Bowie, All Souls College

Editorial Coordinator for French
Dr Nicola Luckhurst, Somerville College

Professor Ian Maclean, All Souls College (French)
Professor Marian Hobson Jeanneret, Queen Mary,
University of London (French)
Professor Ritchie Robertson, St John's College (German)
Professor Lesley Sharpe, University of Bristol (German)
Dr Diego Zancani, Balliol College (Italian)
Professor David Robey, University of Reading (Italian)
Dr Stephen Parkinson, Linacre College (Portuguese)
Professor Helder Macedo, King's College London (Portuguese)
Professor Gerald Smith, New College (Russian)
Professor David Shepherd, University of Sheffield (Russian)
Dr David Pattison, Magdalen College (Spanish)
Professor Alison Sinclair, Clare College, Cambridge (Spanish)
Dr Elinor Shaffer, School of Advanced Study, London
(Comparative Literature)

Senior Publications Officer
Kareni Bannister

Publications Officer
Dr Graham Nelson

LEGENDA

European Humanities Research Centre

University of Oxford

Roger Laporte
The Orphic Text

IAN MACLACHLAN

European Humanities Research Centre
University of Oxford
2000

Published by the
European Humanities Research Centre
of the University of Oxford
47 Wellington Square
Oxford OX1 2JF

LEGENDA is the publications imprint of the
European Humanities Research Centre

ISBN 1 900755 38 6

First published 2000

All rights reserved. No part of this publication may be reproduced or disseminated or
transmitted in any form or by any means, electronic, mechanical, photocopying,
recording or otherwise, or stored in any retrieval system, or otherwise used in any
manner whatsoever without the express permission of the copyright owner

British Library Cataloguing in Publication Data
A CIP catalogue record for this book is available from the British Library

© *European Humanities Research Centre of the University of Oxford 2000*

LEGENDA series designed by Cox Design Partnership, Witney, Oxon
Printed in Great Britain by
Information Press
Eynsham
Oxford OX8 1JJ

Chief Copy-Editor: Genevieve Hawkins

CONTENTS

NOTE

Roger Laporte was born in Lyon in 1925 and for many years taught philosophy in Montpellier. Following three short *récits* published in the 1950s, *La Veille* (1963) initiated a series of works exploring the experience of writing. It was followed by *Une Voix de fin silence* (1966), *Une Voix de fin silence II: Pourquoi?* (1967), *Fugue* (1970), *Fugue: Supplément* (1973), *Fugue 3* (1976), *Suite* (1979), and *Moriendo* (1983). This series was collected as *Une Vie* in 1986. Selections from Laporte's extensive critical writings have been published as *Quinze variations sur un thème biographique* (1975) and *Etudes* (1990). Commentators on his work include Michel Foucault, Emmanuel Levinas, Jacques Derrida, Philippe Lacoue-Labarthe and Jean-Luc Nancy. Laporte was awarded the Prix France-Culture in 1978.

ACKNOWLEDGEMENTS

I am grateful to Adrianne Tooke, who supervised the Oxford D.Phil. dissertation from which this study emerged, for her patience and wise counsel. Michael Holland and Leslie Hill, who examined the dissertation, were most supportive on that occasion and have continued to be so. The publication of this volume would not have been possible without the generous financial support of the Carnegie Trust for the Universities of Scotland and the Arts Faculty Research Committee of the University of Aberdeen. I have always enjoyed a congenial working environment thanks to friends and colleagues at the Universities of Aberdeen, Leicester and Oxford. I should also like to express my gratitude to Roger Laporte for his kind support of my work. Finally, there is no doubt that I would not have found myself in the enviable position of being able to undertake work of this sort without the constant support and encouragement of my parents; this book is dedicated to my mother and to the memory of my father.

ABBREVIATIONS

The following abbreviations are used for the works by Roger Laporte referred to most frequently.

i. Une Vie (Paris: P.O.L, 1986)

The works collected in this volume are referred to according to the pagination of *Une Vie*, but preceded by the following abbreviations to indicate the individual works collected therein:

V	*La Veille*
VFS	*Une Voix de fin silence*
P	*Une Voix de fin silence II: Pourquoi?*
F	*Fugue*
FS	*Fugue: Supplément*
F3	*Fugue 3*
S	*Suite*
M	*Moriendo*

ii. Other abbreviations

B	'Bief' in *L'Arc* 54 (1973), 'Jacques Derrida', 65–70.
C	*Carnets (extraits)* (Paris: Hachette, 1979).
DLMB	Laporte and Noël, *Deux Lectures de Maurice Blanchot* (Montpellier: Fata Morgana, 1973).
E	*Etudes* (Paris: P.O.L, 1990).
EDM	*Entre deux mondes* (Montpellier: Gris Banal, 1988).
LP	*Lettre à personne* (Paris: Plon, 1989).
QV	*Quinze variations sur un thème biographique* (Paris: Flammarion, 1975).
SR	'*Souvenir de Reims*' et autres récits (Paris: Hachette, 1979).

CHAPTER 1

Orphic Writing

On 24 February 1982, Roger Laporte ceased to be a writer.[1] Since that time, to be sure, he has written and published a number of critical and occasional texts, but on completing the final 'Post-scriptum' of *Moriendo*, he ceased to write in his sense of the word, bringing to an end one of the most remarkable and distinctive undertakings in post-war French literature.

The aim of this study is to survey the entirety of Roger Laporte's literary enterprise, from the three short *récits* of the 1950s to *Moriendo*, which marked the end of a series of works subtitled *biographie* initiated by *Fugue* in 1970. The publication in 1986 of a collected volume entitled *Une Vie* effectively extended the designation of *biographie* to the three volumes of the 1960s included therein. The term *biographie* is better seen as a marker of genre than as a subtitle, in fact, for Laporte's ambition is to institute a new type of writing; what exactly is at stake in this ambition will be fully explored later,[2] but to situate these texts in terms of existing categories, one might say that they are essays which explore the experience of writing. But one would have to add immediately that, in an important sense, this is not writing *on* writing, but rather, in the words of Philippe Lacoue-Labarthe, it is a question of '*écrire l'écriture*, ce qui n'est pas le réfléchir déjà existante, mais l'inventer encore inconnue, en faire l'expérience nue et primitive'.[3] My exploration of Laporte's invention of writing[4] will draw on all of his published work, but my overriding concern will be with the paradoxically concluded but interminable project of *biographie*.

Laporte's work has attracted a number of commentaries, but predominantly in the form of review-articles on the occasion of a new publication. Only a few of these endeavour to consider the broad itinerary of Laporte's writing, and even then they do so at a length which precludes consideration of that itinerary in any detail. My objective in writing the first full-length study of Laporte's work is therefore to analyse individual works in detail, but at the same time to attend to the progression in Laporte's work, focusing particularly on the transitions between stages of Laporte's writing, which we shall come to regard as ambivalent *brisures*, at once connective and disjunctive.

These commentators have included, from quite an early stage, Michel Foucault, Emmanuel Levinas and Maurice Blanchot and, more recently, Jacques Derrida, Roland Barthes, Philippe Lacoue-Labarthe and Jean-Luc Nancy. But the celebrity of such commentators has not been enough to ensure a large readership for Laporte's work; in his 'Avant-Propos' to *Lettre à personne*, Lacoue-Labarthe describes him as 'un écrivain pratiquement sans lecteurs (ils sont tout au plus un petit millier)' (*LP* 14). This is the case, despite the fact that the publication of *Une Vie* had stimulated a small upsurge in interest, leading even to the first British appreciation of Laporte's work to appear in print, in the form of John Sturrock's full-page review of *Une Vie* in the *Times Literary Supplement*.[5]

The objective of the present study will largely have been fulfilled if, in some form, it is able to play a part in fostering a wider readership for Laporte's work, the importance of which is an implicit, and at times explicit, claim of the pages which follow. This claim is not simply predicated on the eminence of some of Laporte's commentators, although the names associated with Laporte are indicative of a limited—one might say, documentary—interest of Laporte's work. In surveying the itinerary of Laporte's writing, it is possible to trace certain key developments in post-war French thought and writing, beginning with the early *récits* of the 1950s, which reveal the influence of Blanchot and, partly through the mediation of the latter, of German philosophy, particularly that of Heidegger; there follows the transitional phase of the texts of the 1960s, in which these influences are still discernible, along with that of Levinas, for example, but which at the same time mark the development of a more distinctive idiom; the *Fugue* series is most obviously distinguished from its predecessors through a focus on writing which owes much to the work of Derrida; finally, *Suite* and *Moriendo* mark something of a return to the idiom of earlier texts, particularly *La Veille*, but in a manner still informed by a Derridean conception of writing, as well as by a psychoanalytic perspective which had begun to manifest itself in the *Fugue* series. In fact, the stages which I have briefly sketched out here largely account for the structure of my argument.

But if Laporte's writing were simply reducible to a set of influences, its interest would indeed be merely that of a marginal document in French intellectual and literary history. In any case, the question of influence is not quite so simple as my brief outline suggests; it will be my contention in the early part of Chapter 3, for example, that Laporte's texts of the 1960s may be said already to anticipate the influence of Derrida. More importantly, I will also contend that Laporte's enterprise of *biographie*, his attempt to 'écrire l'écriture', gives rise to a writing which promises to outstrip the limits of philosophical or theoretical thought, an impossible transgression which is the only possibility of a certain conception of literature; in making this case, which is particularly to the fore in the latter part of Chapter 3 and in my Conclusion, I am myself, of course, indebted in particular to the work of Blanchot and of Derrida.

I am also indebted to Blanchot for the title of this study, which alludes to Blanchot's use of the myth of Orpheus and Eurydice in *L'Espace littéraire*,[6] which I discuss in the course of Chapter 2, and to which I return intermittently thereafter. I use the term 'Orphic text' to distinguish the reflexivity of works like Laporte's from a more conventional conception of literary reflexivity, applied to works which are seen, in some way, as successfully mirroring themselves or containing their own image, a conception whose mythological counterpart is generally given as Narcissus; it is one of the effects of the Orphic text to reveal such successful self-reflection to be illusory. The Orphic text turns towards its own origin to discover that origin to be ever-receding and yet still to be accomplished, and returns on itself to find itself already other; the reflexivity of the Orphic text turns out to be the impossibility of perfect reflexivity. In this failure of self-coincidence, the reflexive moment of the Orphic text no longer consolidates its integrity as a work, but becomes instead a movement towards the other, sealing its own ruin or *désœuvrement* as a work, but at the same time founding an ethical communication, in the sense of ethics elaborated by Levinas.[7]

For reasons such as these, Laporte's work seems to me to have an importance not presently reflected by the extent of his readership. In particular, it is a body of work which would repay greater attention at a time when discussion in literary theory and contemporary philosophy has increasingly focused on the question of ethics.[8] This tendency, which was already in evidence and received an unexpected impetus from the Paul de Man affair, has cast a welcome light on the ethics of deconstruction and on the ethical dimension of literature in general, and has brought nearer to the foreground figures such as Levinas and Blanchot. Laporte's work has a great deal to offer in such a climate.

To write of Laporte's work under the rubric of the Orphic text is implicitly to place that work in a particular tradition, a tradition which Laporte has clearly indicated in his published *Carnets* and in a number of critical studies; in the case of a number of figures in this tradition, Laporte has also signalled the extent to which these were mediated for him by Blanchot's critical writings. In the 'Post-face, ou un chemin de halage' written for his first collection of critical essays, *Quinze variations sur un thème biographique* (QV 229–46), Laporte offers a simple justification for his critical writing: 'il est juste de payer ses dettes' (QV 235), a sentiment echoed in Laporte's cover-note to his second such collection, *Etudes*, which ends with the last line from René Char's poem 'Qu'il vive!': 'Dans mon pays, on remercie'.

Char himself is of course one of the later figures in this tradition, and was also instrumental in encouraging Laporte's earliest literary efforts, ensuring the first publication of *Souvenir de Reims* in the journal *Botteghe Oscure* in 1954.[9] Laporte's essay, 'Clarté de René Char' (QV 7–15), focuses on two complementary movements in Char's poetry, which find an echo in Laporte's work: towards an originary moment, a movement indicated by the title of Char's collection *Retour amont*, and towards the unknown *as* unknown, which is the very domain of poetry, as Char's famous aphorism, 'Le poème est l'amour réalisé du désir demeuré désir'[10] reminds us, a movement whose counterpart in Laporte's work will be explored, in a Blanchotian context, in Chapter 2. That the two movements are one, the movement towards an unattainable origin at the same time an opening to a perpetual future, as in Laporte's own work, is suggested by the opening lines of the section 'Odin le Roc' of Char's 'Les Transparents', with which Laporte concludes his study: 'Ce qui vous fascine par endroit dans mon vers, c'est l'avenir, glissante obscurité d'avant l'aurore, tandis que la nuit est au passé déjà.'[11]

To restrict oneself to the domain of French literature, the obvious place to which one would look for the beginnings of this tradition is the work of Mallarmé. Laporte has not, in fact, devoted a study to Mallarmé, an omission which he notes in the 'Post-face' of *Quinze variations* (QV 235), but the importance of Mallarmé for him is clear enough from his *Carnets*, and indeed from his study of Blanchot, 'Une

Passion',[12] some of which concerns his reading of Blanchot's essays on Mallarmé. In fact, he ascribes the foundation of his work to a misreading of Blanchot's 'Le silence de Mallarmé',[13] his ambition being, he says, to write 'le Livre' which Mallarmé never achieved, taking Blanchot's article to be 'un appel en ce sens' (*DLMB* 55). However, despite this *contresens* in his reading of Blanchot's article, he adds: '*En fait*, ma position et celle de Blanchot ne sont pas très éloignées puisque Blanchot a dû écrire toute sa vie afin tout au plus d'indiquer l'absence de livre, alors que je passe ma vie à écrire un Livre qui sans cesse se dérobe; il n'empêche qu'*en droit* nos positions sont radicalement différentes' (*DLMB* 56). The position of Mallarmé at the origin of a particular tradition of reflexivity, and the importance of his writing for a view of poetic language, impersonality, and the necessary failure of the work which is central to much contemporary writing and theory, and to Blanchot's work in particular, has already been too well-documented to require further comment here.[14]

Laporte's *Carnets* and critical writings readily suggest other figures in this tradition: Valéry, in particular, for Laporte, *Monsieur Teste* and the *Cahiers* (cf. *E* 305–17), the latter presenting clear parallels with aspects of Laporte's work in terms, for example, of its evocation of the work as mental discipline, such that the construction of the work is inseparable from a reconstruction of the self,[15] and the law of 'self-variance' which describes the mobility essential to the exercise of thought in the work,[16] and which, as we shall see, has its counterparts in the *contre-écriture* and the *écart* of Laporte's later works; Ponge, of whom Laporte notes in his *Carnets* as early as 1954 that what he admires in his works is: '1) (malgré lui) leur aspect *genèse* d'un poème; 2) son amour de la clarté; 3) son refus de la fiction, je veux dire sa mise à nu de l'imagination comme telle' (*C* 35), and to whose work we shall briefly refer in Chapter 3; Artaud, in his exploration of failure, loss and dislocation of the self, which leads Laporte, in his 'Antonin Artaud ou la pensée au supplice' (*QV* 101–12), to ask how one could not dream of a work which would be a transcription of the impersonal drama of the soul, 'qui dénuderait radicalement l'esprit et ainsi le mettrait en jeu, aventure cruelle qui formerait le "thème" unique de la littérature se trouvant enfin avant peut-être de se perdre! Avec Antonin Artaud ce rêve s'est accompli' (*QV* 103). The texts to which Laporte seems to have been particularly drawn are the correspondence with Jacques Rivière, *L'Ombilic des Limbes*, *Le Pèse-*

nerfs and *L'Art et la Mort*; one may readily observe, for example, the affinity with Laporte's literary enterprise of the programme announced at the beginning of *L'Ombilic des Limbes*: 'Là où d'autres proposent des œuvres je ne prétends pas autre chose que de montrer mon esprit. [...] Je ne conçois pas d'œuvre comme détachée de la vie',[17] sentiments which, as we shall see, are closely echoed in the *Fugue* series.

When one adds to these names those of Joubert, Proust, Bataille, and, outside France, Hölderlin and Kafka, for example, one sees to what extent Laporte's pantheon coincides with the recurring figures of Blanchot's critical writing, in which, as Leslie Hill observes, one encounters 'not so much a repertoire of critical concepts as a configuration of proper names'.[18] In the next chapter I shall therefore consider Laporte's earliest works[19] in the light of Blanchot's fictional and critical writings, and in the light of the inheritance shared by Laporte and Blanchot, focusing, for example, on aspects of the work of Heidegger and on other key intertexts, notably in the works of Heraclitus and Hölderlin, to which Laporte's *Carnets* and features of his early work, such as epigraphs, direct us.

Notes to Chapter 1

1. See e.g. *LP* 21, and Philippe Lacoue-Labarthe's 'Avant-Propos' to those notebooks, *LP* 11–18.
2. See Ch. 3, below, in particular.
3. Cover-note to Roger Laporte, *Suite (biographie)* (Paris: Hachette, 1979).
4. I return specifically to the notion of invention in the third part of Ch. 3.
5. John Sturrock, 'The writer as Writer', *Times Literary Supplement* 4357 (1986), 1111. The only substantial studies to have appeared in English are the section '*Fugue*: The Adventures of Metaphors' in Dina Sherzer, *Representation in Contemporary French Fiction* (Lincoln, Nebraska and London: University of Nebraska Press, 1986), 104–17, Andrew Benjamin's much more sophisticated 'The Redemption of Value: Laporte, Writing as *Abkürzung*', in *Art, Mimesis and the Avant-Garde* (London and New York: Routledge, 1991), 197–211, and my own '*Musique-rythme*: Derrida and Roger Laporte', in *The French Connections of Jacques Derrida*, ed. Julian Wolfreys, John Brannigan and Ruth Robbins (Albany: State University of New York Press, 1999), 71–84.
6. Cf. 'Le regard d'Orphée' in Maurice Blanchot, *L'Espace littéraire* (Paris: Gallimard, 1955), 227–34.
7. I explore aspects of Levinas's thought in Ch. 2, and return to this notion of communication in Ch. 5. Clearly, it follows from these remarks that I deplore Fredric Jameson's recent dismissal of Laporte as 'of all contemporary writers the most intransigently formalist in the bad sense of writing about nothing but your own process of writing' ('Marx's Purloined Letter', in *Ghostly Demarcations: a*

symposium on Jacques Derrida's 'Specters of Marx', ed. Michael Sprinker (London and New York: Verso, 1999), 33).

8. Studies such as Timothy Clark's *Derrida, Heidegger, Blanchot: sources of Derrida's notion and practice of literature* (Cambridge: Cambridge University Press, 1992) and Simon Critchley's *The Ethics of Deconstruction: Derrida and Levinas* (Oxford: Blackwell, 1992) are notable examples of this tendency. A stimulating account of the conception of ethics at stake here, which repudiates certain attacks on the supposed ethical and political indifference of deconstruction, is Seán Hand's article 'Reading, "Post-modern", Ethics', *Paragraph* 13:3 (1990), 267–84. More recently, amongst some of Derrida's admirers, there has emerged a converse and equally hasty assumption about the essentially ethical nature of deconstruction, irrespective of the specific sites of deconstructive engagement; for an indication of Derrida's unease about any such assumption, see *Passions* (Paris: Galilée, 1993), 40–1.

9. Laporte indicates Char's role in his 'Correspondance avec Sylviane Agacinski', *Digraphe* 57 (1991), 77–94 (87).

10. René Char, 'Partage formel' XXX, in *Seuls demeurent*, in *Œuvres complètes* (Paris: Gallimard, 'Pléiade', 1983), 162. Laporte slightly misquotes this in his study (*QV* 13).

11. Char, *Œuvres complètes*, 298.

12. In his later study of Blanchot, 'L'ancien, l'effroyablement ancien' (Montpellier: Fata Morgana, 1987; *E* 9–50), Laporte disavowed this earlier study, having indeed withdrawn it from publication, so that a subsequent new edition comprised only Bernard Noël's 'D'une main obscure'. A new version of 'Une Passion', preceded by a note explaining his extreme disquiet about the earlier version, was published by Laporte in *A l'extrême pointe: Bataille et Blanchot* (Montpellier: Fata Morgana, 1994), 33–53. However, the later version omits the very references to Laporte's own work which are of particular interest to us here.

13. In Maurice Blanchot, *Faux pas* (Paris: Gallimard, 1943), 117–25 in the 1987 printing; these page numbers do not correspond to the ones given by Laporte (*DLMB* 55), as the pagination of *Faux pas* has changed since the early printings.

14. On Blanchot's reading of Mallarmé in particular, see Leslie Hill, 'Blanchot and Mallarmé', *MLN* 105 (1990), 889–913. For an account of Mallarmé's relevance to contemporary thinking on literature, which aims to show that Mallarmé's work is not in the end reducible to the categories of such thinking, see Peter Dayan, *Mallarmé's 'divine transposition': real and apparent sources of literary value* (Oxford: Clarendon Press, 1986), particularly 'Part 2: The Vanishing Trick', 109–219.

15. Cf. Paul Valéry, *Cahiers I*, ed. Judith Robinson (Paris: Gallimard, 'Pléiade', 1973), 368: 'Le but ne soit pas de faire telle œuvre, mais de faire en soi-même celui qui fasse, puisse faire—cette œuvre.
Il faut donc construire de soi en soi, ce soi qui sera l'instrument à faire telle œuvre.'

16. Cf. Valéry, *Cahiers I*, 960: 'Mon premier point est toujours la self-variance. Tout ce qui semble stable dans la conscience ou capable de retours aussi fréquents et aussi aisés que l'on voudra, est pourtant soumis à une instabilité essentielle. L'esprit est ce qui change et qui ne réside que dans le changement.'

17. Antonin Artaud, 'L'Ombilic des Limbes', suivi de 'Le Pèse-nerfs' et autres textes (Paris: Gallimard, coll. 'Poésie', 1968), 51.

18. Hill, 'Blanchot and Mallarmé', 889.
19. In the first part of Ch. 2, I shall be concentrating on the three texts of the 1950s which were published at the time: *Souvenir de Reims*, first published in *Botteghe Oscure* 13 (1954), *Une Migration*, first published in *Botteghe Oscure* 23 (1959), and *Le Partenaire*, first published in *Lettres Nouvelles* 7 (1960), 'Jeunes écrivains français'.

CHAPTER 2

Writing the Unknown

i. The early *récits*

Souvenir de Reims relates a visit to Rheims undertaken by a narrator
unable to complete work on the final chapter of a novel. It describes
his initial disappointment on finally seeing the famous cathedral, and
then his discovery of its glory on returning there shortly afterwards.
The latter revelation poses further problems for the narrator, as he
seeks to account for the effect on him of the cathedral's rose window
and to describe the nature of the cathedral's beauty. These endeavours
are suddenly curtailed by the narrator's apparent renunciation of the
artificiality of his narrative, in favour of an admission of the 'real'
situation of writing (Algiers, not Rheims), and a discussion of the
possibility of a description of description and, ultimately, of a sort of
textual self-coincidence, this discussion returning the focus to the final
chapter of the incomplete novel. The narrator ponders the possibility
of an open-ended conclusion to the novel, and the significance such
a concluding silence would have for the reader. The remainder of this
short text pursues this discussion of the novel's ending in terms of the
'Devoir d'écrire' imposed by the inspiration of the cathedral, the
notion of a speaking silence and the impersonality of the writer whose
experience of writing is a failure of self-coincidence and a loss of
identity.

The hiatus between description and its object discovered by the
narrator of *Souvenir de Reims* may be ascribed to language's
generalizing properties which realize the world in abstract terms,
inasmuch as the linguistic sign renders its referential object in its
ideality rather than its materiality. The notion that the linguistic
presentation of an object also signals its 'real' absence can be traced
back to Hegel and beyond, and is most notably observed in French
literature in Mallarmé's famous 'Je dis: une fleur!'. It is also of central
importance to Blanchot's discussion of the language of literature in 'La

littérature et le droit à la mort': 'Le mot me donne l'être, mais il me le donne privé d'être. Il est l'absence de cet être, son néant, ce qui demeure de lui lorsqu'il a perdu l'être, c'est-à-dire le seul fait qu'il n'est pas.'[1] Having noted that language generalizes the specific by transforming the actual, physical existence of its referent into the ideal essence of the sign, Blanchot argues that the goal of literature is precisely this ideal, abstract realm, but that the negation of reality operated by language is vitiated by the material reality of the sign. In a further twist to his argument, Blanchot asserts literature's concern with a reality prior to the negation of language, and with language's inability to realize this elusive realm, which will by definition escape any effort to name it: 'La négation ne peut se réaliser qu'à partir de la réalité de ce qu'elle nie; le langage tire sa valeur et son orgueil d'être l'accomplissement de cette négation; mais, au départ, que s'est-il perdu? Le tourment du langage est ce qu'il manque par la nécessité où il est d'en être le manque. Il ne peut même pas le nommer' (316). In its endeavours to locate what precedes it, language is condemned to propel this element ever forwards beyond the reach of a naming which perforce denies the reality of such an element. But this impossible pursuit is, for Blanchot, precisely literature's quest—'Le langage de la littérature est la recherche de ce moment qui la précède' (316)—and its privileged resource in this quest is that very materiality of the linguistic sign which had previously appeared as an obstacle to the literary ideal, for in addition to being the negating abstraction of reality, language is also part of that which it negates: 'Où réside donc mon espoir d'atteindre ce que je repousse? Dans la matérialité du langage, dans ce fait que les mots aussi sont des choses, une nature, ce qui m'est donné et me donne plus que je n'en comprends. Tout à l'heure, la réalité des mots était un obstacle. Maintenant, elle est ma seule chance' (316). This leads Blanchot to suggest that literary language characteristically foregrounds the physical properties of language at the expense of the transparent signifying function that language appears to have in its everyday usage.

The attempt to discover a realm prior to manifestation is the source of the exigency to write experienced by the narrator of *Souvenir de Reims* as he seeks to convey the joy experienced when the light of the rose window reveals the true glory of Rheims cathedral: 'Joie digne par excellence d'être décrite [...], elle désespère le poète dès qu'il se change en philosophe et veut l'atteindre dans sa source de lumière comme en dehors et avant sa manifestation' (*SR* 31). The attempt to separate source from manifestation is frustrated, since the former is inaccessible in its purity; the ideal essence sought is inextricable from its concrete existence, and although it is in a sense the condition of the latter, it will always escape nomination, as Laporte suggests by the oxymoronic formulations which end the following passage: 'Mais le poète apprend au philosophe qu'il est vain de chercher la source de la lumière, car elle est à elle-même sa propre source, n'existe que par son illumination et qu'elle est le rouge même, mais sorti des limbes, érigé à la toute-puissance d'un vitrail, lumière noire comme l'éclatante musique sourde d'un pays muet' (SR 32). As description proves inadequate to its object, necessarily silencing that which subsists beneath the negation of language, the narrator of Souvenir de Reims endeavours to make language its own object, but in so doing discovers that language as object equally produces a remainder which escapes the negating distance of nomination, condemning the attempted reflexivity to the infinite regress mentioned earlier. He then envisages an impossible double writing, which would simultaneously ac-complish the negative interval of description and the presentation of description's negation: 'il serait impossible de décrire un motif et de décrire en même temps sa description. Pourtant, maintenant, je vais tenter de décrire sur le vif, au cœur d'un même travail, ce que j'ai ressenti le 6 juin à Reims, et la description de cette description, que je vais faire à Alger le 19 décembre' (SR 39). This initiative returns the narrative to the moment at which the narrator renounced the fictional situation of writing in Rheims, when the revelation of the cathedral imposed a 'Devoir d'écrire' on the writer, at which point the narrative broke with the words: 'Et c'est alors que ...' (SR 37). The narrator is now tempted to conclude his novel with the truncated phrase 'C'est alors que ...', ending in the silent interval of three points of suspension. Most of the rest of Souvenir de Reims is devoted to a discussion of the significance of such an ending, and to slightly varying versions of a description of this final silence. Two fundamental motifs may be extracted from the latter· first, a characterization of this silence in terms of a movement which turns back on itself before its culmination, like an ebb-tide before high tide, and secondly, the evocation of a speaking silence in a time irreducible to linear temporality. We may see the first motif as a figure of the movement of language turning back on itself in reflexivity, as the writer, faced with the impossibility of describing the object in its totality given the subsistence of a remainder beneath language's negation, tries instead to perfect this negation by turning language away from the world and onto itself: unable to say all, he will attempt to say nothing, as Blanchot remarks: 'Le langage aperçoit qu'il doit son sens, non à ce qui existe, mais à son recul devant l'existence, et il subit la tentation de s'en tenir à ce recul, de vouloir atteindre la négation en elle-même et de faire de rien tout. Si des choses on ne parle qu'en disant d'elles ce par quoi elles ne sont rien, eh bien, ne rien dire, voilà le seul espoir d'en tout dire' (314). But beneath the silence of negation imposed by language, there is still something which escapes negation, and this remains true when language takes itself as object, as we have already observed, for now the materiality of language assumes the status of object in the world, and likewise produces a remainder which escapes nomination. Instead of achieving a perfect self-coincidence, which would, so to speak, cancel language out, reflexivity produces the linguistic sign as 'la possibilité même de signifier':

Quand [la littérature] refuse de nommer, quand du nom elle fait une chose obscure, insignifiante, témoin de l'obscurité primordiale, ce qui, ici, a disparu—le sens du nom—est bel et bien détruit, mais à la place a surgi la signification en général, le sens de l'insignifiance incrustée dans le mot comme expression de l'obscurité de l'existence, de sorte que, si le sens précis des termes s'est éteint, maintenant s'affirme la possibilité même de signifier, le pouvoir vide de donner un sens, étrange lumière impersonnelle. (318)

The concluding silent interval imagined for the end of the novel in *Souvenir de Reims*, represented by the image of a tide turning on itself, proves to be an imperfect silence, beneath which there remains the impersonal murmur of signification itself which defeats the writer's attempt at a voluntaristic appropriation of the silence of self-coincidence ('C'est alors que ...'). This defeat, and the vanity of the writer's quest to master silence, is represented in *Souvenir de Reims* by the narrator's anxiety about the reader's response to this inconclusive ending: 'Si le roman se terminait par: "c'est alors que ..." le lecteur ne saurait pas si, seul, le hasard le prive de la suite' (*SR* 43). The writer's concern lest the reader attribute this silence to chance rather than design is itself indicative of the subordination of the writer's design to the impersonal chance of a generalized signification which resists appropriation.

However, in a turn itself reminiscent of Blanchot's text, the impersonal murmur beneath silence which had frustrated the narrator's attempt to achieve a self-coincidental writing which would, as it were, erase itself, provides the very resource the narrator had sought to translate his ineffable experience before Rheims cathedral. That experience itself is consistently described in terms of a communicative silence or absence, and a potentiality which always appears to approach realization without achieving it. Even before the narrator's arrival at Rheims, the quality of light in the Ile-de-France is one of inspirational purity which never fully manifests itself to the onlooker: 'Cependant, discrète et pleine d'humour, [la lumière] fait s'écrier: "Que l'air est pur!", bien que, tel le Dieu d'Israël, on ne la voie jamais face à face' (SR 26). The revelation of the cathedral's rose window is, as has already been noted, expressed in oxymoronic terms which combine illumination and darkness, music and silence: 'lumière noire comme l'éclatante musique sourde d'un pays muet' (SR 32). When the narrator returns his focus to the cathedral, now at nightfall, the fascination it exerts is described first of all in terms of potentiality: 'Seule la cathédrale est là. Hypnotique, dure et féline, mais comme la promesse d'un poing fermé juste avant de s'ouvrir ...' (SR 36). The Calvary on the gable above the cathedral's portal is partly ruined, but this absence seems to constitute the Calvary's perfection: 'Pourtant, par cette absence même, obsédante comme le silence blanc d'une page du *Coup de dés*, la vérité du calvaire seulement alors est accomplie' (SR 37). Following the renunciation of fictional artifice, and the abortive attempts to qualify the projected silent ending of his novel, the narrator returns to his vision of the cathedral, and in particular to its soaring towers first evoked just before the interruption of the narrative (SR 37). The apparent movement of the towers is now the focus of the ineffable experience with which the narrator is struggling: 'Je vois les tours s'élever dans leur essor. Comment faire voir ce que j'ai vu? Comment dire l'impossible?' (SR 46).

The attempt to describe this experience, which coincided with the imposition of a 'Devoir d'écrire', involves a series of paradoxical juxtapositions—of sound and silence, motion and fixity, mystery and revelation, past and future—in a Heraclitean 'harmony of opposites' which the narrator adduces at one point (SR 47). The temporal fusion at first appears to derive from the workings of memory on the original experience, bringing the past into the present, and the project of transcribing that remembered experience into the text, past through present into the future: 'Je ne pense plus à Reims, je suis à Reims. Je vois les tours s'élever dans leur essor. Ma dernière mésaventure m'a rendu prudent. Néanmoins, si je pouvais dire ce que signifie: "Je suis à Reims", on commencerait, peut-être, à comprendre l'essence de la mémoire' (*SR* 45). However, such a schematic and linear account is misleading since the experience to which the narrator is trying to bring expression is irreducible to a commonplace notion of linear temporality, belonging rather to a time in which past and future communicate in the Nietzschean moment of eternal recurrence—'la cathédrale même [...] m'accueillit au séjour de la vraie vie, dans la fulguration stable d'un éternel retour' (*SR* 31)—a moment which contains past and future in the retention and protention which are the very possibility of memory. Fundamentally, however, the experience involves an element which escapes memory despite intangibly haunting it, and which belongs at once to an immemorial past and an ever-impending future, leaving a trace in the evanescent present. The narrator tries to name this temporality, but not at first to his satisfaction: 'Comment exprimer une idée aussi "illogique": un avenir qui devient passé sans jamais être présent et qui pourtant est la Présence même. Temps qui passe et ne s'écoule pas. Je me refuse à tout ce langage philosophique' (*SR* 47). However, he retains the notion of a point in time containing past and future, origin and end, expressing it a few lines later in the image of a midnight sun which is reborn at the very instant of its death. The narrator envies Breton's invention of the term 'explosante-fixe', which appears at the end of his first chapter of *L'Amour fou* in a new definition of the 'beauté convulsive' invoked in the final line of *Nadja*.[2] Such a term combines the sense of an endless temporal diffusion coexisting with an intense compression to an infinitesimal point in time with the idea of motion within stasis, as suggested by the apparent movement of the cathedral's towers. The revelation of the cathedral is not the simple manifestation of an object to consciousness, for it involves an element which violates the negative interval of consciousness and object, whose modality is not that of manifestation but is rather an approach which has always already begun and is always still impending, and which is discernible in the impersonal murmur of signification of literary language, as described by Blanchot: '[La littérature] n'est pas au-delà du monde, mais elle n'est pas non plus le monde: elle est la présence des choses, avant que le *monde* ne soit, leur persévérance après que le monde a disparu, l'entêtement de ce qui subsiste quand tout s'efface et l'hébétude de ce qui apparaît quand il n'y a rien' (317).

In *Souvenir de Reims*, this impersonal, ineffable element is given the name of the 'sacré' which inspires the writer through 'une Parole, puissante mais au loin et captive et pourtant sur le point de se désentraver' (*SR* 49). Both terms of this 'sacred Word' are contained in the first epigraph of *Souvenir de Reims*, taken from Hölderlin's poem 'Wie wenn am Feiertage ...': 'Et ce que je vis: Le Sacré, soit ma parole'. In his essay on 'La Parole "sacrée" de Hölderlin', Blanchot notes that Heidegger, in his celebrated exegesis of this poem, reads the sacred as Being in its immediacy, an immediacy which represents the very possibility of communication, but is itself incommunicable, aligning it with the primordial chaos which is the source of the poet's inspiration, the 'sacred chaos' evoked a few lines later in Hölderlin's poem. However, just as Heideggerian Being is inaccessible except in the mediated form of existent beings, so this immediate, undifferentiated chaos is not experienced by the poet as such; in Hölderlin's poetry, Blanchot argues, the sacred is experienced rather as an illumination or opening to vision: 'Le Sacré, [...] [c]'est le jour, mais antérieur au jour, et toujours antérieur à soi, c'est un avant-jour, une clarté d'avant la clarté et de laquelle nous sommes le plus proches, quand nous saisissons l'éveil, le lointain infiniment éloigné du lever du jour, qui est aussi ce qui nous est le plus intime, plus intérieur que toute intériorité' (124).[3] The divine illumination thus described is clearly not the manifestation of an object to consciousness, although it is the very principle of the latter; in Heideggerian terms, it is the primordial Being which underlies the false dichotomy of consciousness and object. It is the 'présence des choses, avant que le *monde* ne soit', that unnameable remainder which subsists beneath the negative interval between language and world, the speaking silence which literature seeks to recover, and which pervades the language of literature as the mute, impersonal signification of words become things, described by Blanchot as 'parole vide de paroles, écho toujours parlant au milieu du silence' (320).

This speaking silence is evoked by the narrator of *Souvenir de Reims* in his final attempt to describe the inspirational epiphany of the cathedral, a passage which I quote in full:

ET C'EST ALORS QUE j'ai vu l'invisible. Immobiles les tours dérament, se reculent sur la nef, se replient sur elles-mêmes, se distendent, s'abîment en une agonie dense comme la mort et résurrection du soleil de minuit où l'ivresse lustrale d'une ténue et suffocante blancheur, la musique inouïe du point d'orgue du jour, le Chaos appert au tonnant recueil de la pierre, érige les tours à leur lieu stable, magnifie l'essor de la cathédrale, décèle, mais en une muette exultation, sa toute Présence: à perte de vue, poignant désir solaire d'une encore inhumaine Toison d'or. Devenu fou, on ne sait, éperdu de joie, ébloui, le poète crie: 'LE SILENCE PARLE. LE SILENCE PARLE. LE SILENCE PARLE'. (SR 49)

This 'invisible' revelation is described in terms which combine and develop the paradoxes of the narrator's experience which we have already discussed. The movement within fixity of the cathedral's towers is one which turns in on itself, a reflexive contraction towards the interior, as if in intensification of its inaccessible Being, which is at the same time an expansion outwards, initially suggested by 'se distendent' and underlined in the 'essor de la cathédrale' which is the climax of the revelation. This movement is situated in the impossible temporality we have earlier encountered, signalled here by the reappearance of the image of the simultaneous death and rebirth of a midnight sun, representing a moment of perpetual advent, the experience of which the narrator has already characterized as 'poignant', exploiting an ambiguity provided by the root of this epithet: 'le déjà là, le ne pas encore, mais sur le point de' (SR 49).

In this time of endless imminence, the revelation afforded by the cathedral's towers is of that ineffable element which escapes consciousness and language, although silently informing them: Heidegger's Being or, as it is named here, Hölderlin's 'Chaos'.[4] We should note that this 'sacred Chaos' is never fully manifest to the narrator, who has already observed that the cathedral was 'révélée dans toute sa plénitude et en même temps comme un mystère encore une fois à découvrir' (SR 49). The persistent obscurity of the inspirational 'Chaos' is marked grammatically here by its position as subject of the verb 'apparoir', normally used only in impersonal constructions. This latter feature contributes to a broader strategy of linguistic defamiliarization undertaken in this paragraph; the use of such words as the uncommon regionalism 'déramer', meaning to row by pushing the oars, the relatively rare 'lustral', which none the less has significant sacramental associations here, and 'recueil' to describe the stone of the towers, although again its literary connotations are important in this context, combines with the syntactical complexity of the sentence which occupies most of this paragraph to foreground language in its materiality, as if to reveal the quiddity of language—words as things—in order to reproduce within the text the obscure revelation of immediate Being which constituted the narrator's experience in Rheims: to show without naming.

But this showing also necessarily names, as is already apparent in my attempt to outline the meaning of this passage. The revelation of that which escapes language must take place in silence, the silence which for Heidegger characterizes the poet's vigilance before Nature.[5] However, the poet cannot communicate the incommunicable in silence; here again is the dilemma we have noted earlier: if the poet cannot say all (including that which language silences in order to name), neither can s/he say nothing. In the essay on Hölderlin, Blanchot remarks that

le silence est marqué de la même contradiction et du même déchirement que le langage: s'il est une voie pour s'approcher de l'inapprochable, pour appartenir à ce qui ne se dit pas, il n'est 'sacré' qu'autant qu'il rend possible la communication de l'incommunicable et aboutit au langage. Se taire n'est pas une supériorité. 'Que le Sacré soit ma parole', voilà l'appel du poète, et ce sont les mots qui sont des 'sanctuaires', les temples du Sacré, non pas le silence. Parler, il le faut, c'est cela, cela seul qui convient. Et pourtant parler est impossible. (129)

The narrator of *Souvenir de Reims* likewise encounters the dilemma posed by the impossible exigency which the revelation of the cathedral has exerted upon him, and, having rejected a recourse to silence in the form of concluding his novel with the aposiopetic 'C'est alors que ...', finds that language too is necessarily inadequate to his task. As he goes on to remark, this experience has brought him 'au seuil du sacré', still faced with the impossibility of expressing the ineffable, of fulfilling 'le seul DEVOIR: celui d'écrire, de nommer l'innommé, l'être, l'immobile fulguration éternelle du Temps' (*SR* 50).

At this point, it may be helpful to note the second epigraph to *Souvenir de Reims*, '... ne parle pas, ne cache pas, mais fait signe' (*SR* 25), being the conclusion of Heraclitus' fragment: 'The Lord whose oracle is in Delphi neither speaks out nor conceals, but gives a sign'.[6] On one reading of this fragment, the Apollonian oracle is neither a revelation nor an impenetrable enigma, but a veiled indication whose sense will become clear to those who know how to interpret it. As Clémence Ramnoux says of it, '*signifier*, c'est dire en cachant, cacher en disant. [...] Ce serait manière d'avertir: que l'on sache entendre en écoutant, que l'on sache lire en regardant, et viser un sens que les mots masquent autant qu'ils le donnent'.[7] The emphasis here on the interpreter's vigilant approach to the oracle recalls Heidegger's characterization of the poet as a silent and attentive listener to the voice of Being. Equally, the paradoxical nature of the oracular sign suggested here may be compared with Heidegger's description of language as that which both gives access to Being and conceals it: 'Language is the clearing-concealing advent of Being itself.'[8] This is to be understood in the sense that the nominating power of language, rather than merely reflecting what is, is that which originally brings what is to light.[9] Indeed, in the later Heidegger, Being and language become quite inseparable as *logos*, which brings to light what is as the *aletheia* of beings. Yet immediate Being is not known in its immediacy, but only through the mediate form of beings; equally, in language, Being as *logos* or aboriginal illuminating utterance retreats as it reveals in a movement which is the very scission of beings and Being, of the ontic and the ontological, designated by Heidegger as the ontological difference. The inseparability of Being and language as *logos* is also evoked in Heidegger's reading of Hölderlin's 'Wie wenn am Feiertage ...', wherein, as we have already noted, the 'Sacred' may be equated with Being: 'The Sacred bestows the word and comes itself in this word. The word is the event [*Ereignis*] of the Sacred.'[10] Even by the standards of the later Heidegger, the notion of *Ereignis* is peculiarly difficult of access; we will perhaps gain a clearer picture of what it involves when we come to consider Laporte's later work. For the moment, we can say that it appears to be the source of the ontological difference which constitutes the ambivalent articulating-disjunctive relation between beings and Being. It therefore represents a moment of aboriginal unity, which would contain even that negative Being which absconds in the revelation of beings, and which silently pervades language,[11] the *lethe* that persists in *aletheia*.

It is this 'event' of Being in its original plenitude that tantalizes the narrator of *Souvenir de Reims* as he seeks the source of the light which reveals the glory of the cathedral's rose window 'comme en dehors et avant sa manifestation', or as he searches for a language which would articulate its own speaking silence. But he discovers that every attempt to reveal Being necessarily conceals it, for what is brought to light is always being as manifestation, the ontic rather than the ontological. This remains true when he tries to turn language onto itself to disclose Being in language—word as thing—for what is shown in self-referential language is, by definition, never that Being which is the hidden ground of what is made manifest, never that which must remain in oblivion for *aletheia* to take place. As Blanchot says of

Hölderlin's poet: 'il parle mais ne parle pas, il laisse inexprimé ce qu'il a à dire, non manifesté ce qu'il montre' (130).

The ecstatic description of the cathedral as epiphany of a primordial 'Chaos' whose silence speaks is therefore condemned to miss the existential in favour of the existent and, at best, to record the wake of the 'event' as it recedes or to herald the approach of Being in its perpetual advent, and this in a language which can only echo the originary *logos* as founding unity. His description is, then, but a 'pre-text' and, recognizing his inability to respond to the exigency imposed on him by the revelation, the narrator goes on to enumerate some more mundane pretexts: 'Mais, volontairement imprévoyant, je n'ai pas sur moi le moindre carnet où écrire' (*SR*, 50)—by now it's too late to buy a *carnet* and, in any case, there will be no time to write before returning to Paris, where there is an oral examination to prepare, essays to mark.

But it is also in these final paragraphs of *Souvenir de Reims* that the narrator envisages what the approach of Being in language demands of the writer: to recall a term used just now to characterize the description of the cathedral, it would be a writing that is properly 'ec-static'. Just as language as *logos* is not the mere reflection of what is, but is that which brings beings to light, neither is it the simple means of expression of some pre-linguistic subject. If *Dasein* is privileged in Heidegger in so far as its linguistic faculty makes it the 'shepherd of Being', language and, therefore, Being retain ontological priority. *Dasein* only *is* in language, through which it is brought into being and apprehends its being. However, what is named in language is only revealed as being on the ground of Being as concealment. *Dasein*'s relation to Being in language is an ec-static one, for it is only there that it achieves identity, but that identity is also outside itself, in the withdrawing Being which is inseparable from its being. To approach Being in language, the writer must therefore abandon the stable notion of identity as it appears in everyday language in pursuit of the originary *logos* to which hidden Being silently calls him/her; to do this, the writer will relinquish the illusion of language as a secondary instrument of self-expression in recognition that 'language speaks'[12] and, by granting language its autonomy, let Being be.

An uncertainty about his identity has haunted the narrator intermittently in the course of *Souvenir de Reims*. Dissatisfied with the opening of this very narrative, he asks: 'N'est-ce pas un autre que moi qui l'a écrit?' (*SR* 44). Before embarking on another attempt to convey his vision of the cathedral, he announces a sense of impersonality redolent of Mallarmé: 'Maintenant, je renais à moi-même. Mais vague, gratuit, et à la fin nul comme un pur possible' (*SR* 46). Now, in these final pages, having accounted for his failure to respond to the exigency to write, he manages at least to reconceive the lines along which his novel should develop, since he has realized that 'ce roman est, sur un point, petitement traditionaliste: il est humaniste; bien loin de la peinture de Cézanne, mais comme celle que je n'aime pas, il grouille d'hommes. Quelle place faite au regard! La nature est presque absente. Il est temps, non pas de promouvoir un art anti-humaniste, mais de retrouver la Terre non-humaine' (*SR* 50).[13] The attempt to 'retrouver la Terre non-humaine', to approach in writing that inhuman Being or originary *logos*, which has necessarily been occluded in humanistic thought, will necessitate the disappearance of the writer as master of language, in favour of an impersonality which will let language speak itself. As Blanchot says of 'La Parole "sacrée" de Hölderlin': 'Impossible, la réconciliation du Sacré et de la parole a exigé de l'existence du poète qu'elle se rapprochât le plus de l'inexistence' (132).

It would seem that the quest for 'la Terre non-humaine' announced at the end of *Souvenir de Reims* is initiated in Laporte's next published work, *Une Migration*, which eschews the overt reflexivity of the former work in favour of an ostensibly symbolic narrative more akin to some of Kafka's short stories, and indeed to the early *récits* of Blanchot. With reference to Laporte's own work alone, the transition from *Souvenir de Reims* to *Une Migration* can be seen in terms of a rejection of the former's combination of narrative and metanarrative, in which the attempt to reproduce the ecstatic experience of Rheims cathedral was frustrated by the delay between fictional discourse and theoretical discourse on the one hand, and between language and event generally on the other, in favour of a symbolic exploration of the experience of the writing subject which would align *Une Migration* with the tendency Blanchot notes in Kafka's symbolic tales, in which literature constitutes 'une expérience qui, illusoire ou non, apparaît comme un moyen de découverte et un effort, non pour exprimer ce que l'on sait, mais pour éprouver ce que l'on ne sait pas'.[14]

Une Migration opens with the narrator's return from a journey and his postponement of a new journey, remaining instead in sickness in his shuttered room. The gathering winds outside constitute a first *invitation au voyage*, which he resists, although resolving immediately to respond to the next call. The latter takes the form of a passing comet, and as he is preparing to depart the narrator is asked his name by the voice of a young girl. He can only laugh in reply, and, as he turns the question instead to that of the name of the 'Pays' which will be his destination, he is almost instantly transported, seemingly by sea. Hurriedly leaving a mysterious port, he finds himself in a deserted wasteland, searching for a 'Pays' whose very name is unknown to him. He follows the bank of a small waterway which progressively widens, only to find he has come full circle around a lake. However, when he tries to set out on the same route again, he finds that the path he thought he had already followed is untrodden. He takes to the water on a raft of reeds, but the stream seems only to connect two lakes, and he has made no progress. He determines to walk unerringly in one direction, but encounters nothing except the unchanging landscape of this wasteland whose very neutrality seems to undermine his efforts to reach the 'Pays', a destination to which he still feels enjoined, despite feeling at the same time exiled. In the meantime, a host of small flowers has appeared; he resists gathering any, and the avoidance of an act he qualifies as violence seems to him to indicate he is pursuing the right path. He feels rejuvenated by the terrain and, stretching out in a bed of flowers, again feels transported, and arises to note the trail of the comet. As he proceeds, his evaluation of his predicament continues to swing between hope and despair and, following a particularly low ebb, he once again feels transported, now to a place characterized only by fading light, in which he feels estranged from himself and definitively expelled from his path, condemned to an ever greater exile for somehow having failed to respond appropriately to the initial injunction. In the process, destination and identity have become intertwined, as his 'Patrie' which constantly awaits in the future is also his origin, his 'Terre natale'. Another identity he imagines for himself is the 'Fiancé', whose 'Fiancée' will follow his phantom presence as he submits to an endlessly unfulfillable 'Loi d'exode'. Finally, he wonders whether his 'Fiancée', who is also the child who asked his name at the outset, might have preceded him, so that he would see her before reaching the 'Pays'. When the 'Loi d'exode' seems to have outlawed any direction or position for the narrator, his narrative breaks off, and there follows an italicized coda which notes the narrator's disappearance. A plural voice asks what has become of him, and wonders whether he has died, but also reached the 'Pays'. These and other questions cannot be answered, says the voice, which concludes enigmatically: 'Alors nous avons fait un vœu!' (*SR* 98).

Laporte's indebtedness to Blanchot is made explicit in the dedication to him of *Une Migration*, although once again we should note the background of Heidegger's work common to both. In a sense, *Une Migration* is concerned with the same pursuit of primordial Being which we discovered in *Souvenir de Reims*, although this is never as overt as it was in the earlier work. However, the peregrinations of the narrator in *Une Migration* may clearly be assimilated to the notion of 'errancy' (*die Irre*), which Heidegger introduces in his essay 'On the Essence of Truth'.[15] Errancy describes the condition of *Dasein*, being amongst beings but with some understanding of Being, structurally both ontic and ontological,[16] as it passes from one being to another in its quest for Being itself, compelled to 'wander in onticity' as Richardson puts it.[17] This sense of never being 'at home' and of ceaselessly wandering is present from the very beginning of *Une Migration*, which suggests the transience of any place of abode for the narrator: 'Dès que je fus rentré chez moi, je commençai aussitôt à préparer un nouveau voyage' (*SR* 67). Once his journey is underway, every strategy the narrator employs to orientate himself and to set out for the 'Pays' serves only to lead him further astray: 'M'étais-je même éloigné? Où étais-je donc? Loin? Près? A la circonférence? Au centre de cette contrée? Et où était le Pays? Comment le savoir! Moi, ce fameux voyageur, je m'étais complètement égaré' (*SR* 73). This errancy, every peripety of which is a further *dépaysement*, is a condition of perpetual exile: 'A peine étais-je ici, déjà j'étais ailleurs, puis ailleurs, puis encore ailleurs, et toujours ailleurs, mais quand donc arriverais-je au Pays? De ce lieu où je me trouvais j'avais été chassé pour un autre lieu dont je suis chassé et le lieu où je vais arriver lui aussi me chassera, mais pourquoi donc n'entrais-je pas au Pays?' (*SR* 93).

However, Heidegger's account of errancy suggests not only that it is intrinsic to *Dasein*, but also that, in tandem with the 'mystery' which is the concealment of Being, errancy constitutes a 'non-essence' of truth which is part of the essence of truth, that negativity of withdrawing Being which is the necessary ground for truth as *aletheia*. It is because of this negative rapport of errancy to Being that the experience of errancy affords *Dasein* the possibility of reflecting on the mystery of Being's concealment—which is habitually forgotten—

and, thereby, of beginning to think of Being.[18] This positive aspect of errancy is observed from time to time by the narrator of *Une Migration*. At first, this possibility is raised most tentatively in respect of the neutrality of the 'lande': 'Cette lande je ne pouvais même pas l'accuser! Elle n'avait jamais rien fait ni pour moi ni contre moi: elle était neutre. Etait-ce bien une chance?' (*SR* 76), a hope which is dispelled a few lines later. After resisting gathering the flowers which appear on the hitherto desolate 'lande', the narrator feels he has made definitive progress through a discovery which would not have been possible elsewhere: 'Je m'étais cru tout à fait perdu, égaré dans un voyage supplémentaire, mais j'en avais à présent la certitude: depuis le début, j'avais commencé mon vrai voyage et même j'avais avancé, car cette découverte: la violence sans pouvoir, jamais je n'aurais pu la faire en dehors de cette contrée. Sans chemin, elle était le Chemin. J'avais joué à qui perd gagne!' (*SR* 79). I shall explore the significance of this discovery later. For the moment, we should simply note the narrator's belief, albeit just at this juncture, that his very wandering constitutes the path, just as errancy may show the way to Being, so that, in a commonplace that will recur in Laporte's work, 'qui perd gagne'.

That the positive movement which the harnessing of errancy may allow will never give rise to a triumphant arrival, at Being itself or at the 'Pays' of *Une Migration*, is made clear by the systematic thwarting of the narrator's every optimistic impulse. The endlessness of the narrator's quest is again prefigured in Heidegger's thought, in a way which also illuminates the narrator's eventual identification of the 'Pays' with his 'Terre natale'. In his commentary on Hölderlin's late poem 'Andenken', Heidegger writes that 'the thinker thinks on the condition of ex-patriation which for him is not a state of passage but the condition in which he is "at home". The thoughtful interrogation of the poet on the other hand poetizes the condition of re-patriation.'[19] We might say that the thinker is 'at home' in the homelessness of expatriation, because it is the experience of errancy for what it is which inspires the interrogation of Being, the constant posing of the *Seinsfrage*. The true poet, on the other hand, as we saw in Heidegger's discussion of 'Wie wenn am Feiertage ...', is one who has received the 'Sacred word' and, with it, the duty of communicating this word through a poetic language which should approach that originary *logos* in which Being and language are united. The poet must therefore journey in onticity on the way to the ontological, in an attempt to return once more to Being, which, although unknown, was always his/her 'home' as *Dasein*. In discussing Hölderlin's 'Heimkunft', Heidegger describes this poetic movement as a return towards a source (*Ursprung*), noting, however, that '[Being-as-source] remains to that degree far-off as there belongs to itself an essential self-withdrawal'.[20] By dint of the withdrawal of Being in revelation, with which we are now familiar, the poet never appropriates this source, and never finally arrives home: 'Indeed, even homecoming is only the beginning of the return to what is the proper domain [of the poet] [...]. Therefore upon arrival he longs [...] to be able to abide [there].'[21] The repatriation described by the poet is not, then, a final accomplishment but is rather an endlessly renewed beginning which alone can maintain the poet in proximity to the source, to the 'Terre natale'.

It is the sense of expatriation which is most readily apparent in *Une Migration*. As soon as the narrator finds himself in the 'lande', he stresses its strangeness and inhospitability: 'Aucune ruine, aucune trace ne laissaient penser qu'un homme eût jamais vécu sur cette terre écartée' (*SR* 70). Indeed, such is his feeling of expatriation that his exile seems to him the only condition he has known: 'Jamais je n'avais vécu au Pays, je ne connaissais que l'exil et c'est pourquoi j'ai envié le sort du banni, car du moins il peut se souvenir de sa patrie' (*SR* 75). However, as we have already observed, the narrator at times sees his errancy as a positive resource in his quest, but only fleetingly; indeed, it is after such moments of optimism that his situation appears to him in its bleakest light, we might say because he forgets the poet's duty, as described by Heidegger, constantly to begin his journey again: 'Je m'étais laissé séduire par les fleurs trop belles de cette terre que j'avais crue mon amie, et tout à ma joie j'avais fini par croire que cette plaine des fleurs violettes était le Pays. Malheur à moi! Juste au moment où j'avais cru jouer à qui perd gagne, j'avais joué à qui gagne perd. Quelle cruauté!' (*SR* 82). Elsewhere he remarks precisely on this need endlessly to start out afresh, when for instance he imagines his journey as a passage from one 'ponton' to another of an interminable 'Ville-flottante': 'mais, si cette Ville-flottante avait envahi toute la mer et toute la terre par-delà tous les horizons même futurs, l'espace de ma fuite serait toujours moins grand que l'immensité de cette plaine rase et branlante, je répéterais indéfiniment le premier pas' (*SR* 95). Despite the narrator's frequent assertions that the 'Pays' he seeks is unknown to him, his errancy in expatriation is increasingly a quest for repatriation, albeit it to a 'Terre natale' which he has never inhabited. Indeed, from the outset the narrator's migration is bound up with questions of origin and identity. The young girl's question to the narrator, 'Quel est ton nom?', is immediately linked with the name of the 'Pays', an association which is underlined in the narrator's first frantic attempts to orientate himself: 'A la terre j'ai confié mon message; "Quel est mon nom?" Je n'ai même pas entendu l'écho de ma propre voix. Alors, debout, j'ai hurlé: "Quel est ton nom? Quel est ton nom?"' (SR 70). Later, when the narrator is transported to a sort of limbo which is neither the 'lande' nor the 'Pays', his uncertainty about his situation accentuates his lack of identity: 'Et dans quelle sorte de lieu est-ce que je me trouvais? Je ne pouvais l'identifier: je ne me voyais plus moi-même, je ne savais plus du tout qui j'étais' (SR 89). With this, the association of 'Pays' and identity is again recalled: 'Jamais je n'avais su où était le Pays, j'avais toujours ignoré mon nom' (SR 89). It is in the darkness of a forbidden zone, where the narrator is an 'exilé de l'exil', that the migration is most clearly linked with a return to a 'Terre natale', although this is a paradoxical return to a place never before visited, which will none the less be a source of identity: 'Je n'étais pas d'ici, je ne pouvais y habiter, et c'est pourquoi au Pays, où jamais je ne vécus, je migrais pour recevoir la pureté de mon nom: celui de la Terre natale. Alors je retrouverai l'enfant et cette fois je la verrai, car je pourrai lui donner mon nom' (SR 92).

In the Heideggerian terms already outlined, this migration is an errancy which produces a sense of exile or expatriation, but which also, when recognized for what it is, affords a path to repatriation for the poet, back to the source which is Being, the 'home' for *Dasein*, in so far as *Dasein* is inconceivable without it, but a 'home' or 'Terre natale' where it has never dwelt, given the withdrawal of Being in the very beings of which Being is itself the ground. The narrator's migration to the 'Terre natale' will therefore be endless, as he pursues a future home which will always elude him, whilst it belongs at the same time to an immemorial past. The narrator describes this plight as he imagines himself to be on an interminable 'Ville-flottante': 'je n'étais pas encore le ressortissant d'un Pays, ma patrie future me réclamait, et c'est pourquoi cette ville étrangère, mais alliée au Pays, ne pouvait abroger sa Loi d'expulsion, car je n'avais pas encore accompli la migration prénuptiale de ma propre naissance' (SR 94–5). The impossible pursuit of this futural source or origin implicates the narrator's identity for, as we saw in relation to *Souvenir de Reims*, it is also a pursuit of the coincidence of the ontic and the ontological in *Dasein*, which the withdrawal of Being precludes. This failure of self-coincidence will haunt Laporte's later work, expressed at times in an image which first appears early in *Une Migration*, as the narrator tries to retrace his steps: 'Par jeu, j'ai avancé en posant régulièrement mes pas dans mes anciens pas. Ce jeu est devenu impossible: pendant mon absence, l'écart entre mes pas s'était agrandi. J'étais déjà passé par là, mais je foulais une terre vierge' (*SR* 72).

However, the passage cited earlier which first describes the migration as a return to the 'Terre natale' indicates that it will also be a return to the child whose question had apparently sent the narrator on his way, and this at least adumbrates an identity for the narrator, who observes that 'sur ce fond de Pays je lisais le négatif de ma présence future: le Fiancé' (*SR* 92), and that the child will be his 'Fiancée'. She is to follow him in his errancy, or rather to follow his ghostly passage as he endures successive exiles: 'Elle était sur le point de me rejoindre, mais en ce nouveau lieu elle ne pourrait plus recueillir ma trace, mais seulement lire le vestige de mon passage: le coup de fouet qui m'avait chassé au dehors. J'ai brûlé l'étape suivante d'un pas si léger que ma promise y verrait seulement l'ombre creuse de ma ligne de fuite' (*SR* 92). The narrator's transitions reduce him to invisibility, threatening any chance of his rejoining his 'Fiancée', as she will lose his trace and he is forbidden to turn back to seek her—'Le Chemin ne me donnait pas le droit de revenir en arrière' (*SR* 93)—unless she should somehow have overtaken him, as he imagines in the final paragraph of his narration, so that he might transgress the relentless 'Loi de proscription' and 'dans ce monde où je n'en avais pas le droit, me présenter devant ma Fiancée, et, avant le Pays, la voir pour la première fois mais dans un rapport criminel' (*SR* 96).

This imagined transgression of a narrator wandering in what he had earlier qualified as a 'zone morte' recalls the transgressive act of another wanderer in the underworld, namely Orpheus, who was allowed to lead his wife Eurydice out of the abode of the dead provided that he did not turn back to look at her. But Orpheus was unable to resist glimpsing Eurydice in her nocturnal, otherworldly state, and, in looking back, lost her. This parallel, which is underscored in a number of ways which we shall explore shortly, throws further light on the symbolic dimension of *Une Migration*, for it is this part of the myth of Orpheus and Eurydice which Blanchot utilizes to describe the experience of the writer in 'Le Regard d'Orphée', the section which Blanchot himself identifies as central to *L'Espace littéraire*. The descent of Orpheus, by analogy with the literary work, is the quest for the obscure domain which precedes and secretly subsists in the language of literature, already outlined by Blanchot in 'La Littérature et le droit à la mort': the brute reality of things which escapes nomination, or the materiality of words which exceeds the interval of language and reality, in other words, that silent remainder in language which is neither the latter's affirmation of ideality nor its negation of materiality. In *L'Espace littéraire*, Blanchot suggests that the search for this inaccessible origin is characteristic of modern literature: 'L'œuvre n'est plus innocente, elle sait d'où elle vient. Ou, du moins, le rechercher, dans cette recherche se rapprocher toujours plus de l'origine, dans cette approche se tenir et se maintenir là où la possibilité se joue, où le risque est essentiel, où l'échec menace, c'est ce qu'elle semble demander, c'est là qu'elle pousse l'artiste, loin d'elle et loin de son accomplissement.'[22] In our discussion of *Souvenir de Reims*, we have already observed the impossibility of this 'recherche de l'origine' which is reiterated throughout *L'Espace littéraire*, although it is precisely to this quest that what Blanchot terms 'l'exigence de l'œuvre' constantly calls the writer: 'Le point central de l'œuvre est l'œuvre comme origine, celui que l'on ne peut atteindre, le seul pourtant qu'il vaille la peine d'atteindre' (56).

The impossibility of the 'recherche de l'origine' for the writer is linked, most notably in Blanchot's reading of the myth of Orpheus and Eurydice, with a more fundamental impossibility: that of dying. The connection between the literary work and death, perhaps the central theme of *L'Espace littéraire*, is already made in 'La Littérature et le droit à la mort', where the negation effected by language on the specific reality of that which it names is described as an 'assassinat différé', an index of our individual finitude which is the ground of our existence as separate beings, and at the same time, of the possibility of communication between beings:

Il est donc précisément exact de dire, quand je parle: la mort parle en moi. Ma parole est l'avertissement que la mort est, en ce moment même, lâchée dans le monde, qu'entre moi qui parle et l'être que j'interpelle elle a brusquement surgi: elle est entre nous comme la distance qui nous sépare, mais cette distance est aussi ce qui nous empêche d'être séparés, car en elle est la condition de toute entente. Seule, la mort me permet de saisir ce que je veux atteindre; elle est dans les mots la seule possibilité de leur sens. Sans la mort, tout s'effondrerait dans l'absurde et dans le néant. (313)[23]

However, in turning towards its origin, literature discovers that this death, the annihilation of reality, is never complete; the alternative ideals of saying all or saying nothing are equally unavailable, for in seeking absolute illumination of reality it encounters the residual specificity of things which evades language's generalization, and in seeking a pure oblivion of material reality it discovers its own materiality:

[La littérature] n'est pas la nuit; elle en est la hantise; non pas la nuit mais la conscience de la nuit qui sans relâche veille pour se surprendre et à cause de cela sans répit se dissipe. Elle n'est pas le jour, elle est le côté du jour que celui-ci a rejeté pour devenir lumière. Et elle n'est pas non plus la mort, car en elle se montre l'existence sans l'être, l'existence qui demeure sous l'existence, comme une affirmation inexorable, sans commencement et sans terme, la mort comme impossibilité de mourir. (317)

The interminable errancy of the narrator in *Une Migration*, echoing Blanchot's discussion of the literary work and death in this essay and in *L'Espace littéraire*, marks the divergence of a movement in French thought, evident also in the work of Bataille and Levinas, away from the Heidegger of *Being and Time*, for whom death is the 'ownmost possibility' of *Dasein*, which may achieve authenticity by resolutely embracing its own finitude, or 'Being-towards-death'.[24] Blanchot may share Heidegger's view of death as a limit which, marking the finitude of *Dasein*, thereby also permeates mortal existence, but where Heidegger observes that 'death is the possibility of the absolute impossibility of *Dasein*',[25] Blanchot is suspicious of that possibility and, in common with Levinas and Bataille,[26] conceives death as an impossibility which one cannot appropriate in Heidegger's sense, and whose only reality is its approach: 'Tant que je vis, je suis un homme mortel, mais, quand je meurs, cessant d'être un homme, je cesse aussi d'être mortel, je ne suis plus capable de mourir, et la mort qui s'annonce me fait horreur, parce que je la vois telle qu'elle est: non plus mort, mais impossibilité de mourir' (*La Part du feu*, 325). Death as the impossibility of dying is the abyssal ground of that failure of negation which literature discovers in its exploration of the imperfect interval between language and reality, in the quiddity of things which survives the annihilation of naming, and in the quiddity of language which prevents the perfection of a silent interval between words and things.

That the narrator's journey in *Une Migration* may also be read as an exploration of the endless space of death as impossibility is indicated by the epigraph from René Char: 'Mourir, c'est devenir, mais *nulle part*, vivant?' (*SR* 67).[27] The inaccessibility of the 'Pays' sought by the narrator, inaccessible both because its only reality is its approach, and because at the same time, as 'Terre natale', it belongs to an immemorial past, and the inefficacy of power and will in the neutral dimension in which the narrator undergoes successive exiles, these aspects of *Une Migration* recall very clearly the terms in which Blanchot describes the impossibility of death in 'La Littérature et le droit à la mort': 'la mort, c'est là-bas, le grand château que l'on ne peut atteindre, et la vie, c'était là-bas, le pays natal que l'on a quitté sur un faux appel; maintenant, il ne reste plus qu'à lutter, à travailler pour mourir complètement, mais lutter c'est vivre encore; et tout ce qui rapproche du but rend le but inaccessible' (325). The death which literature discovers in its quest to perfect the negation operated by language is not, then, that death which for Hegel sustained the life of the spirit, in so far as it founded the power of the negative,[28] but rather an affirmation of the absolutely other which subtends negation, and which forestalls our attempts to mobilize it in projects of power or will. The writer who seeks to transgress the limits of language, that is, to attain the death promised by the annihilation effected by naming, finds a limit that is not susceptible to transgression,[29] for s/he has taken one death for another, impossibility for the ultimate possibility, just as the suicide, who seeks to master death by resolutely embracing it, finds his/her project suspended inconclusively in a death which admits no mastery or appropriation: 'Même là où je décide d'aller à [la mort], par une résolution virile et idéale, n'est-ce pas elle encore qui vient à moi, et quand je crois la saisir, elle qui me saisit, qui me dessaisit, me livre à l'insaisissable?' (*L'Espace littéraire*, 118).

Wandering in the space of death as impossibility, the narrator of *Une Migration* likewise finds that every initiative he takes to free himself from exile and make his way to the 'Pays' apparently only serves to lead him away from his goal, not because he encounters insuperable obstacles, but, on the contrary, because this a-phenomenal space of exile offers no resistance, no limit that may be transgressed: '[ce no man's land] s'étendait indéfiniment devant ma marche, je serais toujours dehors et ainsi jamais je n'avais pu ni ne pourrais l'attaquer: il était impossible d'en sortir par effraction. Cette neutralité était ma perte, car, sans avoir à se battre, elle triomphait de moi' (*SR* 76). This, in turn, leads the narrator to imagine the construction of a vast fortification, extending beyond the horizon, in the impenetrable heart of which he would imprison himself, as a recourse against the limit-less neutrality which disempowers all action, in other words, to reconstruct death as a possibility, as the following passage makes explicit: 'Lorsque la cellule royale serait elle-même toute close, je serais si encastré dans cette demi-sphère d'une seule coulée que mes jambes seraient tout à fait immobiles, et lorsque ma poitrine nue rencontrerait le métal noir, alors, alors enfin je serai prisonnier, je pourrai me battre et d'un seul coup d'épaule, Lazare, j'aurai triomphé du tombeau!' (SR 77). But this is the illusory death of the suicide who imagines a self which would somehow survive to witness the completion of such an appropriative project, not death as impossi-bility, whose dispossession of the self renders initiative powerless.

Shortly after this passage, the narrator makes the discovery, to which we have already briefly alluded, of the inefficacy of violence in the quest for the 'Pays'; pondering his reluctance to pick any of the flowers which have suddenly appeared in this barren wasteland, he observes that, had he done so, 'j'aurais été coupable, car sur cette terre la violence était interdite. Jamais on ne pouvait l'exercer. Elle n'avait point cours pour aller au Pays. On ne pouvait s'en emparer d'assaut' (SR 79). This discovery, which he owes to the neutrality of the 'lande', leads him to suppose that this very neutrality may be his greatest ally, in so far as his failures to overcome it have kept him on the right path. However, his acquiescence in the wasteland's neutrality and the refusal of violence prove no more effective in his quest than resolve and resistance, and the game of 'qui perd gagne' becomes one of 'qui gagne perd' (SR 82).

Once again, there is a parallel between the 'Pays' of Une Migration and Blanchot's conception of death as impossibility, which approaches endlessly but cannot be approached, and which one experiences, though we cannot really conceive it as 'experience', as a pure 'passion' or 'souffrance',[30] as the narrator indicates in willing an end to his ordeal in these terms: 'Migrateur-en-souffrance, incapable d'obéir à l'amicale mais impérieuse nécessité, n'étais-je pas sur le point de mourir!' (SR 87). Acquiescence offers the narrator no greater purchase on his goal than resistance, because the 'Pays', like death as impossibility, permits no complicity in its approach; as Joseph Libertson writes of the dilemma of suicide in Blanchot: 'There is no alternative to the paradox of suicide, that is, to the mobilization of the unavailable, to the passivity of resolution. Passivity cannot be assumed.'[31] The death which approaches but does not arrive is an impossibility which none the less concerns the subject, not as the ultimate possibility which is the negation of life, but as an alterity whose approach, already begun in an immemorial past, constitutes life as an incompletion, the Bataillian *inachèvement*, which makes of subjectivity 'la sauvage *impossibilité* que je suis, qui ne peut éviter ses limites, et ne peut non plus s'y tenir'.[32] To this extent, the narrator of *Une Migration* is right to say of the limitless neutrality of the wasteland that 'sans chemin, elle était le Chemin' (*SR* 79), but not to imagine that this path will make possible any arrival.

At this point, we may return to Orpheus, forever turning towards Eurydice. Orpheus' descent into the night of the underworld takes him away from the world of action into the darkness which is the realm of literature, the darkness of the negative interval between language and reality. In this realm, Eurydice is the ultimate goal which Orpheus' own art has allowed him to approach, 'le point profondément obscur vers lequel l'art, le désir, la mort, la nuit semblent tendre. Elle est l'instant où l'essence de la nuit s'approche comme l'*autre* nuit' (227). She is the other night which the night, as negation of day, conceals, and Orpheus' *œuvre* is to bring her back to the light, to restore death to life as a possibility, respecting the interval between the silence of the underworld and the language of the world of action. This is the sense of his *œuvre* as accomplishment, which may only be achieved by turning away from the nocturnal Eurydice. But the world of possibility and achievement is haunted by an affirmation of impossibility and *inachèvement*, which subsists beneath the negations which make initiative, decision and action possible. The *œuvre* harbours another desire, for the accomplishment of the impossible, the knowledge of night as the other night, rather than the negation of day, of death as impossibility, and, for the writer, the mastery of that inaudible murmur which persists when language has annihilated reality, 'le sens, détaché de ses conditions, séparé de ses moments, errant comme un pouvoir vide, dont on ne peut rien faire, pouvoir sans pouvoir, simple impuissance à cesser d'être' (*La Part du feu*, 320). The suicide who mistakenly thinks death may be mastered by resolution is mirrored by the writer, who takes the completion of the *livre* to be the accomplishment of the *œuvre*, for the *œuvre* has another face, which demands the impossible, and which compels Orpheus to look back at Eurydice: 'Il perd Eurydice, parce qu'il la désire par-delà les limites mesurées du chant, et il se perd lui-même, mais ce désir et Eurydice perdue et Orphée dispersé sont nécessaires au chant, comme est nécessaire à l'œuvre l'épreuve du désœuvrement éternel' (230). For Blanchot, the impatience of Orpheus is not simply the opposite of patience, but is rather the renunciation of accomplishment in a pursuit, dictated by the *inspiration* which founds the *œuvre*, of death as impossibility and of the *œuvre* as *désœuvrement*; this impatience is also, then, an endless patience: 'L'impatience d'Orphée est donc aussi un mouvement juste: en elle commence ce qui va devenir sa propre passion, sa plus haute patience, son séjour infini dans la mort' (230).

The narrator of *Une Migration*, condemned to an interminable errancy in the space of death as impossibility, imagines he might finally encounter his Eurydice, if she had lost his trail and had somehow overtaken him to await him 'dans un lieu futur', where he might see her 'pour la première fois'. But the impossibility of such a future meeting is also the impossibility of a 'first time', for he already knows her from an immemorial past, they are already 'Fiancé' and 'Fiancée', just as Orpheus has already turned to Eurydice: 'S'il ne l'avait pas regardée, il ne l'eût pas attirée, et sans doute elle n'est pas là, mais lui-même, en ce regard, est absent, il n'est pas moins mort qu'elle, non pas mort de cette tranquille mort du monde qui est repos, silence et fin, mais de cette autre mort qui est mort sans fin, épreuve de l'absence de fin' (229). The impossibility of an ending for the 'souffrance' of the narrator of *Une Migration* is also the impossibility of a beginning, for his migration has always already begun: the endless quest for the 'Pays' is also the unaccomplished 'migration prénuptiale de ma propre naissance' (*SR* 95). The endless quest for death as impossibility is the pursuit of an alterity whose approach has always already constituted life as incompletion, and has therefore compelled that quest from its unattainable origin. In the final section of 'Le Regard d'Orphée', which I quote in full, Blanchot suggests that the interminability of writing is also commensurate with its absent origin:

Ecrire commence avec le regard d'Orphée, et ce regard est le mouvement du désir qui brise le destin et le souci du chant et, dans cette décision inspirée et insouciante, atteint l'origine, consacre le chant. Mais, pour descendre vers cet instant, il a fallu à Orphée déjà la puissance de l'art. Cela veut dire: l'on n'écrit que si l'on atteint cet instant vers lequel l'on ne peut toutefois se porter que dans l'espace ouvert par le mouvement d'écrire. Pour écrire, il faut déjà écrire. Dans cette contrariété se situent aussi l'essence de l'écriture, la difficulté de l'expérience et le saut de l'inspiration. (234)

Blanchot characterizes the 'inspiration' which compels the writer to renounce accomplishment in the pursuit of the impossible as the movement of a 'désir'. This desire does not, we should note, find its origin in the initiative of the subject; it is not Hegel's desire, which proceeds from an already constituted self-consciousness, but is rather a desire deriving from an alterity which always already conditions subjectivity: a desire without origin. It is the aboriginal silent murmur beneath language which the writer vainly seeks to master in accomplishing the *œuvre*, the impossible death which compels its own pursuit by its constitution of subjectivity as *inachèvement*. This desire, as an affirmation which always precedes our own decisions and initiatives, and makes them never quite 'our own', has decided the journey of the narrator of *Une Migration* before he takes a step, and is an affirmation which has already preceded his initiative: 'Déjà j'étais débusqué et c'est alors que ... / OUI. J'ai dit Oui' (*SR* 68). Thus, in his migration, the narrator's own initiatives are always too late, he is always 'en partance', and the impossibility of arrival is the impossibility of eradicating this originary delay. At the outset, his own desire is pre-empted—'J'avais vu passer une comète. / Las! Je n'avais pas eu le temps de faire un vœu' (*SR* 68)—and after his disappearance in the aposiopetic conclusion of his narrative, the coda, which leaves his fate as an open question, ends with an enigmatic wish that returns us to the intransitive desire which was the absent origin of the migration: 'Alors nous avons fait un vœu!' (*SR* 98).

If the narrator's quest in *Une Migration* reveals the impossibility of a final accomplishment in response to the injunction issuing from the affirmation of an alterity which always precedes and conditions the subject, constituting subjectivity from the outset as an incompletion, then Laporte's next published *récit*, *Le Partenaire*, reveals the impossibility of refusing such an injunction, or of taking a distance on this constitutive alterity.

The opening sentence, 'Quelqu'un est là, dehors' (*SR* 101), immediately sets the essential situation of this short narrative, and highlights the two key characteristics of the narrator's 'partenaire': *anonymity*, and an association with the *exterior*. We discover straightaway that, in an as yet undefined sense, the narrator already knows this visitor,[33] and has already refused him entry—has already pronounced a 'NON' which he will not and, it seems, cannot now reverse. The narrator is satisfied with his decision, and it is only some days later that he happens to notice that his door is still bolted. On unbolting it, he looks through the spy-hole and senses that he is being watched, and indeed that the visitor has been maintaining a constant watch over his house. As he considers how to safeguard his house from attack, it occurs to the narrator that he has not even drawn the bolt across again. The visitor has not taken advantage of this, and furthermore, the narrator remarks that he cannot enter without his consent. However, the narrator cannot leave either, as he presumes the visitor is now by the door; the narrator therefore resigns himself to a war of attrition, which he is confident he can win. Some time later, the narrator finds he has moved from his table, and is now near the door with his back to the wall. The visitor still seems powerless to enter, but none the less exerts such a fascination over the narrator that the latter finds himself with his back to the door, his finger on the latch. He even wonders whether he has not already opened the door and let the visitor in. But the door remains closed and, at the end of this episode, the narrator, trembling with fear, is once again at his table. Since the 'Non' with which the narrator refused the visitor has not rid him of the latter, nor broken the spell of his fascination, he now wonders whether the only way of keeping him at a distance is to say 'Oui'. The narrator continues to fluctuate between acceptance and refusal, 'Oui' and 'Non', even wondering whether winning the war of attrition might be a form of 'qui gagne perd', until the root of his dilemma strikes him: either alternative requires opening the door and confronting the visitor, who could even be dismissed once and for all with a simple 'Va-t-en' to his face, a solution which the narrator had never contemplated 'car il m'était impossible de le voir' (*SR* 108). In the final short section of the *récit*, the narrator imagines he may have killed the visitor, or almost done so, leaving him waiting to enter the house in order to die. The narrator both desires and fears this death, which he is unable to consummate. It occurs to him that his initial 'Non' had, in fact, established a bond with the visitor, but a bond which precluded direct contact. Finally, the narrator realizes he wanted to kill the visitor before ever seeing him.

The entries in Laporte's *Carnets* before and after the composition of this *récit* reveal the importance of his reading of Kafka at this time, particularly the tale *The Burrow* in which relations between interior and exterior closely parallel those which obtain in Laporte's text. However, I want to focus on the impact of Laporte's continuing reading of Blanchot by considering the epigraph of *Le Partenaire*, taken from a text which Laporte was reading at the time of this text's composition, *Celui qui ne m'accompagnait pas*: 'Celui qui ne répond pas, plus que tout autre, est enfermé dans sa réponse' (*SR* 101).[34] The sentence comes from a passage in which the narrator, as so often in this *récit*, is meditating the relations between himself, the other—the non-accompanying companion—and writing, and is in particular exploring the impossible demand which the other appears to make in respect of the narrator's writing. Indeed, this whole section of Blanchot's *récit* leaves an illuminating imprint on *Le Partenaire*, for it is shortly after the passage from which Laporte takes his epigraph that we find a description of the status of the other which could readily be applied to the ambivalent 'partenaire' of Laporte's text (or indeed to a number of non-oppositional figures of alterity throughout his work, from the *lande* of *Une Migration* to the *contre-écriture* of the *Fugue* series): 'Il ne me presse pas, ce n'est pas un adversaire, il ne s'oppose pas à moi, c'est pourquoi je ne puis me défendre en combattant, le combat n'est même pas ajourné, il est lui-même l'ajournement incessant du combat.'[35] In Laporte's text we find both this perpetual deferral of combat and the concomitant powerlessness of the 'partenaire', who may indeed provoke both fascination and dread in the narrator, but disposes of no force with which to enter or draw the narrator outside. This is indicated a number of times in the *récit*, most clearly when the narrator realizes he has been fortunate in having nothing with which to barricade the door, for 'à trop bien renforcer la porte, j'aurais risqué de la défoncer et de me retrouver dehors, car aucune force ne se serait opposée à la mienne, et du reste nulle machine de guerre ne venait ébranler les murs de la maison, je n'avais pas à repousser la moindre attaque' (*SR* 103). As the terms used here to describe the narrowly avoided accident suggest, the 'partenaire' exerts such fascination not despite his powerlessness, but rather *because* of it, as it were in the manner of a vacuum. To account for this, we shall have to consider the significance of the epigraph: that is, the response which is refused, and the silent demand of the other, to which, it will transpire, no response is adequate.

On the evidence of Laporte's *Carnets*, the refusal to answer the call of the other was central to the conception of *Le Partenaire*, which, in this respect, turns out to form a kind of diptych with *Une Migration*: 'J'ai écrit toute une œuvre sur un Oui initial et ses développements, il est possible d'écrire une œuvre sur le Non initial et ses non moins nombreux développements' (*C* 62). Whereas *Une Migration* traces the erring peregrinations of a narrator who has accepted the invitation

outside, *Le Partenaire*, as Laporte also remarks in the *Carnets*, constitutes a sort of continuation of the refusal which opened the earlier *récit*
(cf. *C* 63). It is also this aspect of *Le Partenaire* which, for Laporte, was
its claim to originality. In the course of a discussion of Kafka's
treatment of the 'outside' in various texts, Laporte observes that 'le
héros de Kafka ne dit jamais non. (Blanchot non plus; suis-je le seul à
avoir exploré cette voie dans *Le Partenaire*?)' (*C* 75–6). It will perhaps
become clearer why this should have been so important to Laporte if
we consider what exactly is being refused, by looking more closely at
the epigraph to *Le Partenaire*.

First of all, we should consider the context of the passage from
which Laporte takes his epigraph, a passage in which, in respect of
his own writing, the narrator of *Celui qui ne m'accompagnait pas*
experiences the impossible invitation of the other, the non-
accompanying companion, and thereby endures an 'épreuve' which,
in the paragraph which concludes with our epigraph, is described
thus: 'Elle n'a pas de limites, elle ne connaît pas de jour ni de nuit,
elle ne se soucie ni des événements ni des désirs; ce qui est possible,
elle l'écarte; ce qui ne se peut pas, de cela seulement elle se satisfait; à
qui n'a rien, elle demande; celui qui répond à sa demande ne le sait
pas et, à cause de cela, ne répond pas.'[36] We should note that the key
terms here, demand and response, are effectively cancelled out in this
same part of the *récit*, as the narrator has already indicated that what is
asked of him 'ne m'est pas demandé', and in the passage which follows
he describes the call as always taking place, but never taking place
'réellement'. The predicament of the narrator here is the one which
literature poses to the writer, as we saw in our discussion of *Une
Migration*, for it places on him/her the demand of inspiration as desire
of the other (a double genitive which will be further explored in the
context of Laporte's later works), that is to say, it exposes the writer
to the interminable murmur of language—to a call, therefore, which
does not 'really' take place (for it is concealed in the world of action,
decision and possibility), but violates the negations which ordinarily
make possible such a world and, most significantly here, assure the
self-identity or closure of the subject.

For the writer, then, inspiration thus conceived constitutes the lure
of 'l'*autre* nuit', of which, in his discussion of Kafka's *The Burrow* in
L'Espace littéraire, Blanchot remarks that 'celui qui l'entend devient
l'autre, celui qui s'en rapproche s'éloigne de soi, n'est plus celui qui
s'en rapproche, mais celui qui s'en détourne, qui va de-ci, de-là' (224).

The dislocation of self-identity announced by this call of the other is indeed experienced by the narrator of Laporte's *récit*, for he remarks of the 'partenaire' that 'il exerçait sur moi une passion dont je n'étais pas le maître' (*SR* 106). Moreover, the relation of the other to the subject is as an inaccessible outside which is already within; this, too, is suggested in *Le Partenaire*, when the narrator realizes that the other 'ne me demandait point de venir dehors, mais d'entrer chez moi, non pas un piège, mais *son lieu*' (*SR* 108; my emphasis). The refusal of the 'partenaire' in Laporte's *récit* may be seen as an attempt to ensure the closure of subjectivity, but it transpires that what was to be excluded was always within. The *other* night being inaccessible, one must work for the day but, says Blanchot, 'travailler pour le jour, c'est trouver, à la fin, la nuit, c'est alors faire de la nuit l'œuvre du jour, faire d'elle un travail, un séjour, c'est construire le terrier et construire le terrier, c'est ouvrir la nuit à l'*autre* nuit' (225).

To summarize the impossibility of a response to the other, then, we may say that the alterity which subsists beneath the world's negations has, as we saw in relation to *Une Migration*, constituted subjectivity as an incompletion from the outset, thereby compelling its impossible pursuit without regard to the will of the subject; it thus constitutes a demand to which the subject cannot respond, yet cannot *but* respond. As Laporte remarks, returning much later to the same sentence from *Celui qui ne m'accompagnait pas* in 'Une Passion': 'Répondre Oui à l'appel, devenir écrivain, ce serait donc entrer dans le "piège" tendu par l'*autre* nuit, mais on n'aurait même pas la liberté de répondre Non, car "celui qui ne répond pas, plus que tout autre, est enfermé dans sa réponse"' (*DLMB* 126). The call of the other is furthermore one which no response can ever answer, for it is a call which never takes place in the present. By the same token, in *Le Partenaire* no explicit demand is made of the narrator by his unseen visitor: 'Depuis qu'il était là, jamais ce quémandeur ne m'avait interpellé par mon nom, il n'avait lancé aucun appel, mon refus de lui ouvrir ne lui arrachait aucune supplication, pas même un gémissement: je l'avais réduit au silence' (*SR* 103). The call which silently haunts the present is one which either resounds from an immemorial past or is approaching in a future which will never arrive, like the inhuman song of the Sirens which always causes the sailors it enchants to drop anchor too soon or too late.[37]

The call of the other therefore takes place in what Blanchot calls, in *L'Espace littéraire*, the 'temps de l'absence de temps', the time to which the writer is drawn in his/her 'solitude essentielle', and in which the pre-originary inextrication of alterity with the subject is discovered in the form of an anonymous 'Quelqu'un': 'Quand je suis seul, je ne suis pas seul, mais, dans ce présent, je reviens déjà à moi sous la forme de Quelqu'un' (24). This, says Blanchot, is the domain of fascination, a term which he amplifies with reference to the *image*, which is not the object, but neither is it nothing; it is, in a formula which recurs in Blanchot's work, the presence of absence.[38] The subject's relation to it is not as to an object assured by the negative interval of consciousness, but equally it is clearly not identical with the subject: 'Quiconque est fasciné, on peut dire de lui qu'il n'aperçoit aucun objet réel, aucune figure réelle, car ce qu'il voit n'appartient pas au monde de la réalité, mais au milieu indéterminé de la fascination' (26). We might say that what fascinates here, what compels but eludes the gaze, is at once too distant and too close to objectify; this is what Blanchot suggests when he refers to the relation to the image in fascination as a 'contact à distance'. This element which begins to appear in essential solitude is necessarily maintained in 'oubli' in the world of action and decision, in the 'jour', or more precisely, in 'oubli de l'oubli', for even under the fascinated gaze it remains in oblivion.

The fascination exerted by the 'partenaire' is due to his invisibility and silence; he is compelling precisely because he is powerless, an alterity irreducible to the powers and negations of the world. After refusing the anonymous 'Quelqu'un' at nightfall ('au moment où j'allais tranquillement me coucher', *SR* 101), the narrator of *Le Partenaire* had for some time gone about the actions of the day ('les jours suivants, je vaquai à mes occupations habituelles qui toutes me retinrent chez moi', *SR* 102), but the 'partenaire' had awaited the moment for this 'oubli de l'oubli' to be interrupted ('ainsi, pendant que je l'avais oublié, il avait continué de me surveiller', *SR* 102), and for the narrator to enter the realm of fascination: 'Cependant cet être sans aucun pouvoir exerçait sur moi une telle attraction que je me trouvais à présent le dos à la porte, le doigt sur la clenchette' (*SR* 105). Thus, this powerless anonymity remains as a presence of absence which cannot be dismissed, for it cannot be encountered or even held as an object of vision: 'le chasser, cette solution si simple, je ne l'avais jamais même envisagée, car il m'était impossible de le voir' (*SR* 108).

The narrator's relation to the other is a 'contact à distance' or 'relation sans relation', as the question of the penultimate line implies: 'Pourquoi tout au début, en disant Non, bien loin de m'en défaire, l'avais-je manqué et me l'étais-je lié, mais sans jamais pouvoir l'atteindre?' (*SR* 109). It is also a dissymmetrical relation, as is evidenced by the fact that, whilst it is impossible for the narrator to face the other, we are told that 'lui, à coup sûr, ne me tournait pas le dos', and that 'tout son être devait se concentrer dans son regard avec un étonnement presqu'ahuri' (*SR* 105).

The dissymmetry of this relation and the powerlessness of the other are both strikingly reminiscent of Levinas's descriptions of the other as absolutely other, the relation to whom is not a reciprocal one of same to same, ego to alter ego (as in most models of intersubjectivity), but a fundamentally dissymmetrical one: '[La collectivité du moi–toi] est le face-à-face redoutable d'une relation sans intermédiaire, sans médiation. Dès lors l'interpersonnel n'est pas la relation en soi indifférente et réciproque de deux termes interchangeables. Autrui, en tant qu'autrui, n'est pas seulement un alter ego. Il est ce que moi je ne suis pas: il est le faible alors que moi je suis le fort; il est le pauvre, il est "la veuve et l'orphelin".'[39] It is, furthermore, a relation which places upon the subject a responsibility for the other which cannot be denied but can never be fulfilled. The narrator's refusal of a response, or of responsibility, is the vain effort to deny a relation which has constituted subjectivity from the outset, hence the narrator's ultimate realization of an impossible wish to return to a point before this aboriginal relation in order to ensure the closure of subjectivity: 'J'avais voulu le tuer avant de l'avoir vu' (*SR* 109). This brief introduction to an aspect of the relation of Levinas's thought to Laporte's work will be developed in the next section on *La Veille*, which Laporte retrospectively dedicated to Levinas on its inclusion in *Une Vie*.

ii. *La Veille* to *Pourquoi?*

La Veille marks an important shift in Laporte's writing, its inauguration of a new phase being marked retrospectively by its inclusion as the first text in the collected volume, *Une Vie*. Its appearance was greeted by enthusiastic review-articles from Blanchot,[40] for whom it was a 'livre majeur', and from Michel Foucault,[41] who wrote of its language as 'un des plus originaux qu'il soit donné de lire en notre temps'. From the earliest stages of preparation of *La Veille*, Laporte's *Carnets* (where the proposed title of this new work is 'Le Guet') reveal a determination to move towards a more direct work, at times described as an 'œuvre pure'. Early in

1959, he writes of 'La recherche d'une œuvre directe: pas de transposition, ou traduction, ou symbole, mais le langage même de l'expérience', and in the same entry, with reference to a *logos* which we may read as that of both Heidegger and Heraclitus, he envisages a unity of language and truth: 'Langage du langage si l'on veut, c'est-à-dire expression, manifestation du langage, langage en même temps sujet et objet de l'œuvre, vraiment langage pur, relation directe de la relation de l'être à l'homme' (*C* 68–9). In keeping, then, with the goal of greater directness, all pretence at a conventional narrative is now abandoned, and writing itself is placed firmly in the foreground, so that within the opening few lines the three strands from which the text is woven are introduced: 'Je', '*Il*' and 'écrire'.

From the outset, the *Il* which opens the text is linked with the narrator's writing, in so far as its[42] disappearance seems to offer the possibility for that writing to be undertaken. However, this relationship is immediately shown to be ambivalent, for the writing which is thereby permitted proves inadequate: '*il* s'était tout à fait effacé, mais, contrairement à mon attente, mon projet, au lieu d'être enfin exécutable, s'était décoloré de tout attrait à tel point que ce n'est pas par désir, mais par dépit, que j'ai commencé d'écrire' (*V* 13). The inadequacy of this writing is then linked to another ambivalence, this time in the relationship between the narrator and *lui*. Earlier, *il* had been too close for the narrator to begin writing, but now, on the other hand, the narrator finds that it is no longer accurate to say that *il* is distant, 'car le terme d'éloignement est impropre: la distance ne peut ni diminuer, ni augmenter, car aucun espace ne nous sépare. Je ne peux même pas me plaindre d'être délaissé, car je dois dire seulement: je n'ai avec *lui* aucun rapport' (*V* 14). There then follows the first of a number of breaks which will punctuate the text of *La Veille*, following which the narrator records the experience of a renewed proximity to *lui*, and in addition suggests that there are two distinct modes of writing, as, surveying his efforts up to that point, he remarks, 'j'écrivais sans écrire' (*V* 14); this notion will become a constant in Laporte's work from now on.

The enigmatic *il* of *La Veille* turns out to possess a number of characteristics which will by now seem familiar. *Il* is unknown to the narrator, who, as an individual, has no relation with *lui*—'il n'y a aucune relation directe entre ma vie d'homme et *lui*' (*V* 15)—and cannot encounter *lui*—'il est celui que l'on ne rencontre pas' (*V* 15). But, at the same time, the narrator writes of 'mon unique relation avec *lui*' (*V* 16), and later suggests that his own sense of self-identity depends on this relation: 'loin de *lui*, ne suis-je pas en exil de moi-même!' (*V* 38). The notion of an alterity at once utterly alien to the subject yet at the same time bearing on its very constitution is one we have encountered in a number of different guises already. In *La Veille*, the narrator summarizes the situation thus: 'Sa nature n'est pas seulement différente de la mienne, mais elle est radicalement autre à tel point que toute relation est inconcevable, et pourtant je ne pourrais point le dire si je n'étais effectivement en relation avec *lui*' (*V* 39). At times we are reminded of the problems of expression encountered by the narrator of *Souvenir de Reims* in his attempts to find a language adequate to a radically unnameable experience. Early in the text, the narrator confesses his dissatisfaction with the simple use of the pronoun *il*, and in the course of the text a number of other possibilities are rehearsed, but none satisfactorily; these include 'l'Inconnu', 'l'Etranger', 'l'Indicible', 'le Solitaire', 'la Solitude', 'l'Unique', 'le Non-transparent' and in one passage both 'le Favorable' and 'le Redoutable'. The anonymity of the other in *Le Partenaire*, belied by the title but strongly suggested in the body of the narrative, is clear from the outset of *La Veille*, and is underlined by the inapplicability of this series of names. The narrator makes this explicit—'En *le* désignant par "*il*", n'ai-je pas toujours sous-entendu qu'*il* était, non par accident, mais fondamentalement anonyme?' (*V* 25)—and concludes the same paragraph with an indication that this anonymity in fact marks an other irreducible to individuality: 'je ne sais quelle chose impersonnelle'. None the less, it is precisely in the context of the impersonality of *lui* that the narrator stresses again that his own self-identity in language is bound up with the other: '*Lui* seul me donne mon nom et me révèle à moi-même, et pourtant *il* est anonyme!' (*V* 25).

It is not surprising, given the new focus on writing in *La Veille*, that the anonymity of *lui* gives rise to a number of passages exploring the ways in which the other is incommensurable with language. The relationship between the other and language seems destined to thwart any attempt by the narrator to offer an account of *lui* in his work, for, although *il* resists nomination, the only approach to *lui* is through language, of which *il* is at once, in some sense, the foundation and the foe: '*il* est au-dessous et en dehors de toute manifestation; le langage *lui* appartient, mais *il* n'appartient pas au langage' (*V* 40). This situation would seem to be the ruination of the work, and indeed the most part of *La Veille* is an account of failure, but it is nevertheless only through the *œuvre* that *il* can be approached: '*Il* est en dehors de tout langage, pourquoi donc est-ce seulement par une œuvre qu'*il* peut se manifester?' (*V* 26). But even in the *œuvre* one cannot say that *il* is revealed, or at best one would have to say that *il* is revealed negatively, as it is only there that *il* is discovered as the absent origin of a language which is still inadequate to *lui*: 'Seule notre liaison, cette œuvre, montre notre irréductible opposition, et ainsi *il* est lui-même dans la mesure où contre le langage, mais dans le langage dont *il* est incompréhensiblement l'origine, *il* se manifeste comme l'ennemi du langage' (*V* 38). The origin evoked in this last quotation is crucial, for, notwithstanding the aporia encountered as a consequence of the paradoxical relations between *lui* on the one hand and the subject, language and the *œuvre* on the other, the narrator of *La Veille* resolutely awaits the approach of the other, and this interminable *attente* or *veille* is also a quest to return to an origin—of the subject, of language, of the *œuvre*—in which the inaccessible *il*, which in the time of writing appears only to promise loss and dislocation, will finally be revealed as an original, founding unity: '*lui* seul est à l'origine de ce temps premier qui fonde mon pouvoir d'établir entre nous une relation transparente' (*V* 32).

If such assertions only occur in the text hedged with qualifications pointing to the unattainability of this origin, the two epigraphs of *La Veille* strongly direct our reading towards the notion of a primordial unity. The first is a fragment from Heraclitus, No. 51 in the Diels-Kranz arrangement: 'Ils ne comprennent pas comment ce qui s'écarte s'accorde avec soi-même: ajustement à rebours comme de l'arc et de la lyre' (*V* 11). The phrase translated here as 'ajustement à rebours' is the *palintropos harmoniè* which Laporte had already quoted to qualify the paradoxical experience of the veiled epiphany of Rheims cathedral in *Souvenir de Reims* (*SR* 47). This harmony which turns back on itself points to the cycle of nature in which the warring opposites that natural phenomena appear to be are reconciled in the harmonious order of the cosmos.[43] However, the fact that 'they do not understand' this underlying harmony is no accident, for it is not a harmony which is manifest in the world, but rather the concealed one evoked in fragment D.K. 54: 'The hidden harmony is superior to the apparent one' (*harmoniè aphanès phanerès kreitòn*). It is the context suggested by this epigraph, as well as other features of the text, which lead Clémence Ramnoux, in her review of *La Veille*,[44] to read the *il* as neuter,[45] and therefore to assimilate it to 'quelqu'un de ces beaux noms philosophiques que le grec introduit avec l'article to'.[46] Specifically, Ramnoux draws a parallel between *lui* and that other figure of hidden unity which recurs in Heraclitus, the *hen to sophon* (translated by Ramnoux in her study of the fragments as 'l'Un—La Chose Sage'), which opens fragment D.K. 32, for instance: 'The wise is one alone [*hen to sophon mounon*], unwilling and willing to be spoken of by the name of Zeus.'[47] The parallel begins to shed some interesting light on the *lui* of *La Veille*, for not only does it suggest an original unity which cannot be named unequivocally, but it also gives us pause should we be tempted to read *lui* as divine, and thus to place *La Veille* in a tradition of religious mysticism,[48] since *hen to sophon* is a neuter form which, according to Charles Kahn, indicates 'an even more radical break with the anthropomorphic conception of deity, a precedent for the impersonal (or transpersonal) One of Plotinus. And the violence of this rupture with traditional theology is further indicated by the initial negation: the wise one is *not* willing to be identified with Zeus.'[49] In fact, having made the identification between *lui* and *la Chose Sage*, Ramnoux immediately cites fragment D.K. 18, which contains not this locution but another neuter form, *anelpiston* ('the unexpected'), since for her this fragment clearly says something about how one may approach *la Chose Sage*; this is the translation she gives: 'S'il n'espère pas la chose non espérée, il ne la trouvera pas, car elle est introuvable et sans accès.'[50] Ramnoux acknowledges that the fragment is susceptible to a number of interpretations, but, in the context of other fragments, interprets it as suggesting that, however unimaginable and inaccessible *la Chose* may be, failing to attempt any representation of it will certainly preclude any progress towards discovery. The pursuit of wisdom will therefore involve making of it 'une certaine espèce de représentation, non point pour la découvrir, puisqu'elle est indécouvrable, mais pour la découvrir indécouvrable, en effeuillant les illusions sans cesse renaissantes qui en masquent l'impossible vision'.[51]

Similarly, the *il* of *La Veille* remains unnameable and inaccessible, frustrating any attempt to capture it in writing, but its relation to writing and the *œuvre* is not simply negative, for *il* is at the same time the obscure source of an exigency to write, and would be consigned to an irremediable oblivion were it not for the *œuvre*: 'Sans *lui*, jamais je n'aurais eu à écrire; s'il n'y avait l'œuvre, *il* demeurerait inconnu, pourquoi est-*il* donc détaché de toute œuvre?—Comment écrire ne m'aurait-il point paru une énigme?' (*V* 18). The ceaseless questioning, discarded experiments with nomination and metaphor, and para-doxical formulations which constitute the pursuit of the ineffable undertaken in *La Veille*, prove to be another form of 'qui perd gagne', for they are the means by which *il* is revealed as irreducible to revelation: 'J'ai échoué, mais j'ai accusé à tort ma pensée de je ne sais quel manquement puisque toute réussite était impossible, et surtout parce que seule sa carence, dont *il* est l'origine, a effectivement manifesté qu'*il* est en dehors de toute relation' (*V* 47). The first epigraph of *La Veille* turns back to an originary union in which the conflict and tension encountered in the text may appear eventually to promise resolution, and does so by turning back to what might be called a pre-originary text of Western philosophy, from a time before Plato bequeathed the dualism which, for Heidegger and others, was to plague the history of that philosophy. This is also a return to an obscure origin which escapes language whilst silently conditioning it, the primordial *logos* which, as we saw in relation to *Souvenir de Reims*, speaks the harmony of opposites to those who know how to listen to it: 'It is wise, listening not to me but to the report [*logos*], to agree [*homologein*] that all things are one.'[52]

A more equivocal figure of original unity is provided by the second epigraph of *La Veille*, taken from the third, unfinished revision of Hölderlin's 'Der Einzige'. 'Der Einzige', in all three versions, is primarily concerned with the poet's attempt to reconcile Hellenic and Christian divinity. The poet begins by evoking his beloved ancient Greece, a land touched by pagan divinity, and then recalls that he has sung the image of God in its earthly manifestations (in reference, presumably, to his other poems). In addressing the pantheon he has just evoked, he observes that one, indeed the outstanding figure is absent. In the fifth stanza, the absent figure is identified as Christ, and in this part of the poem the poet simultaneously asserts divine unity, by calling Christ the brother of Hercules and Dionysus, and reveals why he is unable to perceive this unity: he is too attached to Christ, and this special affinity threatens to destroy the unity sought. The next stanza in the third version is fragmented (it is even more so in the first, and does not appear in the second) and appears contradictory. On the one hand, the poet is ashamed to associate Christ with 'worldly men' (that is, demigods), yet he goes on to reassert their fraternity and, in an evocation of Christ on earth, to underline the parallel. Laporte takes his epigraph from the beginning of the final, unfinished stanza, citing it in the following version:

> ... A jamais
> demeure ceci: le monde, jour après jour, est tout entier
> toujours lié. Souvent cependant un Grand
> paraît ne pas convenir à un
> Grand. Tout le temps ils se tiennent néanmoins, comme auprès
> d'un abîme l'un
> à côté de l'autre ... (V 11)

These lines, then, assert a unity which the poem hitherto has shown to be precarious, as the image of the divine triad side by side at an abyss underlines. The remainder of the stanza elaborates on the image in a way which stresses the worldly aspect of these divinities, before suggesting that the unity has, in a sense, been achieved by the poem: 'It is beautiful and lovely to draw comparisons' (*Schön / Und lieblich ist es zu vergleichen*). But even now the unity achieved through poetry seems about to be threatened again, as the poem breaks off with the words, 'Always, however ...' (*Immer aber ...*).

The contradictory movements of the poem might well be seen to imply that there is indeed unity from the point of view of the divine sphere on the one hand (Christ, Hercules and Dionysus are all the sons of God), and from that of the human sphere on the other (all three are also supposed to have known a mortal existence), but that that unity is compromised whenever these two spheres are brought together, and that the unity achieved for the duration of the poem is at the cost of a tension which constantly threatens to shatter that unity. This certainly seems to be the significance that the epigraph from the poem had for Laporte. In a later study of Hölderlin, Laporte describes Hölderlin's eventual rejection of the poet's role as mediator for the divine, since the divine only is divine precisely in so far as it remains distinct from humanity, and, to illustrate his remark, he turns once again to the same part of 'Der Einzige': 'Il ne s'agit plus d'unir la sphère humaine et la sphère divine, mais de maintenir fermement l'écart entre les deux mondes: l'homme et le dieu, "les voici en tout temps comme au bord du gouffre, l'un à côté de l'autre"' (QV 94).[53] In his second published study of Hölderlin (E 149–61),[54] Laporte advances an argument which we have already seen is suggested by 'Der Einzige', namely that the union of the human and the divine is accomplished in the poem, and quotes Heidegger's remark from his exegesis of 'Wie wenn am Feiertage ...', which we have already cited in respect of *Souvenir de Reims*: 'The Sacred bestows the word, and comes itself in this word. The word is the event of the Sacred.' However, he adds that the union thus achieved is a harmony of opposites, citing the very same Heraclitean fragment which is *La Veille*'s other epigraph, and concludes that 'la conciliation des contraires: les dieux / l'homme, n'est en effet acquise qu'au prix d'une tension permanente, à la longue ruineuse, jamais assurée de maintenir ensemble deux mondes non seulement différents, mais opposés' (*E* 152).

Writing in his *Carnets* late in 1963, Laporte suggests that he envisaged a similar goal for *La Veille*, in that he conceived the *œuvre* as an icon, in other words something which 'est non seulement la représentation d'une figure sacrée, mais est elle-même sacrée: non qu'elle s'identifie au sacré lui-même, mais elle en est le véhicule' (*C* 199). He goes on to suggest that, although unnameable and mute, *il* is in a relation with the language of the *œuvre*, the 'rayonnement', of which *il* is the source, being manifest at certain points, so that, to recall Ramnoux's phrase, *il* may be discovered as 'indécouvrable'. The narrator of *La Veille* suggests something similar when he remarks that the space between himself and the other occasionally attains a transparency for which, he says, he is doubtless responsible, without being the master of it, and so, 'l'œuvre que j'écrirai sera semblable à une claire-voie composée de parties transparentes et vives qui devraient laisser passer le rayonnement dont *il* est l'origine, mais aussi de parties à peine translucides, et enfin de longues parties mortes, car tout à fait opaques' (*V* 23–4). We can achieve a fuller understanding of the tension which accompanies the discordant union of the human and the divine if we consider some other passages from Hölderlin's late work (before his madness) which were important texts for both Laporte and Blanchot.

The first passage I want to look at restates the necessity for a distinction to be maintained between the human and divine spheres, so that the identity of each may be preserved. It is taken from one of the prose commentaries which Hölderlin wrote to accompany the translated poems in his *Pindar-Fragmente*, the passage in question being the first paragraph of the commentary to 'Das Höchste'.[55] Laporte actually quotes it from Blanchot's *L'Espace littéraire*, reminding us that the impact of Blanchot's critical work on his writing is not confined to direct echoes: 'L'immédiat est, en un sens strict, impossible aux mortels comme aux immortels; le dieu doit distinguer des mondes différents, conformément à sa nature, parce que la bonté céleste, eu égard à elle-même, doit rester sacrée, non mélangée. L'homme lui aussi comme puissance connaissante, doit distinguer des mondes différents, parce que seule l'opposition des contraires rend possible la connaissance' (*C* 158–9). This is cited in 1962, after the completion of *La Veille*, with reference to Laporte's pursuit of 'une voie plus directe'. The impossibility of immediacy stated here finds expression in *La Veille*, in a passage where the narrator dreams of a means other than language which would permit an immediate rapport with 'cette chose au-dessous du langage', only to check such an impulse straightaway: '—Il est temps de prendre garde que, si je parvenais jusqu'à cette chose close sur elle-même, je mourrais à l'instant même' (*V* 47). However, having quoted this passage from Hölderlin in his *Carnets*, Laporte avows that he has in mind to pursue the very path that it forbids, adding that Hölderlin's text suggests that 'la très héraclitéenne "opposition des contraires" est seulement un mode de connaissance, et non point le réel lui-même' (*C* 159), and that such an opposition must therefore be avoided if one is to approach *lui* more directly through the creation of an *œuvre*. Now, it may well be true to say that *Une Voix de fin silence* and *Pourquoi?* do indeed constitute this attempt at a more direct approach, which, as we shall see, helps to explain Laporte's subsequent dissatisfaction with them, and the creative *impasse* in which he found himself between *Pourquoi?* and *Fugue*. As regards *La Veille*, however, I would want to argue that an approach to *lui* which eschews the opposition of contraries as a 'mode de connaissance' is already undertaken there, and to illustrate what I mean by this I would like to turn to another passage from Hölderlin cited by both Laporte and Blanchot.

In 1961, Laporte identifies a passage which, he says, is at the origin of *La Veille*, and could indeed be used as its epigraph. The version he gives is as follows: 'Le divin est alors sans ménagement, il est l'esprit de la sauvagerie inexprimée et éternellement vivante, l'esprit de la région des morts' (*C* 115). The passage is taken from the *Anmerkungen zur Antigonæ* which Hölderlin wrote to accompany his translation of Sophocles' tragedy, the spirit of savagery, which describes the divine here, being a reference to the time when the gods turn away from humanity.[56] Laporte immediately goes on to say that, in his own writing, the situation is rather the reverse, in that the time of 'allégresse' occurs when *il* is absent but awaited, whilst 'la sauvagerie c'est le temps de la proximité' (C 116). It is certainly the case that the moments when *il* is felt to be at its closest in *La Veille* represent what appears to the narrator as a mortal danger, and, commenting for instance on the necessity of the *œuvre* for the relation to *lui* to be apprehended, he remarks that 'elle seule *lui* permet de se montrer dans sa sauvagerie primitive' (V 39). None the less, it seems to me that in *La Veille* Laporte is faithful to the Hölderlin text from which he quotes in a way which his contemporaneous remarks in the *Carnets* fail to recognize, but which is signalled, albeit without reference to his own work, in his later studies of the poet, as well as in Blanchot's essay 'L'Itinéraire de Hölderlin', one of the texts appended to *L'Espace littéraire*. To explain why I think this is the case, I shall have to say a little more first of all about Hölderlin's commentaries on his translations of both *Œdipus Rex* and *Antigone*, although it is beyond the scope of the present study to consider all the implications, not to mention the conflicting interpretations, of these difficult texts.[57]

Hölderlin's remarks in these commentaries treat, in interrelated fashion, the relationship between mortals and the gods in Sophocles' tragedies, and the problems of translating these plays into German in such a way as to communicate their tragic vision to a contemporary public. For Hölderlin, the situations of *Œdipus Rex* and *Antigone* are, like Sophocles' and his own times, moments of disturbance and upheaval, when the gods desert humanity, condemning mortals to live 'in dürftiger Zeit', to cite the famous expression from the elegy 'Brot und Wein'. In *Œdipus Rex*, according to Hölderlin, it is Œdipus who, in bringing the human and divine spheres into too great a proximity, provokes the gods' wrathful desertion. Towards the end of his discussion, he argues that it is in precisely such times that man, too, must turn away 'certainly in a sacred way, like a traitor'.[58] This is the celebrated 'kategorische Umkehr', the paradoxically faithful infidelity, which Hölderlin identifies at the end of his commentary, and which also informs his approach in translating Sophocles. Beginning with the view that we learn best what is foreign to us, Hölderlin argued that the Greeks, in whom Apollonian passion was innate, excelled in the clarity and sobriety which they acquired, and for which we now celebrate them, whereas Hesperian (Western) poets such as he were naturally sober, and therefore had to compensate by acquiring more of the passion which was natural to the Greeks; a true translation from one tradition to the other would therefore involve a degree of 'faithful infidelity'.[59]

What is primarily significant from the point of view of Laporte's creative relationship with Hölderlin's texts is the notion that the mediation of the human and the divine is not only prohibited by the need to maintain the distinction between the two spheres, as was already suggested in our reading of the epigraph from 'Der Einzige', but that in the time of the absence of the gods, fidelity to the absent divinity will involve a parallel turning away by humanity. Laporte and Blanchot, in describing the consequent position of the poet, follow Heidegger to an extent, before diverging significantly. Whereas, for Heidegger, the holy infinite requires the mediation of the poet in order to be known, albeit in the mediated finitude of the poem, for Laporte and Blanchot what the poet mediates is the void created by the double infidelity of the gods and humanity, and it is in the rift provoked by this double infidelity that the trace of the divine may be preserved; as Blanchot writes in 'L'Itinéraire de Hölderlin': '[le poète] doit accomplir le double renversement, se charger du poids de la double infidélité et maintenir ainsi distinctes les deux sphères, en vivant purement la séparation, en étant la vie pure de la séparation même, car ce lieu vide et pur qui distingue les sphères, c'est là *le sacré*, l'intimité de la déchirure qu'est le sacré' (375). The time of *sauvagerie* in *La Veille*, viewed from this perspective, is therefore not the time of proximity to the divine, but rather of proximity to an absence or, as Laporte says in respect of Hölderlin, to an 'écart, antérieur à toute présence' (*E* 157).

I shall shortly elaborate on this absent other in *La Veille*, but before leaving Hölderlin I should like to say something more about the application of the 'kategorische Umkehr' to the problem of translation. Both Laporte and Blanchot apply an additional twist to the notion of 'faithful infidelity' which I outlined earlier, since for them what Hölderlin had to learn in order to translate Sophocles was precisely the 'Junonian sobriety' which was originally innate to Hesperian poets, but from which they had departed to such a degree that this supposedly native disposition was once again foreign to them.[60] For Laporte, the re-acquisition of this native sobriety is a move in parallel with the 'kategorische Umkehr' which humanity must make in response to the defection of the gods: 'c'est donc se détourner des dieux et du même coup s'éloigner du trop brûlant feu du ciel' (*E* 157).

Of course, this is written much later than *La Veille*, but the *Carnets* reveal a similar concern with simplicity and sobriety of expression during and immediately after the composition of *La Veille*, and Laporte's own practice of writing in this and subsequent texts bears out the notion that the approach to an absent other which threatens the subject and the *œuvre* with dislocation and fragmentation is to be made not in a language which would imitate the disruptive effects of the other, but in a sober, muted style which faithfully turns away from the other. In the final chapter of this study, I return to a comparison of Laporte's work with some of his contemporaries, but it is worth noting here that, in a period of literary activity marked most characteristically by experimentation and formal extravagance, Laporte eschews many of the procedures of, for example, fragmentation, lexical and syntactic disruption and parody, adopted by writers who, in other respects, share similar concerns. The approach to the ineffable in *La Veille* is undertaken largely by means of paradox, rhetorical questions, rejected nomination and sparing use of aposiopesis; in other words, by means similar to those used to convey states and phenomena irreducible to rational discourse in many of the texts of French neo-classicism, for instance.

The originary union which at first seemed to be indicated by the epigraphs from Heraclitus and Hölderlin, in which a harmony of opposites was only maintained at the cost of a tension that constantly threatened to fracture that unity, began to sound very much like a version of Heidegger's ontological difference, which both articulates and distinguishes Being and beings, and describes an original unity obscured by the history of philosophy, but recalled to us by poets such as Hölderlin who respond to the originary and unifying *logos*, and which we may discover in pre-Socratic philosophers like Heraclitus, for whom thought had not yet been fundamentally split from *physis*. Certainly, there is a deployment of Heideggerian terminology at times in the *Carnets* which might support an approach to *La Veille* in this light. However, the new perspective on the origin suggested by our reading of the Hölderlin texts to which Laporte was drawn at this time, and Laporte's actual practice in *La Veille*, rather than his writings about it, elicit another reading of his text. Like the absence of the gods in Hölderlin, of which Blanchot writes that it is not 'une forme purement négative de rapport' (376), the *il* of *La Veille* is an absent alterity whose relation to the subject and the *œuvre* is not simply negative, an other which cannot be constituted as a presence but which none the less concerns the subject. There are recognizable parallels with an experience which Laporte has struggled to bring to expression since *Souvenir de Reims*, but whereas the concerns of that early text still revolved primarily around the relationship between consciousness and object, and the approach to Being, in *La Veille* the concern is with something which precedes and exceeds ontology. The *il* of *La Veille* cannot be constituted as an object of consciousness; it therefore defies the opposition of contraries as a mode of knowledge, of which Laporte is rightly distrustful in the *Carnets*, and it demands instead a response which would not seek to assimilate this alterity, but would faithfully turn away. It is in this context, I think, that we should understand Laporte's remark, after the completion of *La Veille*: 'Ecrire doit toujours être une ouverture et non point un écran' (*C* 159).

Blanchot opens his review of *La Veille* by describing the work as an attempt to 'conduire la pensée jusqu'à la pensée du neutre'.[61] What he goes on later to say about the *neutre* is very revealing about the notion of an origin, and indeed about the entire itinerary mapped out by *La Veille*:

> Le neutre n'est pas unique, ni ne tend à l'Unique, il nous tourne non pas vers ce qui rassemble, mais aussi bien vers ce qui disperse, non vers ce qui joint, mais peut-être disjoint, non vers l'œuvre, mais vers le désœuvrement, nous tournant vers cela qui toujours détourne et se détourne, de sorte que le point central où il semble qu'écrivant nous soyons attirés ne serait que l'absence de centre, le manque d'origine. Ecrire sous la pression du neutre: écrire comme en direction de l'inconnu.[62]

We should be careful here to resist the idea that the other to which the *neutre* turns us is such that there is an absence of any relation with it, for if this were the case the *œuvre* would no longer be compelled by an impossibility: 'L'œuvre prend son origine dans ce qui est à l'écart de toute communication, et c'est pourquoi j'ai le sentiment que si je parvenais à dire dans sa vérité: *il* est en dehors de toute relation, je trouverais alors l'origine de toute relation' (*V* 52). The duplicity of the other in *La Veille* resides precisely in the fact that, although inaccessible to the subject, it has always already compelled an approach which will never attain it, and that, although incommunicable, it is the condition of communication: '*Il* est et fermé sur lui-même et ouvrant toute transparence: est-*il* donc un être double?' (*V* 53). This other which poses itself as impossibility for the subject is none the less the very condition of experience, 'car il n'y a expérience au sens strict que là où quelque chose de radicalement *autre* est en jeu', as Blanchot remarks in an essay which also played an important part in the conception of *La Veille*.[63] The '*autre* rapport' which the subject entertains with the other is an endless *espoir* or *désir*, and the *œuvre* is a response to the other which, irreducible to nomination, demands an interminable response: 'Tel est le partage secret de toute parole essentielle en nous: *nommant* le possible, *répondant* à l'impossible.'[64]

The writing of *La Veille* must, then, be a perpetual approach to the endlessly futural other which has compelled that approach from an origin lost in the immemorial past, from which the *œuvre* must faithfully turn away in order to approach. The writing is therefore generated by a void which is not simply nothing, a presence of absence which is not pure negativity. On a superficial level, this is evidenced by the generative force of the interruptions in the text, which in the instances of aposiopesis mark the narrator's sense of greatest proximity to *lui*, and in other instances constitute the reference point for the recommenced writing, and are therefore interruptions with a connective and motive force. Alternatively (and here we anticipate Laporte's practice from *Fugue* onwards) we can consider this void as the *espacement* which is the condition of writing without being present in writing, and which opens the possibility of reading without being reduced by reading to a 'theme'.

It is perhaps in the context of this notion of *espacement*, as well as in respect of the broader movement of the text between proximity to and distance from *lui*, that we should understand the idea of *rythme* introduced towards the end of *La Veille*. The narrator writes of 'cette alternance d'espoir et d'effacement dont *il* est l'origine' (*V* 57), going on to bemoan his inability to welcome the other 'selon son rythme propre'. The rhythm thus described might, in fact, be said to be compelled by the other, since the approach which it demands must always be frustrated, as it discovers only the indiscoverable, the other as absolutely other. This notion of rhythm therefore describes a repetition which violates the economy of the same, a repetition in which the same is discovered to be traversed by an endlessly renewed alterity; hence the interminability of the *attente* or *veille*: 'l'attente est inséparable d'une perpétuelle fraîcheur, car, je peux l'affirmer, d'une reprise à l'autre le temps ne s'écoule pas: l'histoire ne recommence pas, mais à chaque fois commence' (*V* 55–6).

This repetition, far from securing the self-identity of the subject, therefore constitutes a 'mouvement sans retour' towards the other, a phrase which returns us to the very beginning of *La Veille*: the dedication to Emmanuel Levinas introduced by Laporte on its appearance in *Une Vie*.[65] Levinas describes the relation of the subject to the other as a movement without return, for the other is not an alter ego to the ego in which the experience of the 'hors du moi' would reinforce ipseity. In 'La trace de l'autre', an essay published after the completion of *La Veille*, but to which Laporte refers in the *Carnets* in respect of *lui* (C 207), he writes that the other is beyond Being, not relatively but absolutely other: 'Il est l'Irrévélé; irrévélé non pas parce que toute connaissance serait trop limitée ou trop petite pour en recevoir la lumière. Mais irrévélé parce que *Un* et parce que se faire connaître implique une dualité qui jure déjà avec l'unité de l'Un. L'Un est au delà de l'être non pas parce que enfoui et abscons. Il est enfoui parce qu'il est au delà de l'être, tout autre que l'être.'[66] This offers us a new perspective on the question of original unity in *La Veille*, for the other is a unity which can only be known as duality, appearing between affirmation and negation, between subject and object, but precisely because this 'between' is in fact 'before', conditioning not conditioned. It is therefore a unity which is not the product of a harmony of opposites, a transcendence which is not an *Aufhebung*, because it is prior to ontological categories, and exceeds them. The other consequently cannot be comprehended, in the sense of adequation to consciousness, but can, indeed must be experienced. Levinas cites as examples of this 'expérience hétéronome' those movements without return, generosity without recompense, which we call *bonté* and the *œuvre*: 'L'Œuvre pensée radicalement est en effet un mouvement du Même vers l'Autre qui ne retourne jamais au Même' (191). The *œuvre* is therefore a movement of generosity which sustains the impossible relation with the other with nothing to show for it, so to speak; it is therefore also *désœuvrement*, the impossibility of accomplishment: 'L'avenir pour lequel l'œuvre s'entreprend, doit être d'emblée posé comme indifférent à ma mort. L'œuvre à la fois distincte de jeux et de supputations—c'est l'être-pour-l'au-delà-de-ma-mort' (191). The movement without return of the *œuvre* is compelled by an other, to which the subject cannot finally respond, yet cannot but respond; this movement may be called an interminable desire: 'C'est cela le Désir: brûler d'un autre feu que le besoin que la saturation éteint, penser au delà de ce qu'on pense. A cause de ce surcroît inassimilable, à cause de cet au delà, nous avons appelé la relation qui rattache le Moi à Autrui—Idée de l'Infini' (196). *Il* is the absolutely other which compels this response, and which draws the subject beyond Being in an inescapable experience of impossibility: '*Au delà de l'Etre est une troisième personne* qui ne se définit pas par le Soi-Même, par l'ipséité' (199). *Il* is the third person which cannot be subsumed in a symmetrical economy of reciprocity. The interminable approach undertaken in *La Veille* destroys the self-sufficiency of the work, making the *œuvre* always the site of *désœuvrement*, an endless preparation for the 'nouvel art d'écrire' sought by the narrator (*V* 58). The generosity of *La Veille*, which makes the work *ouverture* rather than *écran*, signals a writing which cannot be placed under the sign of Narcissus, as a text reflecting and answering to itself, but must be placed under the sign of Orpheus, in which the work pursues its own ruin in response to a call which it can never answer.

Laporte's entries in his *Carnets* for the period during which *Une Voix de fin silence* and *Pourquoi?* were written, however, reveal a consistent concern for a still greater directness than he felt he had achieved in *La Veille*. The early pages of *Une Voix de fin silence* bear this out, at least in a superficial sense, inasmuch as they explore the narrator's difficulties with his prospective *Œuvre*, now capitalized, without reference to the anonymous other which had haunted that relationship in *La Veille*. In 1963, Laporte notes the absence from his future work not only of that *lui*, but also of such terms as *autre*, *étranger*, *au-delà* and *sacré*. However, far from signalling the renunciation of the transcendental realm suggested by such figures, this seems to be a decision dictated by a determination to approach this realm without the intercession of these mediating figures of alterity: 'Il ne s'agit pas de remplacer ces mots par d'autres mots, car le problème tel qu'il a été longtemps posé a disparu. Il ne s'agit plus en effet de "montrer l'invisible", et on pourrait dire que mon mouvement actuel est l'inverse de l'"aletheia" puisqu'il n'est plus question de *le* produire au jour, de *le* manifester, mais d'aller vers *lui* comme tel' (*C* 169). The transcendental realm sought by Laporte is none the less still conceived as inhabiting writing, without ever being manifest in it, and the approach to this realm is also still a return to the origin of writing: 'Ecrire authentiquement c'est à coup sûr écrire de telle sorte que l'origine non humaine de l'écriture ne soit jamais oubliée; bref, il faut écrire de telle sorte que l'origine de l'écriture demeure transparente' (*C* 180–1). Later on, Laporte qualifies this notion of transparency by means of the image of the work as 'vitrail', an image which also finds a place in *Une Voix de fin silence* and *Pourquoi?*. In a note written at the very end of 1963, Laporte points out that the 'vitrail' is not transparent, but diaphanous, allowing light to pass through but not permitting the source of that light to be seen.

Despite changing approaches, the consistency of Laporte's fundamental concerns is once again apparent here, as we are reminded of the wish of the narrator of *Souvenir de Reims* to attain the source of light which has revealed the glory of the cathedral's rose window to him. To complete the analogy with the *œuvre*, Laporte recalls Ramnoux's remark in her interpretation of Heraclitus' fragment D.K. 93: 'le langage cache en disant'. The *œuvre*, then, may be unable to make the transcendental origin manifest, but it can signify it: 'L'œuvre renvoie à autre chose, autrement dit est un langage (ne faut-il pas dire plutôt est un *signe*?)' (*C* 200). Shortly after this, in a note concerned with the sense of something surpassing, yet immanent in humanity, which he detects, for instance, in Beethoven's late quartets, Laporte further qualifies the signifying relation of the *œuvre* to the transcendental realm onto which it opens: 'Bref, je ne crois plus que l'œuvre soit *son* langage, mais je crois que par sa non-coïncidence avec elle-même, l'œuvre est un signe' (*C* 206). Once again, we are reminded of *Souvenir de Reims*, in our discussion of which we saw that the impossibility of linguistic self-coincidence, which frustrated the attempt to turn language entirely onto itself in order to perfect the negative interval between language and the world, comes to the narrator's aid inasmuch as reflexivity yields the sign as the very possibility of signification, allowing the narrator at least to approach a way of communicating the 'speaking silence' which had inspired him at Rheims cathedral; in other words, recalling the terminology inspired by Hölderlin via Heidegger and Blanchot, the poet may not be able to name the holy, but is able to signify it, indeed, in another form of 'qui perd gagne' it is precisely the failure of nomination which opens up the possibility of signification.

The signifying failure of self-coincidence of the *œuvre* can also be formulated as a 'mouvement sans retour' towards the other—inasmuch as the work's distance from itself, or *espacement*, constitutes a rhythm—of the sort suggested towards the end of *La Veille*, in which repetition, far from accomplishing a return to the self-identical, signals an alterity in identity. That the failures of self-coincidence, or discontinuities, of the *œuvre* may themselves constitute a language signifying the transcendental realm which escapes nomination is suggested by the narrator of *Une Voix de fin silence*, when he expresses his concern lest the incoherence of his writing be taken for a disorder inherent in the ideal 'chemin' which he wishes to follow, but decides to allow such moments of incoherence to remain, since they will provide 'les marques à jamais visibles des moments plus ou moins longs où j'aurai perdu l'ordre du chemin' (*VFS* 110).

Shortly after this observation, there is a break between the sections into which *Une Voix de fin silence* is divided, the interruption marking, as on numerous other occasions, a moment of 'bonheur', which the narrator indicates at the beginning of the next section, observing that 'le bonheur' has returned, with the qualification that this is a return to what has never occurred before, a repetition marked by alterity: 'Parler d'un retour est inexact tant ce bonheur est chaque fois éprouvé comme pour la première fois' (*VFS* 111). Some pages later, it occurs to the narrator that the discontinuous itinerary of his writing, rather than leading him astray, may instead itself constitute a language which permits an approach to the unnameable: 'L'acte d'écrire laisse une trace derrière lui: cet ouvrage-ci tel qu'il se présente jusqu'à maintenant. Le chemin parcouru, loin de former une ligne droite et continue, ressemble plutôt à une série de hachures dont je me demande pourtant si l'ensemble ne constitue pas un langage' (*VFS* 124). The notion that the discontinuity of the *œuvre* may itself provide an approach to the unknown readily recalls the idea of the 'errancy' which we encountered in respect of *Une Migration*. There, we saw that, in Heideggerian terms, the unattainability of Being itself compelled *Dasein* to 'wander in onticity', but that this wandering, or errancy, although never arriving at Being, could, when recognized for what it is, provide the impetus for the questioning of Being which at least rescues Being from the profound oblivion to which Western philosophy had consigned it. The narrator of *Une Voix de fin silence* concedes that he has made errors, but suggests that these may constitute a direction of sorts: 'je n'ai pas lutté contre cette dérive comme si la mobilité était aussi une loi, comme si peut-être elle me portait vers un embarcadère inconnu' (*VFS* 118). Underlining the parallel with Heideggerian errancy, he later suggests that this awareness of error itself opens up a path, and that his indirection is therefore a direction inspired by some external agency: 'ne faut-il pas [...] qu'il y ait en dehors de moi un repère auquel je reste obscurément lié même dans l'erreur pour que ce sentiment d'erreur soit possible?' (*VFS* 130). As was the case in *Une Migration*, the ceaseless errancy which will never culminate in arrival at a destination (such as Being) is described as an exile, an expatriation which reveals the hitherto obscured goal, and which to that extent is a positive resource for the writer who, in Heidegger's words, cited earlier, 'poetizes the condition of repatriation'.

That this repatriation can never be accomplished is evident in the dilemma of the narrator of *Une Voix de fin silence*, compelled to write but unable to write as he would wish:

Je ne peux ni écrire, ni renoncer à écrire, mais j'en viens à penser que par cette froide exclusion j'entretiens un rapport juste, le seul possible, avec ce malheur dont je voudrais tant parler.

L'exil m'a été imparti: à présent je l'accepte sans aigreur et même avec calme comme si je me confiais à lui. (*VFS* 75)

We may also recall that poetic repatriation was the return towards an unattainable origin, to which the poet only remains in proximity by endlessly beginning his/her journey afresh, with each new beginning once again condemned to become a 'false start', in so far as it will only serve to perpetuate an unaccomplishable exodus. Thus, in the same section in which he wonders whether his apparent indirection is not itself a direction towards the unknown, the narrator of *Une Voix de fin silence* asks himself if he will ever find a stable point of departure, but is inclined to think not: 'Je crois plutôt que je glisserai toujours d'embarcadère en embarcadère et qu'en ce sens je n'en serai toujours qu'à la recherche d'un juste commencement' (*VFS* 188). Instead, the work has constantly to be started again as the *œuvre* as accomplishment is undone by an inescapable *désœuvrement*, with each new beginning bringing the narrator back to zero, 'car, quelle que soit l'œuvre que j'écrive, je repasserai toujours par ce point où je me situe en ce moment et où je peux dire: je n'ai encore rien écrit' (*VFS* 143). This movement is, then, a repetition which violates the economy of the same, and which we might describe, anticipating a Derridean (and Nietzschean) perspective which will be fully elaborated in respect of Laporte's later works, as the eternal return of difference: 'L'expérience à laquelle je me réfère est telle qu'on la fait chaque fois pour la première fois' (*VFS* 143). In *Pourquoi?* the narrator soon feels unable to attain the 'sommet' to which he had hoped his writing might lead, 'alors que je suis incapable de me frayer un chemin jusqu'à ce point de départ dont à vrai dire je sais d'expérience qu'il est le même que le sommet!' (*P* 175). The impossibility of beginning, and hence the need constantly to begin afresh in these works, therefore becomes identified with the impossibility of attaining a goal, echoing the experience of the narrator-protagonist of *Une Migration*, unable to attain the 'Pays' and to rejoin his 'Fiancée' because he has yet to complete the prenuptial migration of his own birth.

On the one hand, then, *Une Voix de fin silence* and *Pourquoi?* are *ouvrages* which signal the impossible *Œuvre*, preparations for a work which must always remain *à venir*, like Mallarmé's projected *Livre*, so that, in a sense, these works are the record of a writing which never actually begins; thus it is that, roughly midway through *Une Voix de fin silence*, the narrator can observe that 'j'ai la conviction que je pourrais écrire dès maintenant la dernière phrase de cet ouvrage: j'ai parlé, mais je n'ai rien dit' (*VFS* 124). On the other hand, these works are at the same time the attempt to recover a lost origin which has compelled the interminable *approche* which they constitute from the outset; or rather, they are the response to a call which demands the response of a writing which it will always elude: the call of the 'voix de fin silence'. This is how Levinas, in his review of *Une Voix de fin silence*, delineates this dilemma: 'Venue d'une parole qui ne dit rien d'autre que cette venue, d'une voix blanche; mais pour "écrire juste" il faut l'avoir entendue, alors que pour l'entendre il faut déjà "écrire juste". Cercle sans issue ou sans entrée.'[67] The dilemma is once again demonstrably parallel to the dilemma faced by the narrator-protagonist of *Une Migration*, unable to complete a quest compelled from and directed towards an unattainable origin, which we examined in the context of Blanchot's treatment of the myth of Orpheus and Eurydice. The turning of Orpheus to the nocturnal Eurydice figures the turning of writing to its obscure origin, but it was Orpheus' art which permitted the descent into the underworld in the first place: 'Cela veut dire: l'on n'écrit que si l'on atteint cet instant vers lequel l'on ne peut toutefois se porter que dans l'espace ouvert par le mouvement d'écrire' (234). The writing of the *œuvre* has to be begun repetitively, yet each time *as if* it were the first time, precisely because of the impossibility of a 'first time', since writing has always already begun. The narrator of *Une Voix de fin silence* can therefore only dream of a truly inaugural writing in which that originary delay would be eradicated, and the *Œuvre*, rather than being perpetually *à venir*, could consequently be accomplished: 'cette écriture foudroyante, d'emblée parfaite, qui seule serait digne de cet instant unique où l'Œuvre fêterait sa propre naissance, son perpétuel avènement' (*VFS* 83).

But even by the time we read this, *Une Voix de fin silence* has begun with at least two false starts. First of all, there is a brief section, preceding the first of the four numbered sequences of which the work is composed, which records an inspirational *événement* that seems to call for an *œuvre*, a challenge to which the narrator feels inadequate, and yet at the end of these two pages he wonders whether he has not already said too much. Then, concluding the first paragraph of the first numbered sequence, the narrator makes explicit the difficulty of beginning and, surveying the unsatisfactory opening he has sketched, remarks that 'c'est précisément parce que ce début sans importance remettait à plus tard le commencement que, sans enthousiasme, je me suis mis à écrire' (*VFS* 73). At the end of this short opening section of the first sequence, the narrator introduces the idea of this work being a preparation for a future *œuvre*, but his dissatisfaction is far from appeased; of the pages written thus far, he asserts, 'elles sont nulles, et je voudrais les détruire' (*VFS* 74). The work as repetition of a blighted beginning is the response demanded and defied by a call, or voice, which we should now look at more closely.

The biblical source of the title *Une Voix de fin silence* is revealed in the work's epigraph, being Levinas's translation of the First Book of the Kings, XIX, 11–13, which recounts Elijah's encounter with God in the cave at Horeb.[68] The passage of the divine is marked by a tempest, an earthquake and a fire, but God is in none of these, and after this there is 'une voix de fin silence'. It should be said, first of all, that the Scriptures do not say that God is present in this voice, for it is only after this that Elijah stands at the cave's entrance and hears the voice of God; the 'voix de fin silence' therefore signals the approach of the divine. The inspirational voice to which the narrator of *Une Voix de fin silence* tries to respond is likewise an approach or opening which says nothing other than itself, a 'pure confidence', to use the phrase which occurs a number of times in the work and which was the working title of the first part of this work (cf. *C* 179):

Personne ne me parle, mais, antérieurement à la première parole, il y a cette confidence: elle ne dit rien, rien d'autre qu'elle même, ou plutôt, confidence pure, elle s'offre seulement, mais ainsi, comme si un secret m'était silencieusement confié, elle s'ouvre en mon cœur, m'ouvre à mon avenir, et c'est pourquoi, par reconnaissance, il est juste de lui donner en retour ce 'oui, j'écris', avènement et pourtant simple écho de l'offrande. (*VFS* 92)

At the risk of stating the obvious, we should also note the paradox of this title; this is a voice which says nothing, a voice which the narrator will never hear: 'cette voix qui n'en est pas une' (*VFS* 115). At the same time, of course, it is also a silence which speaks: 'ce silence qui n'est pas une simple absence de bruit' (*VFS* 111). Furthermore, it is a silence of a certain type, one that can be qualified as 'fin', so that, as Clémence Ramnoux observes in her review-article 'Accompagnement pour *Une Voix de fin silence*', 'il exige l'oreille à l'extrême attentive. Il veut dire quelque chose: mais la chose, assez bien entendue pour ébranler l'acte d'écrire, n'a précisément été dite ni écrite.'[69]

A couple of literary models for this paradoxical voice suggest themselves in the light of Laporte's critical writings, namely, the mysteriously compelling singing, which is not singing, of Josephine in Kafka's *Josephine the Singer, or the Mousefolk*, and the voice of Claudia in Blanchot's *Au Moment voulu*.[70] It is really the latter which presents the closest parallel with the 'voix de fin silence'; the narrator of *Au Moment voulu* writes the following of Claudia's voice:

[elle] était indifférente et *neutre*, repliée en une région vocale où elle se dépouillait si complètement de toutes perfections superflues qu'elle semblait *privée d'elle-même* [...] une petite chose qui ne se souciait pas de la qualité des œuvres, qui se produisait derrière la musique—et cependant un instant de la musique—, *qui laissait entendre ... mais quoi?* justement elle laissait très peu entendre. Son amie lui disait: 'Tu as fait ta voix de pauvre' ou bien, 'tu as chanté en blanc' [...].[71]

The similarities between Claudia's voice and the 'voix de fin silence' may readily be enumerated. First, the poverty and restraint of her voice are characteristics shared by the silent 'parole' to which the narrator of *Une Voix de fin silence* tries to respond, for this is a call which says only itself, but says itself as absence or silence: 'Puis-je assurer qu'il y a une parole retenue qui ne s'affirmerait pas encore, un silence qui se dirait mais comme silence?' (*VFS* 158). The narrator dismisses his question, 'car dans une telle voie il n'y a rien à penser', not that this entirely disqualifies his insight, as he is dealing precisely with the unthinkable, about which, as he goes on to remark, nothing may categorically be affirmed or denied. Here, of course, is another point of comparison; the call or 'parole', like Claudia's voice, is *neutre*: 'je peux tout au plus me demander un instant, mais sans chercher la réponse, si je ne suis pas en liaison avec un langage neutre, mais premier, antérieur à la distinction de la parole et du silence' (*VFS* 158). It is between affirmation and negation, but not as a synthesis of them, since it is prior to and inhabits both, just as Claudia's voice is behind and yet within the music which she sings. The narrator of *Au Moment voulu* wonders whether the reserve he notices in Claudia's voice is due to some recording sessions for which she is now just practising ('peut-être répétait-elle en ce moment'), adding that 'cela expliquait qu'elle ne chantât pas réellement, plutôt à la recherche de quelque chose qui fût le début, l'espoir de son propre chant'.[72] Her voice therefore reveals another characteristic which is familiar from our description of the 'voix de fin silence', in that it is always yet to come, a perpetual futurity which is at the same time an absolute anteriority which, as the following remark from *Pourquoi?* indicates, requires in response a writing which effaces itself to become, as far as possible, a pure 'écoute': 'il me faut écrire en vue de la seule écoute pure afin que ma parole retenue ne soit pas trop infidèle à cette non encore parole dont elle vient, dont elle devrait être seulement l'écho' (*P* 212).

The obstacles to achieving such a writing will already be apparent, and indeed we have already encountered them in *Souvenir de Reims*. Faced with the task of echoing this communicative silence, the narrator of the two texts we are presently considering seems effectively to have the choice of two forms of betrayal: the immodest revelation afforded by a language which endeavours to make manifest and therefore falsifies the ineffable, or the oblivion of silence in which the ineffable is not even known negatively, so to speak, by being revealed as irreducible to revelation. As Blanchot remarks in 'La Parole "sacrée" de Hölderlin', 'le silence est marqué de la même contradiction et du même déchirement que le langage' (129). The communicative silence itself, like its counterpart in *Souvenir de Reims*, resembles that element which violates the negative interval between consciousness and the world described by Blanchot in 'La Littérature et le droit à la mort', which Blanchot there assimilates to Levinas's *il y a*, which is the presence of absence, the absolutely anterior anonymity of being, described by Levinas in *Le Temps et l'autre* in terms of the moment when 'l'absence de toutes choses, retourne comme une présence: comme le lieu où tout a sombré, comme une densité d'atmosphère, comme une plénitude du vide ou comme *le murmure du silence*'.[73] But to recall this is also to recall that, for the writer, the dilemma of a language which makes manifest and a silence which precludes communication is a false one. A language which is not directed at manifestation, but which rather, we might say, turns faithfully away from this unnameable presence of absence and, to pass it over in silence, turns instead onto itself, produces not silence but the impersonal signification of words become things which, Blanchot observes in this essay, characterizes the language of literature, so that 'la littérature [...] est la seule traduction de l'obsession de l'existence, si celle-ci est l'impossibilité même de sortir de l'existence' (320); the imperfect silence of the literary word is the echo of the 'murmure du silence' of the *il y a*. This is to say that language is not simply nomination but signification, and, as we noted earlier, the impossibility of naming the ineffable opens up the possibility of signifying it. If the narrator of *Une Voix de fin silence* and *Pourquoi?* does not envisage this as a solution to the dilemma of responding to the 'voix de fin silence', it is because he is seeking something more than the perpetual approach which signification allows.

What is being sought here may be clarified by considering what Laporte has to say about a text by Blanchot which influenced him greatly at this time. The text in question is 'René Char et la pensée du neutre' in which, starting from Char's question 'Comment vivre sans inconnu devant soi?', Blanchot explores the relation of poetry and thought to the 'inconnu'. This is the crucial passage for Laporte:

La recherche—la poésie, la pensée—se rapporte à l'inconnu comme inconnu. Ce rapport découvre l'inconnu, mais d'une découverte qui le laisse à couvert; par ce rapport, il y a 'présence' de l'inconnu; l'inconnu, en cette 'présence', est rendu présent, mais toujours comme inconnu. Ce rapport doit laisser intact—non touché—ce qu'il porte et non dévoilé ce qu'il découvre. Ce ne sera pas un rapport de dévoilement. L'inconnu ne sera pas révélé, mais indiqué.[74]

In a parenthesis after this passage, Blanchot stresses that the 'inconnu' is not *known* in this 'rapport' as an entity, echoing the final assertion of the passage cited to the effect that the 'inconnu' is indicated (or signified, we might say), not revealed: 'L'inconnu comme neutre suppose un *rapport* étranger à toute exigence d'identité et d'unité, voire de présence.' We should note that the quotation marks around the word 'présence' in the former passage, and the phrase 'voire de présence' in the latter, were absent from the original article as Laporte would have read it prior to writing *Une Voix de fin silence*. These alterations are noted by Laporte in 'Une Passion', as part of his account of how he came to interpret this text 'de manière "mystique"', explaining that at the time these lines 'formulaient avec une netteté exceptionnelle, la relation de l'homme avec l'Inconnu.— Et si l'Inconnu était Dieu?' (*DLMB* 131).

It is the possibility raised by this last question which in part explains Laporte's subsequent dissatisfaction with his writing at this time. In an interview with Jean Ristat in 1972, Laporte remarks that 'j'avais mis un espoir insensé dans cette expérience: et si Dieu était possible?'.[75] However, some of the passages we have already considered demonstrate that the possibility of signification opened up by the failure of nomination, and the concomitant idea of the work as approach rather than a bringing to presence, have not been forgotten in *Une Voix de fin silence* and *Pourquoi?*. The narrator of these texts is equally conscious of the endless futurity of the *œuvre* and the inaccessible anteriority of the call of the origin which compels his impossible quest, as the following passage—one could cite many others—makes very clear:

—Il se peut aussi que je doive écrire cet ouvrage comme en ne l'écrivant pas, que je doive rêver d'une Œuvre toujours future, dont l'irréalité fasse écho à cet événement dont il ne convient peut-être même pas de dire qu'il est suprême dans la mesure du moins où il n'affirme rien. L'Œuvre n'existe pas, et il convient de construire seulement le berceau d'un navire destiné un jour toujours futur à prendre la mer, mais il faut trouver une manière authentique de laisser à l'Œuvre sa réserve, sa liberté, son inexistence. (*VFS* 147)

We have therefore yet to explain fully Laporte's later dissatisfaction with these works, expressed not only in the interview just cited, but also in an interview conducted by Serge Velay in 1980, in which Laporte says that 'j'ai certainement écrit *Une Voix de fin silence* (dont je déteste depuis longtemps la douceur) contre *La Veille* qui m'avait en effet éprouvé',[76] as well as in his *Entre deux mondes*, in which the condemnation is more sweeping: 'toute une partie de *Une Vie*, celle intitulée *Une Voix de fin silence*, est une projection de mes désirs, une marque de mes préférences personnelles, et rien d'autre' (*EDM* 18).[77] The contrast with *La Veille* is also noted by Clémence Ramnoux, who describes the relative serenity of *Une Voix de fin silence*, from which the sense of danger she found in its predecessor is largely absent, adding that perhaps 'l'auteur a vécu dans la crainte et le tremblement un travail dont le rendu, le poli final rayonne l'enjouement'.[78] It seems to me that we can express the contrast with *La Veille* by observing that, rather than being haunted by the spectre of *désœuvrement*, the impossibility of accomplishment, these works are perhaps explorations of the unknown and the impossible which are tempted by the possibility of accomplishment. Notwithstanding the many indications to the contrary contained in these works, of which a number have already been cited, the narrator of these texts does not, in the end, relinquish the ambition of bringing to presence that which can only be signified and, by restoring to the present an absolutely anterior *événement*, of completing the unaccomplishable *Œuvre*, the Book in which the Word will be made flesh.

The originary *événement* is apparently recorded in the opening lines of *Une Voix de fin silence*, where it is identified as the source of the wish to write a work, but at the same time as defying expression. Although, at the outset, this event does seem to have occurred, within a few lines it appears rather to remain *en deçà* of occurrence, as suggested by the narrator's evocation of his experience: 'J'étais ouvert à une fraîcheur qui jamais ne se fanait, qui mettait ma sensibilité à vif, et pourtant à peine puis-je parler d'une émotion tant elle était non seulement fine et retenue, mais comme suspendue' (*VFS* 69). The accomplishment of the event is said to require a passive 'letting-be' on the part of the narrator: 'Rien ne m'était demandé si ce n'est de laisser s'accomplir, selon son temps propre, ce que je n'ose appeler un événement' (*VFS* 70). This hesitancy in speaking of an 'événement' is clarified a little later by the observation that the only evidence of the event is its absence, a trace of the event which itself then disappears: 'Je sentis bientôt qu'un départ sans retour venait de se produire, puis cette amère impression d'absence, preuve du moins d'un événement, cette dernière trace elle-même disparut' (*VFS* 70). The event hesitantly described as the original impetus of the work recurs in the course of the work, but according to the same modality, whereby it is never said to be present, and can either be recorded retrospectively (and even then, cannot unequivocally be said to have occurred), or is anticipated as a perpetual advent. The alternation of tenses in *Une Voix de fin silence* and *Pourquoi?* corresponds broadly to these two forms of relation to the *événement* with, naturally enough, past tenses predominantly in the retrospective passages, and present tenses (along with future and conditional) in the anticipatory passages. There are likewise two fundamental affective relations to the *événement*: the *bonheur* which immediately precedes and succeeds those interruptions in the text which correspond to the silent passage of the *événement* and the *malheur* provoked by the withdrawal of the *événement*. It should be said that the *bonheur* and the *malheur* do not simply mark the positive and the negative poles of the narrator's experience, since the *malheur* which accompanies the withdrawal of the *événement* none the less offers the narrator the possibility of sustaining his relationship with the inaccessible *événement*. More than that, the *malheur*, described as 'sans nom' or 'sans voix', is itself assimilated to the *événement*, the presentation of which would enable the accomplishment of the *œuvre*. In fact, neither affect has, as its site, the self-identity of the subject, for the *bonheur* too takes the form of an impersonal visitation: 'Oui, je suis le lieu d'un bonheur, bonheur comme impersonnel et que pourtant l'on peut aimer, seul digne d'être aimé ...' (*VFS* 109). Both *bonheur* and *malheur* rather describe a relation of which the subject is not the master, since this relation conditions the subject from the outset, and repetitively disrupts its self-identity; *bonheur* and *malheur* might best be described in Catherine Backès-Clément's formulation as 'l'affect de l'écriture'.[79]

We have already noted features of these works which invite a Heideggerian reading, and this is also true of the *événement*, as Levinas remarks: 'L'événement ressemble tantôt à celui de l'être ou, en donnant au mot *essence* la valeur d'un nom abstrait d'action, l'événement ressemble à l'*essence* de l'être, au fameux *être de l'étant* heideggerien.'[80] Levinas goes on to remark that, in Blanchot, this takes the form of 'un ressassement impersonnel et neutre, comme un remue-ménage incessant', and the rest of his description of the *neutre* in Blanchot reminds us how close this is to his own conception of the *il y a*. The proximity of Laporte to Blanchot and Levinas has already been amply illustrated and we have seen that it is still readily discernible in these works. However, Levinas immediately adds that, in respect of the *événement*, Laporte appears closer to Heidegger and to that leading French Heideggerian, with whom Laporte had studied, Jean Beaufret: 'Il parle d'avènement, de sommet, tout en ayant soin de séparer ces notions des bruyants triomphes des vainqueurs. Cette voix qui vient en s'éloignant, comme un écho ou une rime, se tient au bord du silence et de l'oubli.'[81] The *événement*, which stands at the origin of the work, and whose bringing to presence in the work, were it possible, would appear to promise the resolution of the dilemmas faced by the narrator, recalls Heidegger's *Ereignis*, to which we alluded briefly in discussing *Souvenir de Reims* and which we must now outline in greater detail, although it is beyond the scope of this study to offer a thoroughgoing account of what, according to Heidegger, we should not even call a 'concept'.[82]

The *Ereignis* is where Being and time are disclosed to each other in mutual appropriation, as Albert Hofstadter remarks in his article

'Enownment', the title of which is his neologized translation of *Ereignis* in place of the more conventional rendering 'event of appropriation': 'In *On Time and Being* [Heidegger] presents enownment as the source which gives Being and gives time, as gifts are given. It sends the destiny of Being and extends time, expropriating itself so that man can stand in appropriation—enownment—with Being within time.'[83] The *Ereignis* 'gives time' inasmuch as the expropriation which allows appropriation *is* the temporality of Being. Hugh Silverman observes that '*Ereignis* is the ecstatic happening of a being's difference from itself, namely, the time of its relation to Being—which is another "time" than the time of everyday being'.[84] This other time is the 'always already' of the withdrawal of Being and the 'not yet' of its advent. This is also the temporality of the *événement* in the two volumes of *Une Voix de fin silence*, in which the narrator always finds himself before or beyond the *événement*, as is suggested in the following passage which reveals another echo of the *Ereignis*:

L'événement a eu lieu: son passage a non seulement fait tourner le temps du futur au passé, mais il a donné naissance à une histoire qui ne cesse de s'éveiller, de me porter au bonheur de pouvoir enfin parler presque au présent. L'intervalle entre ce que je vis et ce que j'écris est si ténu que l'écriture n'est pas un écho, mais la résonance de ce que j'éprouve, l'espace hospitalier où se déploie le don qui ne cesse de m'être fait. (P 180)

The idea that the *événement* is a gift is one that recurs in both volumes, and it is a characteristic shared by the *Ereignis*, which might be glossed as the *es* of *es gibt*, and which in that sense bestows the truth of Being by its generous withdrawal—the *lethe* which permits *aletheia*.

We noted in passing, in our earlier consideration of *Souvenir de Reims*, that the *Ereignis* is an event of language. In *Identity and Difference*, Heidegger identifies language as the site of the mutually appropriative disclosure in which man and Being each come into their own:

To think of appropriating as the event of appropriation [*Das Ereignis als Er-eignis denken*] means to contribute to this self-vibrating realm. Thinking receives the tools for this self-suspended structure from language. For language is the most delicate and thus the most susceptible vibration holding everything within the suspended structure of the appropriation [*des Ereignisses*]. We dwell in the appropriation in as much as our active nature is given over to language.[85]

It is precisely the faculty of language which accords an existential privilege to *Dasein*, and it is, at the same time, through language that the truth of Being is discovered in *aletheia*. However, if Being requires the mediation of language in order to come to presence in the mediated form of beings, it none the less remains the case that, in the process, Being must withdraw into the *lethe* at the heart of *aletheia*. To attend to the call of Being in language, for Heidegger, means to attend to the silence from which language comes forth, for the differentiating rift between language and silence corresponds to the rift, elsewhere known as the ontological difference, between beings and Being. In the later works—and here the connection with Laporte's work becomes most evident—this silence which is part of the autonomous speaking of language is known as the 'peal of stillness' (*das Geläut der Stille*).[86]

The *Ereignis* as event of language gives Being in a communicative silence which is clearly akin to the 'voix de fin silence' which resounds from the originary *événement* in *Une Voix de fin silence* and *Pourquoi?*. For the narrator of *Pourquoi?*, neither language nor silence represents an adequate response to the 'voix de fin silence', and so he asks: 'Un langage qui parle sans dire ni taire est-il possible?' (*P* 197). In *Identity and Difference* Heidegger is concerned with the same question, inasmuch as Western languages are permeated with metaphysical thinking and therefore cannot echo the 'peal of stillness' which is the call of Being to thought, unless 'these languages offer other possibilities of utterance—and that means at the same time of a telling silence [*des sagenden Nichtsagens*]'.[87] The notion of a 'telling silence', or more literally a 'saying not-saying', is often echoed in Laporte's work when the narrator envisages that, in a form of 'qui perd gagne', the failures of his work themselves constitute an opening to the unnameable. However, at least as frequent are negative assessments of the achievement of such an opening, such as the following: 'Depuis bien longtemps je rêve d'écrire un ouvrage qui soit l'équivalent d'un vitrail ou, mieux encore, d'une vitre si transparente qu'on l'oublie comme telle, mais ce présent ouvrage ressemble plutôt à un mur opaque' (*VFS* 147). Such assessments have been amplified by Laporte's own subsequent remarks, in which he has often been scathingly dismissive of both volumes of *Une Voix de fin silence*.

One of the sources of their perceived weakness might be Laporte's inability at this stage to resolve the nature of the originary *événement* and its consequent relation to his writing, but this failure, in another form of 'qui perd gagne', may be seen to open the way to Laporte's later work. The pursuit of the originary *événement* reveals what had frequently been taken to be the founding unity of this event to be at the same time a rift: 'L'unisson, s'il y a unisson, est en effet aussitôt déchirure: la voix vient à me manquer, mais ainsi par cette entrouverture sur le vide ne suis-je pas alors en rapport direct avec la partie manquante?' (*P* 226). The discovery of a rift as the original event is in keeping with Heidegger's conception of the *Ereignis* as the differentiating moment of beings and Being. But the discovery that, at the origin, lies an event which is not an entity but a relation, for Heidegger the 'relation of relations', brings with it the realization that an origin which is not identity or plenitude, but is rather difference, entails the abandonment of any notion of a unitary origin. The movement from origin as unique event to origin as a difference which effaces any origin might be taken to be the movement from Heidegger to Derrida. In the words of Timothy Clark: 'More accurately, the movement of a relation that has always already borne away the relata, and that withdraws from every attempt to grasp or objectify it, could never have been single. It is the value of *one*, in the supposed unique site that must be questioned. This rhythm is a primordial difference from itself, inherently diverse and disseminated, "beginning" as its withdrawal, etc.'[88] The narrator of *Pourquoi?* notes the impossibility of thinking the *neutre* according to a binary logic and asks: 'Comment penser une différence qui ne serait pas encore une séparation?' (*P* 207). The attempt to do just this leads away from the conception of the text as 'self-vibrating realm' in which the play of forces is held in check by an originary and unitary event, or a transcendental signified, and leads instead to a conception of textual play traversed by a non-oppositional difference or *différance*, that is, to writing as *fugue*.

Notes to Chapter 2

1. In Maurice Blanchot, *La Part du feu* (Paris: Gallimard, 1949), 293–331 (312); further references to this essay and to 'La Parole "sacrée" de Hölderlin' in the same volume (115–32) will be given in the text.
2. *Nadja* is also the source of the other allusion to Breton in *Souvenir de Reims*, when the narrator echoes the call to 'vivre à perdre haleine'.
3. An excellent analysis of Blanchot's reading of Heidegger's exegeses of Hölderlin, particularly in this essay, may be found in Leslie Hill's *Blanchot: Extreme Contemporary* (London and New York: Routledge, 1997), 77–91.

4. A chaos which, as becomes most apparent in this passage, is also that of Nietzsche, whose name has already been invoked in the course of the *récit* (*SR* 37). The writer's ecstatic vision of a primordial chaos is the affirmation of the flux of becoming over the stasis of being.

5. e.g. 'Der eine Dichter verwahrt die gestillte Erschütterung des Heiligen in der Stille seines Schweigens' (This one poet safeguards the calmed tremor of the sacred in the stillness of his silence), Martin Heidegger, *Erläuterungen zu Hölderlins Dichtung*, 3rd edn. (Frankfurt: Klostermann, 1963), 66.

6. Fragment No. 93 in the Diels-Kranz ordering.

7. Clémence Ramnoux, *Héraclite ou l'homme entre les choses et les mots*, 2nd edn. (Paris: 'Les Belles Lettres', 1968), 304; this edition also contains a preface by Blanchot, based on a review of the first edition, which ends with the very quotation Laporte had used for his epigraph.

8. From the 'Letter on Humanism', in Martin Heidegger, *Pathmarks* (Cambridge: Cambridge University Press, 1998), 239–76 (249).

9. 'Language, by naming beings for the first time, first brings beings to word and to appearance' ('The Origin of the Work of Art', in Martin Heidegger, *Poetry, Language, Thought* (New York: Harper and Row, 1971), 73).

10. Heidegger, *Erläuterungen zu Hölderlins Dichtung*, 74.

11. 'Every original and authentic naming expresses something unsaid, and, indeed, in such a fashion that it remains unsaid', from *Was heißt Denken?*, cit. William J. Richardson, *Heidegger: through phenomenology to thought*, 2nd edn. (The Hague: Martinus Nijhoff, 1967), 609. My understanding of Heidegger owes a particular debt to Richardson's study. I am less concerned with demonstrating the influence of Heidegger on Laporte than with providing an intellectual context which allows us to read Laporte's early work with a view to anticipating subsequent directions in his writing. Thus, here and elsewhere I occasionally refer to publications by Heidegger which post-date the works by Laporte under consideration.

12. Heidegger, *Poetry, Language, Thought*, 190.

13. The reference to Cézanne in conjunction with a programme for an art which would recover 'la Terre non-humaine' recalls the painter's discussion of art in his late correspondence: '*Pénétrer ce qu'on a devant soi*, et persévérer à s'exprimer le plus logiquement possible', he wrote in a letter of 1904 to Emile Bernard (Paul Cézanne, *Correspondance*, ed. John Rewald (Paris: Grasset, 1978), 303; my emphasis). A year earlier, in a letter to Ambroise Volland, he had famously evoked a Promised Land: 'Je travaille opiniâtrement, j'entrevois la Terre promise. Serai-je comme le grand chef des Hébreux ou bien pourrai-je y pénétrer? [...] L'Art serait-il, en effet, un sacerdoce qui demande des purs qui lui appartiennent tout entiers?' (292).

14. Blanchot, *La Part du feu*, 83; this quotation indicates why I have, with some hesitation in respect of Laporte's *récits*, used the term 'symbolic' here and near the beginning of this paragraph, where the term 'allegorical' might have been expected. For a brief account of the distinction between the symbolic and the allegorical, in Blanchot's sense, see Clark, *Derrida, Heidegger, Blanchot*, 76–8. Laporte's eventual renunciation of the form of the *récit* might in fact be explained by the extent that he was unable to transcend allegory.

15. Heidegger, 'On the Essence of Truth', in *Pathmarks*, 136–54.

16. On this conception of *Dasein*, see Heidegger, *Being and Time* (Oxford: Blackwell, 1962), 32.

17. Richardson, *Heidegger*, 226.

18. Cf. Heidegger, *Pathmarks*, 150–2.

19. Cited in Richardson, *Heidegger*, 472.

20. Cited in Richardson, *Heidegger*, 452.

21. Cited in Richardson, *Heidegger*, 453.

22. Blanchot, *L'Espace littéraire*, 248; further references to this volume will be given in the text (distinguishing them from references to *La Part du feu* wherever necessary).

23. As attested in his footnotes to this essay, Blanchot is close here to the thinking of Levinas. We will return to this affinity later, but for the moment let us note these remarks from Levinas's essay, first published in 1948, *Le Temps et l'autre* (Paris: Presses Universitaires de France, coll. 'Quadrige', 1983): 'Cette approche de la mort indique que nous sommes en relation avec quelque chose qui est absolument autre, quelque chose portant l'altérité, non pas comme une détermination provisoire, que nous pouvons assimiler par la jouissance, mais quelque chose dont l'existence même est faite d'altérité. Ma solitude ainsi n'est pas confirmée par la mort, mais brisée par la mort' (63). Blanchot's conception of communication is also close to that of Bataille, e.g.: 'La communication demande un défaut, une "faille"; elle entre, comme la mort, par un défaut de la cuirasse. Elle demande une coïncidence de deux déchirures, en moi-même, en autrui' (*Le Coupable*, in *Œuvres complètes*, v.(Paris: Gallimard, 1973), 266).

24. Cf. Heidegger, *Being and Time*, § 53; e.g. 'Death is Dasein's *ownmost* possibility. Being towards this possibility discloses to Dasein its *ownmost* potentiality-for-Being, in which its very Being is the issue. Here it can become manifest to Dasein that in this distinctive possibility of its own self, it has been wrenched away from the "they"' (307). The later Heidegger's thoughts on death and the negativity or mystery of Being seem to bring him closer to these French thinkers; cf. 'Death is the shrine of nothing, that is, of that which in every respect is never something that merely exists, but which nevertheless presences, even as the mystery of Being itself' ('The Thing', *Poetry, Language, Thought*, 178). But even here, mortals are distinct in the 'Fourfold' of Being 'not because their earthly life comes to an end, but because they are *capable of death as death*' (179; my emphasis).

25. Heidegger, *Being and Time*, 249.

26. Levinas, *Le Temps et l'autre*, 62: 'La mort n'annonce pas une réalité contre laquelle nous ne pouvons plus rien, contre laquelle notre puissance est insuffisante; des réalités dépassant nos forces surgissent déjà dans le monde de la lumière. Ce qui est important à l'approche de la mort, c'est qu'à un certain moment nous ne *pouvons plus pouvoir*; c'est en cela justement que le sujet perd sa maîtrise même de sujet.'

   Bataille, *Le Coupable*, in *Œuvres complètes*, v. 241: 'L'angoisse n'est pas vraiment le possible de l'homme. Mais non! l'angoisse est l'impossible! elle l'est au sens où l'impossible me définit. L'homme est le seul animal qui de sa mort ait su faire exactement, lourdement l'impossible, car il est le seul animal qui meurt en ce sens fermé. La conscience est la condition de la mort achevée. Je meurs dans la mesure où j'ai la conscience de mourir. Mais la mort dérobant la conscience, non seulement j'ai conscience de mourir: cette conscience, en même temps, la mort la dérobe en moi.'

27. The line is from the poem 'Les Compagnons dans le jardin', first published in the *Cahiers du Sud* 338 (1956), collected in *Œuvres complètes*, 381–3. When *Une Migration* was reprinted with *Le Partenaire*, it was also preceded by a 'Lettre-Préface' by Char.

28. Cf. Hegel's Preface to the *Phenomenology of Spirit*: 'Death, if we care to call this unactuality by this name, is what is most terrible, and to hold on to what is dead requires the greatest strength. That beauty which lacks strength hates the understanding because it asks this of her and she cannot do it. But not the life that shrinks from death and keeps itself undefiled by devastation, but the life that endures, and preserves itself through, death is the life of the spirit' (*Hegel: selections*, ed. M. J. Inwood (New York and London: Macmillan, 1989), 115–51, 130).

29. The terms which I use here further underline Blanchot's affinity with Bataille, a bond which Blanchot has consistently signalled throughout his critical writings. The best introduction to the aspect of Bataille's thought adumbrated here remains Foucault's article 'Préface à la transgression' (*Critique* 195/196 (1963), 751–69) where, for instance, Foucault writes: 'Le jeu des limites et de la transgression semble être régi par une obstination simple; la transgression franchit et ne cesse de recommencer à franchir une ligne qui, derrière elle, aussitôt se referme en une vague de peu de mémoire, reculant ainsi à nouveau jusqu'à l'horizon de l'infranchissable' (754–5).

30. Blanchot turns to the term 'souffrance' increasingly in later works, such as *L'Entretien infini* (Paris: Gallimard, 1969). 'La souffrance est souffrance, lorsqu'on ne peut plus la souffrir et, à cause de cela, en ce non-pouvoir, on ne peut cesser de la souffrir' (63).

31. Joseph Libertson, *Proximity: Levinas, Blanchot, Bataille and Communication* (The Hague: Martinus Nijhoff, 1982), 76. I am indebted to Libertson's study for my understanding of the relations between these three thinkers.

32. Bataille, *Le Coupable*, in *Œuvres complètes*, v. 261.

33. Significantly, the 'other' in this *récit* is only described as 'Le Partenaire' in the title; I use the term 'visitor' in this outline of the *récit* for the sake of simplicity; the status of this other is discussed later.

34. The sentence is from Maurice Blanchot, *Celui qui ne m'accompagnait pas* (Paris: Gallimard, 1953), 122.

35. Blanchot, *Celui qui ne m'accompagnait pas*, 123.

36. Blanchot, *Celui qui ne m'accompagnait pas*, 121.

37. Cf. Maurice Blanchot, *Le Livre à venir* (Paris: Gallimard, 1969), 10.

38. A notion which may be clarified with reference to the paradoxical status of literary language outlined in 'La littérature et le droit à la mort'.

39. Emmanuel Levinas, *De l'existence à l'existant*, 2nd edn. (Paris: Vrin, 1986), 162.

40. Maurice Blanchot, 'Traces', *Nouvelle Revue Française* 129 (1963), 472–80. The section on *La Veille* (478–80) is subtitled 'Le Neutre', and is reprinted in *L'Amitié* (Paris: Gallimard 1971), 249–51; further references will be to the latter.

41. Michel Foucault, 'Guetter le jour qui vient', *Nouvelle Revue Française* 130 (1963), 709–16. Foucault's interest is particularly significant, since it was he who

introduced Laporte's work to Derrida, providing the foundation of what was to be an important friendship: cf. Geoffrey Bennington and Jacques Derrida, *Jacques Derrida* (Paris: Seuil, 1991), 303.

42. I have to pre-empt myself here by referring to this *Il* in the neuter, a decision which will be explained shortly.

43. My understanding of Heraclitus is indebted to two works; I have already cited Ramnoux's *Héraclite*, which drew the admiration of both Blanchot and Laporte. My principal guide to Heraclitean terminology, and to the significant cross-references between fragments, has been Charles H. Kahn, *The Art and Thought of Heraclitus* (Cambridge: Cambridge University Press, 1979). Kahn's commentary on this fragment is at 195–200.

44. The author of the review is not indicated in the text, but the bibliography in *Digraphe* 18/19 'Roger Laporte' (1979), prepared with Laporte's participation, credits it to Ramnoux.

45. A reading explicitly supported by the text: '*il est neutre*' (*V* 29). As we shall see, there are further grounds for such an interpretation.

46. Ramnoux, '*La Veille*, par Roger Laporte', *Revue de Métaphysique et de Morale* 2 (1964), 232–4 (232).

47. Translation in Kahn, *Art and Thought of Heraclitus* , 83. Kahn adopts a different arrangement of the fragments; I have kept the Diels-Kranz numbers, since they are the ones Laporte uses.

48. Henri Raynal, 'Roger Laporte ou l'écriture angélique', *Courrier du centre international d'études poétiques* 64 (1968), 3–19, in many ways a sensitive reading of *La Veille* and *Une Voix de fin silence*, seems to me to go too far in this direction. One should say, however, that the itinerary marked out by these two works (*Pourquoi?* had only just appeared) does make such a reading particularly inviting; Raynal says of them: 'Tant que nous n'avions lu que le premier, le doute était encore permis. Le second fait tomber nos scrupules. Le climat en est incontestablement mystique' (8). Furthermore, the particular mystical tradition he maps out *is* one to which Laporte is indebted, comprising as it does such figures as Meister Eckhart, Angelus Silesius and even Heidegger.

49. Kahn, *Art and Thought of Heraclitus* , 269.

50. Ramnoux, '*La Veille*, par Roger Laporte', 233.

51. Ramnoux, '*La Veille*, par Roger Laporte', 233.

52. Heraclitus, D.K. 50; cf. also Kahn's comments, made in respect of D.K. 32: 'wisdom in the full sense is accessible only to the divine ruler of the universe, since it means mastering the plan by which the cosmos is governed. For human beings such wisdom can serve only as an ideal target, a goal to be pursued by *homo-logein*, by agreement with the *logos*: putting one's own thought, speech, and action in harmony with the universal course of things' (268).

53. 'Hölderlin ou le combat poétique' (*QV* 79–99), first published in *Critique* 259 (1968), 1019–40; that the significance of these lines is roughly the one I have just outlined is clear from what appears to be a slight misreading by Laporte of the literal sense of these lines.

54. First published as a separate volume in 1980.

55. The original may be found in the *Kleine Stuttgarter Ausgabe* (Stuttgart: W. Kohlhammer, 1965), v. 309.

56. *Kleine Stuttgarter Ausgabe*, v. 290; Hölderlin writes that here the 'Geist' (which

has already been identified as the divine: 'der Geist der Zeit und Natur, das Himmlische' [the spirit of time and nature, the divine]) at this time appears not 'wie ein Geist am Tage, sondern er ist schonungslos, als Geist der ewig lebenden ungeschriebenen Wildnis und der Totenwelt' (as a spirit in daylight, but rather as the merciless spirit of eternal, unwritten savagery, and of the underworld).

57. The complexity and far-reaching implications of these texts are evidenced by George Steiner's discussion of Hölderlin's translations of Sophocles in his *Antigones* (Oxford: Clarendon Press, 1984), 66–106. In the light of Steiner's survey, it will be clear that Blanchot's and Laporte's readings, mediated by Heidegger's writings on Hölderlin, are unconventional.

58. 'In solchem Momente vergißt der Mensch sich and den Gott, und kehret, freilich heiliger Weise, wie ein Verräter sich um' (at such times, man forgets both himself and God, and turns away, certainly in a sacred way, like a traitor), *Kleine Stuttgarter Ausgabe*, v. 220.

59. These views are expressed in two letters to Böhlendorff and Wilmans, *Kleine Stuttgarter Ausgabe*, vi. 455–8 and 464–5, respectively.

60. Blanchot summarizes this position in *L'Espace littéraire*, 369–71. The idea is supported by two of Hölderlin's letters; in 1801, he remarks to Böhlendorff that 'das Eigene muß so gut gelernt sein wie das Fremde' (that which is native has to be learnt as much as that which is foreign), and in 1804, in a letter to Wilmans about his *Œdipus der Tyrann*, he hopes to have written against 'die exzentrische Begeisterung' (eccentric inspiration) in order to attain 'die griechische Einfalt' (Greek simplicity) (*Kleine Stuttgarter Ausgabe*, vi. 456 and 469, respectively).

61. Blanchot, *L'Amitié*, 249.

62. Blanchot, *L'Amitié*, 251.

63. Cf. 'Une Passion': 'En écrivant *La Veille*, je me référais souvent à un texte, au demeurant voisin de celui que je citais à tort: "Comment découvrir l'obscur?", texte paru en 1959' (*DLMB* 130). The essay appeared in the *Nouvelle Revue Française* 83 (1959), 867–79, and is reprinted in *L'Entretien infini*, 57–69; the passage I have quoted is at 66.

64. Blanchot, *L'Entretien infini*, 68.

65. I refer to Levinas here to shed light on the relation to the other in *La Veille*, not as an influence. Roger Laporte has indicated to me that, at that time, he did not yet know Levinas's work. When *La Veille* was republished in *Une Vie*, Laporte introduced the dedication, as it had been the work of Laporte most admired by Levinas.

66. 'La trace de l'autre', first published in *Tijdschrift voor Filosofie* 3 (1963), reprinted in *En découvrant l'existence avec Husserl et Heidegger*, 2nd edn. (Paris: Vrin, 1976), 187–202 (190); references immediately hereafter are given in the text.

67. Emmanuel Levinas, 'Roger Laporte et la voix de fin silence', *Noms propres* (Montpellier: Fata Morgana, 1976, reprinted in 'Livre de Poche', collection 'Biblio: essais'), 105.

68. The translation arose from a conversation between Levinas and Laporte about Christian mysticism. For details of this, and some remarks on the translation, see Laporte's essay on Levinas, '"Il n'est pas de Présent, non—un présent n'existe pas"' (*E* 235–40).

69. Clémence Ramnoux, 'Accompagnement pour *Une Voix de fin silence*', *Critique* 235 (1966), 990–5 (991).

70. Laporte refers to this part of Blanchot's *récit* in *DLMB* 73, *QV* 27, and *E* 37–8; in the last two of these references, he suggests the parallel with Kafka's *Josephine the Singer*.

71. Maurice Blanchot, *Au Moment voulu* (Paris: Gallimard, 1951), 68–9; my emphases.

72. Blanchot, *Au Moment voulu*, 70.

73. Levinas, *Le Temps et l'autre*, 26; my emphasis.

74. This piece first appeared in *L'Arc* 22 (1963), 'René Char', 9–14; an amended version appears in Blanchot, *L'Entretien infini*, 439–46 (442, and 443 for the subsequent reference).

75. 'Lire Roger Laporte', in Jean Ristat, *Qui sont les contemporains* (Paris: Gallimard, 1975), 281–300 (285) (reprinted from *Les Lettres françaises* 1453 (1972)).

76. 'Entretien entre Roger Laporte et Serge Velay (janvier 1980)', *Autour de Roger Laporte* (Nîmes: Cahiers de littérature 'Terriers', 1980), 11–18 (15).

77. I think these remarks have to be taken to refer to both volumes of the work. Certainly, *Pourquoi?* does not escape Laporte's rebukes; in another interview, Laporte describes it as 'l'ouvrage le plus mauvais, le plus raté que j'ai écrit' ('Entretien entre Mathieu Bénézet, Roger Laporte et Jean Ristat', *Digraphe* 18/19 (1979), 121–55 (145).

78. Ramnoux, 'Accompagnement pour *Une Voix de fin silence*', 994.

79. Catherine Backès-Clément, 'Histoire d'un sourire', *Critique* 276 (1970), 413–37 (436). Clément here analyses *Une Voix de fin silence* and *Pourquoi?* from a Lacanian perspective. I do not discuss it here, simply because, in Ch. 4, I consider Laporte's work from a psychoanalytic perspective.

80. Levinas, *Noms propres*, 106.

81. Levinas, *Noms propres*, 107. For an account of Laporte's part in the 'affaire Beaufret' of 1967, when Laporte insists that he heard Beaufret make anti-Semitic remarks with regard to an impending academic appointment (the target of these remarks being none other than Levinas), see Christophe Bident's *Maurice Blanchot: partenaire invisible* (Seyssel: Champ Vallon, 1998), 463–8. In 'Heidegger, Beaufret et le politique: témoignage et réflexions sur une longue occultation', *Lendemains* 65 (1992), 72–4, Laporte indicated that the dedication of *Pourquoi?* ('A tous mes amis juifs') was prompted by the 1967 affair.

82. Besides Richardson's work, already cited, my understanding of the *Ereignis* has been assisted by Albert Hofstadter's Introduction to his translations of Heidegger collected in *Poetry, Language, Thought*, pp. ix–xxii, and his article 'Enownment', *Boundary 2* 4:2 (1976), 357–77, and by John Llewelyn's *Beyond Metaphysics? The hermeneutic circle in contemporary Continental philosophy* (Atlantic Highlands, NJ: Humanities Press, 1985), 18–29.

83. Albert Hofstadter, 'Enownment', 369.

84. Hugh J. Silverman, 'Derrida, Heidegger, and the Time of the Line', in *Continental Philosophy II: Derrida and Deconstruction*, ed. Hugh J. Silverman (London and New York: Routledge, 1989), 154–68 (159).

85. Martin Heidegger, *Identity and Difference* (New York: Harper and Row, 1969), 37–8.

86. Apart from *Identity and Difference*, see also, e.g., Heidegger, *Poetry, Language, Thought*, 207.

87. Heidegger, *Identity and Difference*, 73.

88. Timothy Clark, 'Not Motion, but a Mime of it: "Rhythm" in the Textuality of Heidegger's Work', *Paragraph* 9:1 (1987), 69–82 (80).

CHAPTER 3

Writing as Fugue

i. *Brisure*

Laporte's literary enterprise is marked through and through by rupture and revision. Within individual works, propositions are advanced, metaphors offered, projects outlined, later to be rejected and, often, later still to be re-introduced in modified form; this is already the case in the texts of the 1960s which we have been considering, and, as we shall see, this process becomes even more manifest in Laporte's later work. Moreover, the process may also be discerned on a broader scale between the individual works which comprise Laporte's *œuvre*. Laporte destroyed his first significant literary endeavour, with the working title of *Genèse d'un roman*, retaining only the chapter later published as *Souvenir de Reims*.[1] We have already noted the transitions between the early *récits* and *La Veille*, and between the latter and the two volumes of *Une Voix de fin silence*, and have seen that in each case the transition contained elements of both continuity and discontinuity. However, the break between *Pourquoi?* and *Fugue* appears to be the least ambivalent of all those in Laporte's literary itinerary, in Laporte's own eyes at least. In the previous chapter, we already noted some of Laporte's scathing remarks about the two volumes of *Une Voix de fin silence*. We might add here that, in answer to Jean Ristat's question as to whether he would like to erase these earlier works, Laporte in 1972 replied, 'Si je le pouvais, en effet',[2] echoing a sentiment expressed in the *Carnets* in 1970: 'A la rigueur, je conserverais *La Veille* (et d'abord *Une Migration*) mais je voudrais *anéantir Une Voix de fin silence 1* et *2*: je suis et ne veux être rien d'autre que l'auteur de *Fugue*; c'est ainsi' (*C* 296). Yet, even at this stage, Laporte goes on to consider the possibility that he might one day regard *Fugue* in an equally disparaging light, adding that, although the possibility seems most unlikely to him at that time, on the other hand '"j'espère" qu'il en sera pourtant ainsi, car cela prouverait le mouvement (le déportement), ma seule et dure loi' (*C* 296).

In point of fact, another major break in Laporte's work does indeed ensue in the transition from *Fugue 3* to *Suite*, so that by the time of the interview with Serge Velay in 1980, Laporte already feels distanced from a good deal of the *Fugue* series,[3] and after the ultimate break of his abandonment of his thirty-year-old literary enterprise following the completion of *Moriendo*, he writes, in the notebooks subsequently published as *Lettre à personne*, of *Moriendo* as 'mon livre ultime, le seul que j'aurais jamais dû écrire' (*LP* 33).[4] From the point of view of our present concerns, it is interesting to note that this more detached perspective on the achievement marked by the *Fugue* series seems to be accompanied by something of a revaluation of the earlier works; later in the same notebooks Laporte observes that

Fugue est le premier de mes ouvrages à s'inscrire dans le genre 'biographie', à fonder ce genre, mais en réalité tous mes livres, par conséquent même *Une Voix de fin silence*, même *La Veille*, et d'une certaine manière même *Souvenir de Reims*, appartiennent plus ou moins à ce genre; il se pourrait, au demeurant, que *Fugue*, *Suite* et même *Fugue 3* (avant le codicille) relèvent bien moins du genre 'biographie' que *La Veille*! (*LP* 55)

The extension of the important generic designation of *biographie*, a term whose significance will be explored later in this chapter, to the works of the 1960s is consolidated by the inclusion of these works in the collected volume *Une Vie*, which also bears the sub-title *biographie*.[5]

In brief, although there are good reasons for regarding the break between *Pourquoi?* and *Fugue* as the most decisive in Laporte's literary career, there are elements of continuity even in this transition. Like all the transitions between the individual works or series of works, and indeed like the divisions between the sequences of which most of Laporte's works are composed, the break before *Fugue* may be described as a *brisure*, in the sense suggested by Laporte to Derrida, whose use of the term in *De la grammatologie* is headed by an extract from a letter from Laporte which signals the useful ambiguity of the word *brisure*, designating both 'la différence et l'articulation'.[6] The *brisure*, then, between *Pourquoi?* and *Fugue* is both disjunction and articulation, in the sense not just that it is a transition containing elements of both continuity and discontinuity, but also that it is a transition whose significance will not be exhausted, witness Laporte's own re-readings of this break and the re-working of the break effected by the publication of *Une Vie*: we shall not arrive at the truth of this rupture, but we can identify some of its constituent elements.

It is of course no accident that I have just invoked the name of Jacques Derrida; *Fugue* is dedicated to Jacques and Marguerite Derrida, and a good deal of this chapter will be devoted to a consideration of the extent to which the transformation in Laporte's writing in the early 1970s is attributable to the impact of Derrida's work. In 'Bief'—one of three pieces by Laporte devoted to Derrida's work and published in the early 1970s, and the one which most clearly signals the consequences of that work for Laporte's own writing—Laporte acknowledges the importance of his correspondence with Derrida, beginning with a letter by Derrida dating from August 1965 which initiated for him a 'cheminement de taupe' (a phrase he borrows from Derrida) leading to his first work on *Fugue* early in 1967 (cf. *B* 68).[7] The severity of Laporte's own judgement on his earlier works which characterizes this period is again apparent in this text, in which he remarks of the three works of the 1960s that 'faute de pouvoir rétroactivement les supprimer, je ne me prive pas du moins de les désavouer' (*B* 65–6), but this remark is made after Laporte has felt obliged, in order to explain Derrida's impact on his work, to record Derrida's own enthusiasm for those earlier works, notwithstanding his preference for *Fugue*. Whatever antipathy Laporte feels for his earlier works at this stage, his account of Derrida's influence on him ends up underlining the ambivalence of the transition which led to *Fugue*, as what he describes as the 'percée' effected by Derrida is recognized by Laporte as having opened up for him 'un chemin jusqu'à "moi-même", jusqu'à mon "archi-projet" d'écrivain, ébauché dès 1945 et resté irréalisé', and Derrida's reading of his earlier works is said to have allowed him to '"passer à autre chose", proposition qui m'amène à admettre que, par un certain biais, il doit y avoir quelque liaison, malgré que j'en aie, entre mon passé d'écrivain et mon présent' (*B* 68). Besides recalling the extent to which the break between *Pourquoi?* and *Fugue* is an ambivalent *brisure*, Laporte's remarks in 'Bief', whilst stressing the importance of Derrida's influence, also signal the extent to which Laporte's earlier work prepared the way for the transformation wrought in part by that very influence. Indeed, it is with some hesitation that I use the term 'influence', since the relationship between Laporte and Derrida, manifested at its clearest in the transition from *Pourquoi?* to *Fugue*, is rather better conceived as the convergence of two almost parallel paths; we should not forget their common inheritance of a philosophical tradition in which Heidegger and Nietzsche loom largest with, inescapably, the figure of Hegel in the background, and of a French tradition of literature and thought comprising the likes of Mallarmé, Valéry, Artaud, Bataille, Blanchot and Levinas. The entries in Laporte's *Carnets* for 1967 include a number of discussions of the achievements and limitations of his earlier works placed under the heading of 'TRACES', which Laporte at one point (*C* 264) suggests will be the generic designation for the new form of writing towards which he is working, and which also of course marks the impact of Derrida's work whilst at the same time recalling the shared inheritance I have just indicated (it is also a term used by Heidegger and Levinas).[8] When Laporte comes to outline his plans for the new work, elements of continuity with his earlier work, going right back to *Souvenir de Reims*, are immediately apparent. The narrator's desire to bridge the gap between language and object, or language and experience, which we noted in that first published *récit*, for instance, is echoed by an entry in the *Carnets*, in which Laporte notes the division which ordinarily obtains between language and referent, and writes of his wish to 'trouver un langage qui [...] ne soit pas en dehors de la "chose" que pourtant il "nommerait"' (*C* 257). In *Fugue* itself we find the scriptor,[9] surveying his work in the ninth and final sequence, recording his failure to fulfil a project which he describes in very similar terms: 'Le langage ordinaire est distinct du référent qu'il désigne ou signifie: j'ai rêvé d'écrire une œuvre où forme, contenu et référent auraient été non seulement inséparables, mais à jamais confondus' (*F* 316). Furthermore, in the same entry in the *Carnets* just cited, Laporte goes on to suggest that the inseparability of language and referent will be partly attributable to a feature which we have already encountered in *La Veille* and *Pourquoi?*, namely a certain conception of language as rhythm: 'Il faudrait que "la chose à dire" = X soit inséparable du langage, entendu non seulement comme vocabulaire, syntaxe, mais surtout comme *rythme*' (*C* 257). The undefined referent, designated here simply as 'X', reveals in turn another aspect of continuity with Laporte's earlier work, in this case an unnameable dimension which is the very condition of a language which can never bring it to expression, and whose metamorphoses we have observed from the ineffable experience of *Souvenir de Reims*, through the *lui* of *La Veille* which is both the impetus and the obstacle of writing, to the silent voice and the unattainable *événement* of the two volumes of *Une Voix de fin silence*. Clearly, this continuity is not lost on Laporte, but he is careful to stipulate the new direction of his projected work, as, having written of his plan to show the relationship between writing, the 'je écrivant', and this unknown 'X', he adds: 'J'ai toujours eu ce projet, mais sur ce point j'ai toujours échoué puisqu'il ne s'agit ni d'un *il* substantiel, ni d'une "voix de fin silence"' (*C* 261). The danger which, it would seem, Laporte finds in the approach adopted in his earlier works is the reification of the unknown 'X', or its reduction to the realm of the author's personal experience, which would then be translated in the work; this approach therefore masks the inseparability of 'X' and the writing itself. Rather than attempting to find another figure for this 'X', then, with the concomitant risk of falsely presenting it as an entity, Laporte proposes both to highlight the *relationship* with 'X', 'ce rapport de liaison et d'opposition entre l'écriture et X' (*C* 262), and to dispel any suggestion that 'X' pertains to some experience prior to writing: 'Peu m'importe, si je puis dire, l'effet sur l'écrivain: je ne veux pas avoir à retraduire ce vécu dans l'œuvre, mais ce qui m'importe c'est l'effet de X *dans* l'œuvre, *sur* l'œuvre, "le mouvement qui déplace les lignes" (Derrida)' (*C* 263).

The importance of this determination to render the unknown referent and the writing itself inseparable can hardly be over-emphasized, and not surprisingly it is a characteristic of the transition between *Pourquoi?* and *Fugue* which has been noted by Laporte's commentators, such as Philippe Lacoue-Labarthe and Jean-Luc Nancy who, having on the one hand asserted the continuity of Laporte's enterprise, observe that in the earlier works 'l'objet, si l'on veut, de l'entreprise—la vie ou l'écriture, la vie et l'écriture, bref, l'inconnu—était encore posé comme quelque chose d'extérieur'.[10] By contrast with what Lacoue-Labarthe and Nancy call the 'forme "poétique"' of the earlier works, which for them inclined towards mysticism and perhaps negative theology, and which defined Laporte's enterprise as a 'quête de l'inconnu', *Fugue* and the later works are instead an 'enquête', 'portant sur quelque chose qui n'a pas eu lieu, ou qui n'a pas de lieu hors de l'enquête même'.[11] That writing will now be placed firmly in the foreground, and that this writing should not be taken for the translation of something prior to the text, such as the lived experience of the writer, is stated clearly enough at the outset of *Fugue*, even though the hesitancy of the opening of this work indicates the scriptor's uncertainty about the consequences of this programme:

Pourquoi ne commencerais-je pas par cette remarque que je comprends mal et qui m'étonne moi-même? J'attends de l'ouvrage à écrire ce que l'on demande d'habitude à la vie, ou même je vais jusqu'à croire que je peux, quant à moi, tenir pour négligeables les événements de ma vie d'homme, voire ceux du monde, en regard de ce qui peut m'arriver en écrivant, de ce qui ne pourra arriver que dans la mesure où j'écrirai. (*F* 255)

The tentative first paragraph concludes with an indication of how far writing and the unknown 'X' discussed in the *Carnets* have become inseparable ('Qu'est-ce qu'écrire? Je retrouve la phrase écartée par laquelle j'aurais pu tout aussi bien commencer: écrire m'est inconnu', *F* 255) and this inseparability is indicated again in the final sentence of the first sequence of *Fugue*, in which Ricardou's famous distinction between the 'écriture d'une aventure' and the 'aventure d'une écriture'[12] is clearly echoed, and in which the qualifying 'en partie' functions as a warning that, inseparable as they may be, writing and the unknown referent are not absolutely coterminous, and that whatever the scriptor is seeking will not be a simple presence in the text; it will, in some sense, remain unreadable: 'Ecrire m'est inconnu, et ainsi la réponse se borne à redoubler la question: ce serait seulement dans le livre que se produirait, et, en partie, pourrait se lire l'aventure d'une écriture inconnue' (*F* 257).

By the time that *Fugue* is written, the new genre proposed in the *Carnets* under the heading of *Traces* has become *biographie*, the subtitle of *Fugue* and subsequent works. We shall have cause to return to this term a number of times in our discussion, but let me begin by noting here the etymological combination of life and writing in *biographie*; this is the feature of the term first noted by the scriptor of *Fugue*, just after the opening lines already cited, when he gives it as the provisional title of his work, with the explanation that his enterprise is linked in some way with the act of writing, 'acte qui ne serait plus subordonné ou accessoire puisque ni en fait ni en droit, ma vie—une certaine vie—ne pourrait en être séparée' (*F* 255). The qualification that writing is inseparable from 'une *certaine* vie' is indicative that the determination to exclude the lived experience of the writer, expressed in the *Carnets*, has not been forgotten; indeed, earlier in this same paragraph, the scriptor has emphasized that this work is not to be an autobiography. Besides foregrounding writing in a work which, without any external reference, will make life and writing synonymous, this new genre is also, we discover, intended to lay bare the processes of thought; in the third sequence of *Fugue*, the scriptor notes that he seems to have been afforded the possibility of fulfilling 'un très ancien projet', which he describes, citing a famous formula from Breton's first *Manifeste du surréalisme*, as 'écrire un livre qui soit à lui-même son contenu, qui produise et inscrive sa propre formation, projet dicté par le souci de mettre à jour *le fonctionnement réel de la pensée*' (F 262; my emphasis). The scriptor's ambition for the work is that it should carry the trace of the very movements of thought, that the blank page should become a 'scriptogramme' inscribed by thought; underlining the inextrication of writing and thought, the scriptor later, in the seventh sequence, reaffirms this project of writing 'un livre où s'imprimerait l'aventure de l'esprit, livre qui serait *un noogramme ou un scriptogramme* dans la mesure où la pensée ni ne parle, ni ne se donne dans aucune appréhension immédiate, mais réserve au lecteur sagace la possibilité de déchiffrer sur texte sa trace multiple' (F 290; my emphasis). The reciprocal illumination of writing and thought in a highly self-reflexive work is central to Laporte's new project, and it is a feature which affords us some insight into the impact of Derrida's work on Laporte.

Time and again Laporte stresses that the new genre he wishes to inaugurate should be such that it could not be subsumed under either of those domains of activity which we associate with the fore-grounding of writing and thought respectively, namely, literature and philosophy. Throughout his career, Laporte has been interested in writing in such a way as to combine or escape existing categories; as early as 1948 we find him asking 'Comment faire la synthèse du mémoire, du journal ... et du roman?' (C 22). In the middle of 1962, therefore after the completion of *La Veille* and before his first work on *Une Voix de fin silence*, Laporte, trying to situate his own writing in respect of existing categories, considers it to be closer to religion than art, but prefers to see himself as inventing 'une forme nouvelle qui ne soit ni philosophie, ni art, ni religion' (C 161). In 1967, as a conclusion to an entry in the *Carnets* devoted to summarizing his ambitions for the new genre of *Traces*, Laporte writes: 'Créer du moins une nouvelle *forme* littéraire, et peut-être parvenir enfin à rompre avec l'art en créant un *genre* autre que la littérature ou que la philosophie mais qui intégrerait certaines de leurs œuvres sous le nouveau concept de TRACES' (C 271). The concern with the instigation of a new type of writing is carried through into *Fugue* itself. At times, the emphasis falls on the reflexivity of the work which, in so far as it does not translate any lived experience prior to the act of writing, renders writing and a certain sort of life inseparable and thereby 'contribuerait à instaurer une nouvelle forme littéraire et—pourquoi pas?—un genre encore presque inconnu, genre qu'à titre tout provisoire on pourrait appeler poème ou récit critique' (*F* 276). At other times, the scriptor focuses on the intertwining of writing and thought as the source of the originality of his project, which is therefore situated on the borderline between literature and philosophy, as in this passage, after which, we should note, the scriptor suggests that his ambition will perhaps never be crowned by achievement, since his errant enterprise proves to be a perpetual process of creation and destruction: 'Mon ambition d'écrivain n'a pas été seulement d'augmenter la littérature d'un genre encore peu connu, mais de participer à l'instauration d'un ordre, ne se réduisant ni à la philosophie ni à la littérature dont il est pourtant issu, nouveau règne que l'on pourrait appeler scriptographie' (*F* 310). In 'Bief', Laporte recalls once again the longstanding ambition to 'faire une "œuvre" qui ne soit réductible ni à la littérature, ni à la philosophie' (*B* 66), and it is through this essay, read in conjunction with another essay on Merleau-Ponty, that we can begin to understand Derrida's role in shaping the guise which this ambition takes in Laporte's later work.

In the essay on Derrida, Laporte says he does not propose to comment on this ambition, adding that he has already touched on it in a study of Merleau-Ponty's 'Hyperdialectique'.[13] In the latter piece, Laporte chooses to focus on a few pages of Merleau-Ponty's *Le Visible et l'invisible* in which the notion of the dialectic is brought to bear on the relation of *l'Etre* and *le Néant* in perception. The application of the dialectic to the problem which Merleau-Ponty has been pursuing in this work is appropriate inasmuch as '"la pensée dialectique [...] admet que chaque terme n'est lui-même qu'en se portant vers le terme opposé, devient ce qu'il est par le mouvement"' (cited in *QV* 160). Moreover, adds Laporte in his summary of Merleau-Ponty's argument, dialectical thought does not describe this movement from a securely transcendental vantage-point, but rather participates in it (we might say, *is* this movement), forging its own path as it proceeds. Given its singular appropriateness to the task in hand, Merleau-Ponty then asks why the appearance of the dialectic should have been delayed until this stage of his discussion. The answer lies in the instability of the dialectic as it has manifested itself in the history of philosophy. This instability does not supervene upon the dialectic but is rather congenital with it, inasmuch as the dialectic is a perpetual process or movement, 'un devenir sans fin' (*QV* 162) as Laporte says, which is inevitably falsified by being fixed in a philosophical thesis about it.

Merleau-Ponty's problem in respecting the endless mobility of the dialectic in a philosophical work may already have suggested parallels with problems of expression in Laporte's own work, from the ecstatic experience of *Souvenir de Reims* to the *événement* of *Une Voix de fin silence*. Such parallels are underlined when, in the face of this difficulty, Merleau-Ponty wonders whether '"Si l'on veut garder l'esprit [de la dialectique], il faut peut-être même ne pas la nommer"' (*QV* 162). If the temptation of silence in the face of such difficulties recalls Laporte's earlier work, the alternative solution adopted by Merleau-Ponty in turn points, as we shall see, to Laporte's practice in the *Fugue* series. Given that the instability of the dialectic is no mere accident inflicted on it by the history of philosophy, but is rather its defining characteristic as ceaselessly mobile thought, then the best means of preserving the dialectic would be to provoke that instability. Laporte remarks that this is precisely what Merleau-Ponty does, as 'loin de se contenter de parler de la dialectique, de survoler ses difficultés, [il] se fraye difficilement un chemin, pratique cette dialectique, la sauvegarde en la contestant, car toute affirmation contredirait son propre contenu: le mouvement, en le figeant en une théorie' (*QV* 163). Merleau-Ponty distinguishes therefore between a 'bonne dialectique' and a 'mauvaise dialectique'. The good dialectic is one which constantly operates a form of auto-criticism and attacks any thesis which would reduce the dialectic to stasis: this is what Merleau-Ponty calls the 'hyperdialectique'. The bad dialectic, on the other hand, is one which is teleologically disposed towards a stable resolution, and is not surprisingly associated by Merleau-Ponty with the name of Hegel, although Laporte in his study sketches the outline of a rehabilitation of the Hegelian dialectic. For Laporte, it is the conception of the 'hyperdialectique' in Merleau-Ponty's unfinished study which points the way forward to subsequent developments in French philosophy, whereas the continued preoccupation with what seems to be an immutable *Etre* threatens to shackle Merleau-Ponty to the tradition he is questioning.

The Janus-like role which Laporte accords to Merleau-Ponty's thought in respect of the philosophical tradition has a striking parallel in the transition in Laporte's own work from the texts of the 1960s, in which the resolution of the dilemmas encountered in those works was constantly sought in the form of a unitary origin, which on many occasions resembled Heideggerian Being, to his later work which shares with the 'hyperdialectique' the constantly renewed process of auto-criticism, as the scriptor's accounts of his activity are repeatedly contested and modified, and which, notwithstanding its reflexivity, resists the paralysis of becoming a thesis *on* writing: 'toute pratique, en particulier une fois que l'on est enfin parvenu à en faire la théorie, est tôt ou tard contredite, du moins partiellement, par une autre pratique, et ainsi indéfiniment, contradiction dont il faut apprendre à se réjouir puisqu'elle provoque cette brusque dénivellation du texte sans laquelle l'écriture, qui aime à remembrer le volume épars, serait condamnée à une oisiveté mortelle' (*F* 305). In the final lines of his study, Laporte wonders whether not only ontology but philosophy in general, in so far as it tends towards totalization, is incompatible with the 'hyperdialectique', and finally expresses his own gratitude to Merleau-Ponty for an answer given twenty-five years earlier to his question about the future of philosophy: '"Il ne s'agit pas de faire une autre philosophie, mais autre chose que la philosophie"' (*QV* 168). With this suggestion of an escape from the *impasse* envisaged by Laporte, we return therefore to the project of an *œuvre* irreducible to literature or philosophy mentioned in 'Bief'. However, before leaving Laporte's study of Merleau-Ponty, we should note an earlier indication of what might constitute 'autre chose que la philosophie'. Just after he first introduces the idea of a form of thought which, in rigorous pursuit of the dialectic's logic of instability, would create its own path as it proceeded, Laporte suggests a parallel for this hyperdialectical thought: 'Cette pensée qui fait elle-même sa route, qui se trace et laisse ainsi une marque, n'est-ce pas ce que notre modernité appelle écriture?' (*QV* 161). This suggestion is then given a more precise orientation, as Laporte makes a *rapprochement* with the work of Derrida, citing a passage in the latter's 'Freud et la scène de l'écriture', which describes the '"travail *itinérant* de la trace, produisant et non parcourant sa route [...] la trace qui trace [...] la trace qui se fraye elle-même son chemin"' (*QV* 161).[14] Of course, in connecting the name of Derrida with the pursuit of 'autre chose que la philosophie', we should not forget Derrida's own insistence on the impossibility of contesting the philosophical tradition simply by stepping outside of it;[15] indeed, it is precisely in the recognition of this impossibility that Laporte locates Derrida's impact on his work.

In 'Bief', Laporte begins his account of Derrida's role in the transition that led to *Fugue* by citing a phrase from Derrida's essay on Mallarmé, 'La double séance', in which, having demonstrated how Mallarmé's text 'Mimique' works against the notion of mimesis as a simple referential correspondence between language and reality (underpinned by the notion of truth as *adaequatio*), Derrida warns against reading Mallarmé's text as anti-referential, since this would permit the return of a notion of mimetic truth, now as *aletheia*, according to which the text would efface itself to allow the unveiling of the thing itself as a pure presence. Laporte cites part of this warning, replacing the word 'mimétologisme' with 'métaphysique': "'A vouloir renverser [la métaphysique] ou à prétendre lui échapper d'un coup en sautant simplement *à pieds joints*, on retombe sûrement et immédiatement dans son système'" (*B* 66).[16] Laporte considers that he made this very mistake in his earlier works, in which, motivated by the project to which he still holds of producing a work pertaining neither to literature nor to philosophy, he thought to have stepped outside of philosophy from the outset; but he now observes that 'le geste par lequel je croyais conquérir l'indépendance était en effet celui qui m'enchaînait le plus insidieusement à un champ culturel dont je demeurais inconscient' (*B* 66). It is in respect of this realization that he feels his greatest debt to Derrida, and he goes on to cite a letter written early in 1966 in which Derrida, in what will be recognized as a characteristic gesture, remarks that "'je ne crois pas à un dedans et à un dehors de l'histoire de la philosophie. Je me sens aussi peu en elle que je vous crois hors d'elle'" (*B* 67). Derrida does not believe in an inside or outside of the history of philosophy because, as he has demonstrated in a series of celebrated readings, in the course of that history the purity of that philosophical domain has always been sought, and therefore the sanctity of its boundaries preserved, by means of the exclusion and debasement of a certain conception of writing; in the 'Exergue' to *De la grammatologie*, for instance, he observes that the history of metaphysics 'a toujours assigné au logos l'origine de la vérité en général: l'histoire de la vérité, de la vérité de la vérité, a toujours été [...] l'abaissement de l'écriture et son refoulement hors de la parole "pleine"'.[17] Philosophy has therefore consistently defined itself in contradistinction to a domain such as literature which accords a privileged status to writing. However, in this defining and, Derrida would argue, necessary gesture of exclusion, philosophy places outside of itself an agency which continues its clandestine work within philosophy, undermining the truths to which philosophy could only lay claim by virtue of the repression of writing. In the very gesture which would seek to preserve its boundaries, therefore, philosophy has established an unstable, chiastic relation between inside and outside. The ambivalent *brisure* which articulates philosophy and non-philosophy, philosophy and literature for example, hinges around writing, the *écriture* which Laporte saw as a parallel for Merleau-Ponty's hyperdialectic which respects the 'devenir sans fin' of dialectical thought, and which is foregrounded in Laporte's attempt, in *Fugue*, to found a new genre irreducible to literature or philosophy. We will better appreciate what is novel in that attempt if we first consider the extent to which Laporte's earlier works are trapped in a tradition he thought to have evaded.

In 'Bief', Laporte suggests that the weakness in his earlier work which was most clearly highlighted by being viewed through a Derridean optic was the reliance on a notion of lived experience which the text sought to translate. We can gauge the importance Laporte attributed to this weakness by the fact that he discusses the Derridean deconstruction of the notion of experience not only in 'Bief' but also in his two other studies of Derrida written in the early 1970s. In 'Une double stratégie', referring once again to the passage in Derrida's 'La double séance' which asserts the impossibility of simply stepping out of the philosophical tradition, Laporte criticizes 'ceux qui prétendent dépasser la métaphysique parce que, disent-ils, ils se fondent sur un vécu',[18] since the attempt to contest the tradition by recourse to such an empiricism remains firmly within the metaphysics of presence. In respect of his own work, Laporte evokes in '"Les 'blancs' assument l'importance"' the writer who imagines that his/her 'expérience littéraire' is an experience which already evades the philosophical domain. In a clear allusion to the two volumes of *Une Voix de fin silence*, Laporte notes that he would never have explored the idea of being 'à l'écoute' in search of the 'voix silencieuse' of an originary experience if he had not read Heraclitus and Heidegger; that is to say that his recourse to a supposedly pre-textual experience is already bound up in the philosophical tradition, and that that experience is not a direct *donnée* but is always already mediated by the tradition: 'il n'y a jamais expérience pure, mais toujours interprétation.'[19] Citing Derrida's *La Voix et le phénomène*, Laporte signals the rapport of a Heideggerian attentiveness to the call of immediate Being, or experience, with the phonocentric privileging of the voice which arises from what Derrida calls the system of 's'entendre-parler'. In 'Bief', as indeed in 'Une double stratégie', Laporte cites the following passage from *De la grammatologie*: '"Expérience" a toujours désigné le rapport à une présence, que ce rapport ait ou non la forme de la conscience.'[20] Laporte goes on to underline the complicity of the notion of experience with the metaphysics of presence by enumerating the systematically interlinked concepts of presence, origin, and 'expérience du proche et du propre' and asserting their common reliance on the idea of an original voice derived from the phonocentrism of the 's'entendre-parler': 'la voix, cette voix, origine du pur signifié, du sens, de Dieu comme Logos, de l'Esprit, puisqu'elle croit s'entendre-parler en l'absence du corps' (*B* 67). When Laporte goes on to write of a voice which one cannot say one has heard or not heard, and of a speaking silence, the reflection on his own earlier work is unmistakably clear. However, before unreservedly consenting to the condemnation of his earlier work invited by 'Bief' by hastily dismissing that work as an acquiescent continuation of the logocentric tradition, we should look more closely at what Derrida writes about experience in the passage cited earlier by Laporte from *De la grammatologie*.

Derrida's remarks on experience are contained in a passage of the chapter 'Linguistique et grammatologie' concerning the work of the Danish linguist Louis Hjelmslev, whose 'glossematics' purported to be the objective science of language as a formal system, excluding from consideration the substance of language: '"Puisque la langue est une forme et non une substance (F. de Saussure), les glossèmes sont par définition indépendants de la substance, immatérielle (sémantique, psychologique et logique) et matérielle (phonique, graphique, etc.)"'.[21] While Derrida is quick to acknowledge the significance of both this bracketing of substance, inasmuch as it evades the phonocentrism to which Saussure falls prey, and of the parity accorded to speech and writing, which opens the way for the study of the specificity of writing, he is also at pains to point out that the conception of writing which emerges from the work of the Copenhagen School cannot be assimilated to what he terms *archi-écriture*. The latter cannot form part of the linguistic system as described by Hjelmslev, although it is the condition of any such system, making possible but at the same time problematizing the distinctions with which Hjelmslev operates (expression/content, form/substance, etc.). Derrida suggests that Hjelmslev would have rejected the notion of an *archi-écriture* underpinning the linguistic system without forming part of it as the very sort of appeal to experience which theory must exclude. This brings us to the crux of the problem of experience, for although Derrida notes the complicity of the notion of experience with the metaphysics of presence, and acknowledges the legitimacy of excluding a certain sort of experience from the field of linguistic theory, he none the less insists on the need to continue to work with the notion of experience in order to discover, by a process of deconstruction, another field of experience, described at one point as 'l'expérience comme archi-écriture'.[22] As with other key terms which underpin the metaphysics of presence, then, Derrida proposes to retain the notion of experience provisionally since it will necessarily harbour the seeds of deconstruction of the very tradition which it has helped to maintain. Simply to reject the notion of experience outright, for example, would give rise to an idealism no less in the thrall of the metaphysics of presence than the empiricism one had sought to avoid.

Returning to the question of Laporte's break with his earlier work, we saw in each of his works of the 1960s that writing was the response to an exigency attributed to some pre-textual domain, whether that took the form of the subject's ambivalent relationship with *lui* in *La Veille*, or the inspirational call of a silent voice in the two volumes of *Une Voix de fin silence*. In this light, it does indeed seem plausible to suggest that writing translated a prior experience, and that the separation of writing and experience was underlined when the return of that experience could only be retrospectively recorded or anticipated in the text. However, we also saw in *La Veille* that the relationship of *lui* to the *œuvre* shared the ambivalence of the relationship between *lui* and the subject, in that it was only in the *œuvre* that *il* could be discovered as 'indécouvrable'. Our discussion of these ambivalent relationships in *La Veille* led us to the conclusion that, if we are to talk of 'expérience' in this work, then it must be in terms of a notion of experience traversed by alterity or, in Levinas's phrase, of an 'expérience hétéronome'; such a conception of experience, far from consolidating the self-identity of the subject or the accomplishment of the *œuvre*, instead reveals the dispossession of the subject in its relationship with the other and the *désœuvrement* at the heart of the *œuvre*. On the other hand, we also saw that, in *Une Voix de fin silence* and *Pourquoi?*, the originary *événement* and the inspirational silent voice are repeatedly characterized as gifts, and this generosity of the extra-textual experience, in tandem with the greater sense of security in these works noted, for instance, by Clémence Ramnoux, does rather suggest, in contrast with *La Veille*, a conception of experience which reinforces the ipseity of the subject and which, more broadly, is complicit with the metaphysics of presence. However, we also noted Levinas's observation that, at times in *Une Voix de fin silence*, 'l'événement ressemble à la sortie de soi, au passage du Même à l'absolument Autre'.[23] Although it seems fair to say that the later two works represent a step back from *La Veille* in this regard, the notion of experience suggested by all three of these works is one which participates in a tradition which was already probing a field of experience that offers a dislocation of the metaphysics of presence.

This tradition, to which both Laporte and Derrida are indebted, includes most notably Bataille, Levinas and Blanchot. Bataille's conception of experience is one in which the incompletion of the subject is revealed in its involvement with the other; he insists that 'l'expérience intérieure est conquête et comme telle *pour autrui!* Le sujet dans l'expérience s'égare, il se perd dans l'objet, qui lui-même se dissout.'[24] We have already noted Levinas's conception of an 'expérience hétéronome' as a movement without return towards the other, which he distinguishes from an experience which involves the other as alter ego only to reinforce the self-identity of the subject.[25] We first noted this conception in our discussion of *La Veille*, and it was in the course of considering the influences on that text that we cited Blanchot's remark in the essay 'Comment découvrir l'obscur?' that 'il n'y a expérience au sens strict que là où quelque chose de radicalement *autre* est en jeu',[26] a remark characteristic of Blanchot's deployment of the term 'expérience' which, as Joseph Libertson observes, 'is not experience, in its familiar and philosophical definition, but precisely the impossibility of the latter'.[27] In 'Bief', Laporte recognizes that the notion of experience which emerges from his earlier works is one which, to varying degrees, is already at odds with the 'expérience du proche et du propre', the deconstruction of which he had credited to Derrida a page earlier. Following an extract from a letter from Derrida which signals the impossibility of the 'Fête' or the 'maintenant' of writing (since writing is 'la rupture même de la maintenance'), and which also asserts that Laporte's own text undermines the lexicon of presence ('attente', 'événement', 'avenir', 'œuvre', etc.) deployed within it, Laporte acknowledges the extent to which the deconstruction of experience was already under way in his earlier texts, 'puisque cette expérience conduite jusqu'au bout, à la condition par conséquent d'en comprendre la logique, se détruit d'elle-même si radicalement que les concepts d'Evénement ou d'Expérience eux aussi sont ruinés, mais cette perte, cet intervalle, ni sensible ni insensible, qui rompt tout "maintenant", qui entame toute présence, c'est justement ce que Derrida appelle espacement ou archi-écriture' (*B* 68–9). The functioning of even these earlier texts, then, comes to resemble the Derridean strategy of deconstruction. Inevitably, a vocabulary is used which is imbued with the metaphysics of presence, but it is mobilized in such a way as to point to the aporia at the roots of such a system of thought. Thus, the conception of experience that arises from these texts, and particularly from *La Veille*, is one in which the subject of experience is involved, by that experience, with an other in a rapport which breaks the circuit of the subject's self-identity, and in which the locus of experience is an event which has always already implicated the subject, but which has never been nor will ever be punctually present; it is an experience, therefore, which has already undermined the 'expérience du proche et du propre' and points instead to 'l'expérience comme archi-écriture'. In his later works, Laporte shifts the focus to the anoriginal[28] source of this deconstruction: writing. I would like to conclude my analysis of this transition by looking at some other interrelated aspects of the earlier work which mark both the limitations of that work and the latent possibilities for the new direction in Laporte's writing, namely, the appeal to an origin and the notion of a silent voice; thereafter, we shall pass on to a detailed consideration of Laporte's recourse to musical metaphors.

As is well known, Western thought, in Derrida's view, has consistently and inevitably taken as its ground one of a series of originary presences: God, *logos*, the Idea, the *cogito*, Being, etc. However, just as a philosophy of absence would only consolidate rather than dispel the metaphysics of presence, of which it would merely be the mirror-image, so the attempt to replace the notion of an originary presence with one of an absence at the origin would replicate a system which can just as easily accommodate an origin with zero-value as one with unitary value. The conception of a generalized writing, on the other hand, is one in which sign leads to sign, and never to a full presence, in a series whose origin is neither absence nor presence but a trace, *différance*, a non-originary origin.

The movement of *différance* refers us backwards and forwards in the production of meaning, towards an origin and an end which will never in themselves be complete and which therefore defy our notions of origin and end. In 'Ellipse', the second study of Edmond Jabès contained in *L'Ecriture et la différence*, Derrida contrasts the metaphysics of the book, which reinforces traditional conceptions of origin and end,[29] with 'l'écriture', which, in a phrase borrowed from Jabès, is a 'passion de l'origine', a movement of *différance* towards the origin, but to an origin which is already implicated in the movement it was supposed to originate: 'L'écriture, passion de l'origine, cela doit s'entendre aussi par la voie du génitif subjectif. C'est l'origine elle-même qui est passionnée, passive et passée d'être écrite. Ce qui veut dire inscrite. L'inscription de l'origine, c'est sans doute son être-écrit mais c'est aussi son être-inscrit dans un système dont elle n'est qu'un lieu et une fonction.'[30] The writing which turns to the origin in the movement of *différance* interminably returns to what is still not yet an origin. The inescapability and the inescapable frustration of writing's return to the origin are, of course, what was signalled by Blanchot by means of the figure of Orpheus, compelled to turn to the nocturnal Eurydice, thereby to lose her to the darkness of the Underworld: 'Mais ce mouvement défendu est précisément ce qu'Orphée doit accomplir pour porter l'œuvre au-delà de ce qui l'assure, ce qu'il ne peut accomplir qu'en oubliant l'œuvre, dans l'entraînement d'un désir qui lui vient de la nuit, qui est lié à la nuit comme à son origine.'[31]

The 'passion de l'origine' is clearly evident in Laporte's work, and his abiding preoccupation with the origin can be traced in a number of remarks in his *Carnets*. In 1959, Laporte forecasts the inexhaustibility of his concern: 'J'en aurai bien pour toute ma vie à chercher, à décrire mon domaine propre: le lieu de l'origine' (*C* 74). That this concern dates from even earlier is suggested three years later, when Laporte observes that '[d]epuis que j'écris je cherche l'origine de l'écriture' (*C* 147). Later again, in 1963 and 1967, Laporte returns to the theme, but now with an important qualification which precludes the identification of the origin of writing with the writer; the origin of writing is non-human or impersonal, and writing therefore is not conceived in terms of self-expression:

Ecrire authentiquement c'est à coup sûr écrire de telle sorte que l'origine non humaine de l'écriture ne soit jamais oubliée; bref, il faut écrire de telle sorte que l'origine de l'écriture demeure transparente. (*C* 180–1) je continue de croire que, pour des raisons obscures, il y a une sorte de 'lieu' impersonnel où l'écriture prend son 'sens' et sa 'source'. (*C* 249)

Of course, this last remark post-dates Laporte's earliest communication with Derrida, and we sense the influence of the latter, joining earlier influences which we have explored, when Laporte summarizes his thoughts on the origin of writing by observing that 'lorsque la "différence" joue, il y a ouverture, liberté, appel, à-venir' (*C* 250).

We have already seen the importance of the notion of an origin in Laporte's works of the 1960s. In *La Veille*, the enigmatic *il* was described as both the origin and the enemy of language, and was identified as the source of an illumination intermittently perceptible in the work. The treatment of *lui* in the text militates against understanding this origin as a presence or a homogeneous unity, however, and this is underscored by the epigraphs from Heraclitus and Hölderlin which, although on first sight suggesting an originary unity, on closer inspection pointed rather towards a heterogeneous origin whose apparent unity disguised a tension between opposing forces. Indeed, we saw that Blanchot had already noted the ambivalence of the origin in *La Veille* when, in describing the work as an attempt to bring us to 'la pensée du neutre', he remarked that the *neutre* turns us towards 'cela qui toujours détourne et se détourne, de sorte que le point central où il semble qu'écrivant nous soyons attirés ne serait que l'absence de centre, le manque d'origine'.[32] Our discussion of the inspirational event recorded in *Une Voix de fin silence* and *Pourquoi?* illustrated the ambivalence of the origin in those works too. The very notion of an *événement* at the source of the work seems to invite the predication of a unitary origin, but this is then cast into doubt by the evocation of the event as never having been simply present, and only discernible as a trace which becomes an absence; the temporality of the event is never that of a punctual presence, belonging as it does to a past which has never taken place and a future which never arrives. We also saw that Levinas, in his review of *Une Voix de fin silence*, found that the *événement* at times recalled Heideggerian Being, but at other times resembled rather the movement from the same to the absolutely other. The proximity we suggested between the *événement* and Heidegger's *Ereignis* hardly simplifies the matter, inasmuch as the *Ereignis* is a moment of both unity and differentiation, appropriation and expropriation, presence and absence; it certainly cannot simply be equated with an originary presence, but the extent to which the notion of *Ereignis* already deconstructs a metaphysical conception of the origin is a question which would require a detailed analysis of the relationship between Heidegger and Derrida beyond the scope of the present study, given the complexity of that relationship and its modifications in the course of Derrida's career.[33] The suggestion, offered on a number of occasions in Laporte's *Carnets* and in the two volumes of *Une Voix de fin silence*, that the failure adequately to name this *événement* opens up the possibility of signifying it certainly appears to posit the *événement* as the transcendental signified standing at the origin of the language of the work. By contrast, the notion of *rythme* which we encountered towards the end of *La Veille* suggests that the ineffable domain sought in that work was not an origin standing apart from the play of the text, but rather a repetitive interruption neither simply within nor without the text, a spacing or *différance*; in other words, what Derrida in 'La double séance' describes as 'l'intervention réglée du blanc, la mesure et l'ordre de la dissémination, la loi de l'espacement, le *rythmos* (cadence et caractère de l'écriture)'.[34] It would none the less remain simplistic to condemn the later two texts as an unequivocal step back into the metaphysics of presence, given the conflicting terms in which the *événement* is evoked, described as it is for example towards the end of *Pourquoi?* as simultaneously 'unisson' and 'déchirure'. Furthermore, the notion of *rythme* introduced in *La Veille* may have disappeared as an explicit theme in the later works, but the contradictory, conflictual movement of these texts which are at variance with themselves itself constitutes a sort of disruptive rhythm so that, as Derrida wrote to Laporte in 1965, 'votre texte est bien la destruction des mots "attente", "événement", "avenir", etc. qui envahissent votre lexique et font le siège de votre écriture' (*B* 68).

Perhaps more telling than the *événement* sought in the two volumes of *Une Voix de fin silence* is the invocation of a silent voice which is also posited as the unattainable origin of the work. Derrida explores the myth of the silent voice, a linchpin of the metaphysics of presence, on a number of occasions, most extensively in *La Voix et le phénomène* in which it is argued that, because of the operation of the 's'entendre-parler', the voice appears to guarantee the uninterrupted self-presence of consciousness, the seamless union of intention and expression, signified and signifier. Indeed, because of the immediacy of the 's'entendre-parler', the voice appears to offer the possibility of expression without substance, an ideal signified silently eclipsing the material signifier: 'Idéalement, dans l'essence téléologique de la parole, il serait donc possible que le signifiant soit absolument proche du signifié visé par l'intuition et guidant le vouloir-dire. Le signifiant deviendrait parfaitement diaphane en raison même de la proximité absolue du signifié.'[35] The evocation of a silent voice is another of Laporte's targets in the condemnation of his earlier works carried out in 'Bief'. Having signalled what he sees as the misguided reliance on the authority of experience, he observes that Derrida's deconstruction of notions of presence, origin and experience highlights the complicity of such notions with 'la voix, cette voix, origine du pur signifié, du sens, de Dieu comme Logos, de l'Esprit, puisqu'elle croit s'entendre-parler en l'absence du corps' (B 67). The theological underpinning of this phonocentrism, to which Laporte alludes here and which Derrida illustrates in the early pages of De la grammatologie, is also recalled of course in the biblical citation which provides the epigraph and title of Une Voix de fin silence. It is also worth noting that the form which this phonocentrism takes—the notion of a silent voice—is not confined to the particular works which bear the brunt of Laporte's criticism in 'Bief'; the continuity of this notion with the speaking silence of Souvenir de Reims, for instance, is clear enough, and has already been discussed here at length in a slightly different context. None the less, it is in the two volumes of Une Voix de fin silence that the notion is most fully explored, revealing for example the complicity of the myth of a silent voice with the transcendental signified, a sign which would be entirely present to itself, an identity without difference. This is made clear enough by the description of the silent voice as a 'confidence pure': 'Personne ne me parle, mais, antérieurement à la première parole, il y a cette confidence: elle ne dit rien, rien d'autre qu'elle-même' (VFS 92).

There is complicity too between the terms in which an origin is evoked in these works, namely as a silent voice and as an event, since the transcendental signified which is concomitant with the phono-centrism of the silent voice represents the possibility of the sign as an event, a sign which would be meaningful in utter isolation. Such a possibility is specifically excluded by Derrida: 'Un signe n'est jamais un événement si événement veut dire unicité empirique ir-remplaçable et irréversible. Un signe qui n'aurait lieu qu'"une fois" ne serait pas un signe.'[36] But just as the événement proved a more problematic origin than it appeared at first sight, so the notion of the silent voice turns out to be less easily assimilable to the metaphysics of

presence than we have so far suggested, given the qualifications with
which it is hedged in Laporte's works. In our earlier discussion of
these works, we noted that, in being qualified by an epithet, the
silence of the 'voix de fin silence' already appears not simply to be
nothing. This impression is borne out time and again in *Une Voix de
fin silence* and *Pourquoi?*, when for example the narrator in the
vigilance of his 'attente' perceives the silence, 'ce silence, qui n'est pas
une simple absence de bruit, qui au contraire écarte tout bruit' (*VFS*
111). In *Pourquoi?*, the narrator remarks that his work appears to
oscillate between the poles of the 'presque rien' and the 'presque
tout', adding that 'ma tâche propre est d'aller toujours du côté du
presque rien, de réduire la marge entre presque rien et rien' (*P*
204–5). Shortly after this the voice of silence is explicitly evoked, with
the observation that 'jamais on ne perçoit la voix du silence comme
silence' (*P* 205). Having again remarked of the silent voice that 'ce
presque rien est un peu quelque chose', the narrator towards the end
of *Pourquoi?* suggests that, in the territory he is exploring, 'parole et
silence forment les deux régions dangereuses dont je dois me garder,
dont je me tiens à l'écart en cherchant l'interstice qui les sépare et les
tient l'une et l'autre en respect' (*P* 234). The silent voice which
inhabits the interval between speech and silence is therefore the mark
of a difference, itself neither the plenitude of sound nor the perfection
of silence, neither presence nor absence, but a trace. This is another
feature of these works noted by Derrida in his letter to Laporte, where
he observes that the rupture of 'la maintenance' effected by writing
implies the destruction not only of the vocabulary of plenitude, such
as *événement* or *œuvre*, but also 'du *Rien*: d'où le *presque rien*' (*B* 68).
The notion of the silent voice, then, can be seen in conjunction with
the treatment of the origin and the event in these works as
participating in a metaphorics of presence whose foundations are
consistently undermined in the text. I turn now to another important
component of this feature of the two volumes of *Une Voix de fin
silence*, the use of musical metaphors, as this provides a clearer
illustration of what is at stake in the transition in Laporte's writing
from *Pourquoi?* to *Fugue*.

ii. *Ecrire la musique*: from harmony to counterpoint

The enormous importance which Laporte accords to music in the
formation of his own work has scarcely been suggested so far in this

study. At every stage of the *Carnets*, one finds musical works cited alongside literary ones, and frequently given prominence over the latter, in Laporte's accounts of the influences on his own writing, with certain works, notably amongst the chamber music of Mozart and Beethoven, recurring as touchstones throughout his career. In 1986 Laporte published a collection of brief essays on musical themes, *Ecrire la musique*, the introduction of which concludes with the hope that these essays will to some extent communicate his passion for music, and 'faire comprendre pourquoi elle constitue non seulement l'expérience majeure de ma vie, mais le paradigme de tout mon travail'.[37] Despite the importance accorded to them by Laporte, I do not propose to pursue any possible links between particular pieces of music and his work, partly for want of musicological expertise, but also because to do so would risk indulging in the crude psychologism of speculating on how the impact of certain musical passages might be translated into Laporte's writing. A more fruitful approach would be to consider the extent to which Laporte's writing aspires to the condition of music. In *Supplément*, for example, the scriptor observes that writing does not give rise to a 'pur signifié' and therefore ventures, in respect of the new genre sought for his writing, that 'il se pourrait que la Biographie se différencie de la philosophie, et au contraire se rapproche de la peinture et surtout de la musique, pour autant qu'elle ne comporte sans doute jamais un véritable contenu' (*FS* 362). This is a line of inquiry to which I shall return later, when there will also be an opportunity to consider how far the notion of rhythm proposed in and by Laporte's texts effects this alignment of writing and music.

Of course, music also leaves a more explicit mark on Laporte's work, from the musical metaphors deployed in *Souvenir de Reims* and the very subject matter of a short text dating from 1954, unpublished at the time, *In Memoriam* (*SR* 53–63) (an account of a recital given late in the career of the violinist Jacques Thibaud), to the titles of the *Fugue* series. More specifically, a musical metaphor used in respect of the unattainable origin in the two volumes of *Une Voix de fin silence* provides an interesting contrast with the fugal metaphors which are so important in the later works.

Musical metaphors play an important part in the third and, particularly, the fourth sequences of *Une Voix de fin silence*. Towards the end of the third sequence, the narrator likens his activity to the composition of a concerto in which the solo instrument, 'centre de l'œuvre, ne jouerait pas sur le proscénium, mais se tiendrait invisible et presque absent en arrière de la scène' (*VFS* 132), an image to which he returns briefly in the fourth sequence (*VFS* 146). It is a few pages after this that the narrator begins to develop a metaphorics of harmony and harmonics[38] which is particularly revealing, and will be further elaborated in *Pourquoi?*. The narrator observes that the inspirational event with which he seeks to remain in contact in his work is not an isolated point but 'au contraire il est le centre d'un domaine qui lui est harmoniquement lié', and the narrator's modest ambition is to occupy that domain, 'être toujours une harmonique du "ton fondamental"' (*VFS* 149). This metaphor then undergoes the transformative process which is characteristic of the auto-critical writing of these works, and which is even more notable in the later works. The complicity of this metaphor of harmony with the notions of an original event or silent voice will be immediately apparent, and like these notions it is subjected to modifications which problematize its status as an origin. So the narrator very soon returns to the metaphor in a moment of apparent proximity to the inspirational event, but now he remarks: 'Je suis une harmonique du "ton fondamental", qui demeure comme tel non entendu' (*VFS* 150). The silencing of the fundamental note is the first step in a transformative process which will deconstruct this metaphorics of harmony, but it does not yet unshackle this metaphorics from the metaphysics of presence for, as we have already noted, such a metaphysics can as easily accommodate an absence as a presence at the origin; indeed, immediately after the remark just cited, the narrator adds that 'pourtant je ne pourrais me dire une harmonique si je ne me sentais déjà en rapport et même en liaison avec je ne sais quelle cime future' (*VFS* 150). In *Pourquoi?* the narrator returns to the metaphorics of harmony, using the analogy of being tuned to the A of a tuning-fork to describe his goal of a writing in keeping with the inspirational event. However, in a paradox which we have already noted and which will be further explored in the *Fugue* series, writing is only 'juste' when it is in harmony with an inspirational event which can only be approached through writing, so that 'l'écriture: l'accordoir, est aussi l'instrument à accorder' (*P* 194). In a further refinement of the metaphor of tuning—a refinement which we have already seen proposed in *Une Voix de fin silence*—the gamut of the narrator's responses to the elusive passage of the event is described as an 'arc-en-ciel sonore [...] formé par les harmoniques d'un *la* fondamental sans aucun timbre, voix blanche dont on ne peut jamais dire qu'on l'ait entendue' (P 197). Later in *Pourquoi?* there is something of a fusion of the metaphor of the absent soloist proposed in *Une Voix de fin silence* with these metaphors of harmony and tuning when the narrator, in respect of his perpetually auto-critical procedure, likens himself to 'ce violoniste exaspérant dont tout le concert ne consistera jamais qu'à accorder son instrument' (P 221), before further qualifying this image with the observation that 'le violoniste doit accorder son instrument sans avoir jamais entendu le *la* du diapason' (P 222). However, as we have already noted, the metaphorics of harmony and attunement, even when the key-note of that harmony is silent, fails to break with a metaphysics of presence which other features of these texts, such as the evocation of the *événement* as a repetitive interruption of the text, promise to undermine. Even an absent key-note of the harmony of the text suggests an origin on which the text is centred, and a *telos* which the text might finally recover; in a passage from *Pourquoi?* which we have already cited, such notions are repudiated since 'on ne peut parler de centre, de sommet, de pôle, voire de passage, à propos de la métamorphose, non immédiate, de l'espace orienté parcouru par l'écriture, en une zone asymétrique où seul le va-et-vient du temps tisse son propre espace' (P 242). It is therefore entirely in keeping with this observation that the metaphorics of harmony should then give way to an evocation of the work as a 'polyphonie à plusieurs voix, dont la plus indiscrète, ou la plus généreuse, car le plus souvent elle couvre les autres, celle qui dit "je", est sans doute la moins importante de toutes' (P 243). The transition from harmony to polyphony is a movement away from the conception of the work as a centred, hierarchical structure founded on a single, unified origin, the recovery of which also provides the *telos* of the work; this unidirectional teleology is further undermined in a final musical metaphor in *Pourquoi?*, when the narrator notes the interminable errancy of his itinerary, which never corresponds exactly with his expectations, adding that 'ainsi la ligne mélodique, elle aussi, a été et sera toujours altérée, voire rompue' (P 248).

In *Fugue*, the metaphors of harmony which had been progressively undermined in the course of *Pourquoi?* are abandoned in favour of the fugal metaphor which provides the work's title and underscores the important motif of *écriture* and *contre-écriture* explored throughout *Fugue* and its two successors. The definition from the *Dictionnaire Robert* which provides the epigraph of *Fugue* might at first sight, in its reference to theme and imitation, suggest that the fugal metaphor will be no less evocative of a work centred on a stable origin than were the metaphors of harmony: 'La fugue est une composition musicale écrite dans le style du contrepoint et dans laquelle un thème et ses imitations successives forment plusieurs parties qui semblent "se fuir et se poursuivre l'une l'autre" (Rousseau)' (F 253). However, even before we consider the relationship between theme and imitation in a fugue in more detail, the terms proposed in this definition may already be seen to indicate that the fugal metaphor will open up a very different conception of the work than that which was implicit in the metaphorics of harmony. First of all, the flight and pursuit of the voices of a fugue evoked here are redolent of dispersal, decentring and incompletion rather than the achieved unity and stability of harmony. In his 1972 interview with Jean Ristat, Laporte stresses above all the idea of 'la fuite' contained in the fugue, adding that this is carried through in *Fugue* itself, for example, in metaphors of 'la chasse'.[39] The scriptor likens the writer to a solitary hunter pursuing 'sans trêve ni pitié une proie invisible, mais en même temps (en même temps?) tout autre chose est cherché ou du moins secrètement attendu' (F 282). The writer-hunter seeks something other than accomplishment—the capture of his prey—for, as the scriptor goes on to remark, he also seeks failure, the tearing of his hunter's net. Shortly after this the scriptor describes writing as 'une chasse éperdue, une quête d'Isis, pour tenter de retrouver le fragment qui manque, une tentative désespérée pour rattraper ce qui fut perdu, pour retrouver ce qui m'échappe et s'échappe' (F 283–4). The connection drawn by Laporte between the 'fuite' of the fugue and 'la chasse' is in fact borne out by the early history of fugal technique; at about the same time that the term *fuga* was first being applied to an imitative vocal technique, the canonic form known in Italian as *caccia* and in French as *chace* was gaining ground and was also sometimes designated by the term *fuga*.[40]

The other key term in the *Robert* definition, counterpoint, will afford us more insight into what is at stake in the transition from metaphors of harmony to the fugal metaphor. It is conventional to regard the history of Western musical composition as dividing roughly between harmonic and contrapuntal thinking. A simple statement of the distinction between counterpoint and harmony underlines the dichotomy: 'Counterpoint may be defined as the element of disagreement between voices or parts in a composition, harmony being the element of agreement.'[41] The distinction between the relative independence of melodic lines in counterpoint and their relative consonance in harmonic writing is clearly a workable one, but of course the detail of musical history and compositional practice would rather attest to the cross-fertilizing interdependence of contrapuntal and harmonic principles.[42] Furthermore, from a more abstract point of view, it is possible for harmony to exist without counterpoint, but the converse cannot be so straightforwardly asserted, since the musical texture produced by contrapuntal writing, whatever its tendency towards dissonance, could not be entirely dissociated from notions of harmony; as Edmund Rubbra remarks, 'independence of parts, which is the root of counterpoint, implies not absolute independence (which would lead to chaos) but relative independence'.[43]

All of this is worth bearing in mind in considering an observation made by Lacoue-Labarthe and Nancy in their discussion of the epigraph of *Fugue*; they too underline the distinction between counterpoint and 'l'harmonie au sens étroit', stressing that counterpoint, in its deployment of imitative voices, consists in 'faire entendre, tout autant que l'accord de ces voix, leur *écart*—leur *écartement*.'[44] Writing as fugue, therefore, implies a conception of the work in which discord rather than unity is the governing principle, and in which the accent falls not only upon the differences between components of the work—the 'écart'—but also upon the movement which produces such differences—the 'écartement'. For what is distinctive about counterpoint is not the melodic lines themselves of course, but the difference, differentiation and deferral—the *différance*—at work between the lines, so that the relation assumes priority over the *relata*, and indeed, in the variations which take place in fugal development for instance, the relation comes to condition the *relata*.

However, the brief observations we have just made about the relationship between counterpoint and harmony should preclude us from regarding the transition from harmonic to fugal metaphors as an unconditional break, and invite us instead to see it once again as a *brisure*, both articulation and disjunction. The relation between terms proposed by the model of counterpoint may not be the perfect unity of harmony, but neither is it polarized opposition; it may better be described as the sort of non-oppositional difference contained in the notion of *différance*. Lacoue-Labarthe and Nancy suggest as much when they say that counterpoint draws attention to the 'écartement' of voices 'tout autant que l'accord de ces voix', and indeed they go on to stress the ambivalent relation suggested by Laporte's deployment of the fugal metaphor. In respect of the contrapuntal treatment of the figures for writing presented by *Fugue*, they suggest that these figures are successively destabilized but without ever being comprehensively negated: 'Il s'agit plutôt de la singulière conjonction de l'*assemblage* et du *désassemblage*—conjonction inassignable, toujours elle-même fuyante ou mouvante—telle qu'on peut l'entendre dans le mot de *désarticulation*.'[45] As if to underline the rapport of disarticulation or *brisure* which we have suggested exists between *Fugue* and Laporte's earlier work, they then suggest that the ambivalent relation implied by the fugal metaphor may also be assimilated to the notion of the *neutre* which Blanchot found at work in *La Veille*. The transition from harmony to fugue does not result in a conception of the work in which the complete disintegration of elements replaces unity, any more than the notion of *différance* replaces a stable relationship between signs with an absence of relationship. It would be more accurate to say that writing as fugue proposes a dynamic rather than a static model of the work, the elements of which are 'disarticulated' by relationships in constant and irresolvable movement, and are thereby themselves constantly modified. We should now consider what happens to one particular element, the notion of origin, in the fugal model.

We saw that the metaphorics of harmony gave rise to a conception of the work as centred on the origin of a fundamental note, a conception resisted by so many other features of the earlier works. Not only did this remain the case when the fundamental note was said to be silent, but this modification of the harmonic metaphor suggests even more strongly the notion of an origin standing outside the play of the text. Given Laporte's ambition to write a work which would not be the translation of a pre-textual experience, whose signification would not be grounded on a transcendental signified, the musical model of the fugue, which Stravinsky described as a 'forme parfaite où la musique ne signifie rien au-delà d'elle-même',[46] has obvious attractions. The text as fugue generates itself from material originated within the text itself. But, as I have already suggested, the 'thème et ses imitations successives' announced in the epigraph of *Fugue* hardly seem to promise an outright rejection of the notion of an origin: a fugue, after all, does have a beginning or origin in the form of its theme or subject. In this respect we should recall first of all a point which has already been made in our discussion of Derrida, that is, that to seek a simple elimination of the notion of an origin would involve replacing the metaphysics of presence with a metaphysics of absence which would be the mirror-image of the former. The deconstruction of the origin rather involves revealing what is taken to be an origin as not being originary in an absolute and immutable sense, and this deconstruction may already be said to be initiated in the transition to a fugal model of the work, in which the origin is included in and comes to be reworked by that which it is supposed to originate. Moreover, the metaphorics of harmony suggested that a unique, pre-textual origin could be retrospectively inferred from the text, and that that origin equally stood as the summation or *telos* of the text, thus producing the circularity of *archè* and *telos* which, for Derrida, is characteristic of the metaphysics of presence.[47] On the other hand, whilst any fugue undeniably has a beginning in the form of the subject, the particular melodic line which starts such a piece is only belatedly revealed as the origin of a fugue by the subsequent entry of other voices in imitation and variation of the subject. In a fugue, then, there is a sort of originary delay, inasmuch as the subject which originates a fugue has to be supplemented by imitative voices in order to become an origin.[48]

We have already seen that the notion of an originary delay can be traced back not only to the works which immediately preceded *Fugue*, but even to an early text like *Une Migration*, whose narrator could find no end to errancy because he had yet to complete the prenuptial migration of his own birth. In *Une Voix de fin silence*, the attempt to remain in proximity to the unattainable origin (represented, for example, by the silent note at the root of the harmony of the text) involved the repetition of a beginning which could never be truly inaugural (as evidenced, for instance, by the series of 'false starts' in the opening pages of that work). Earlier in this chapter, we noted the hesitancy with which *Fugue* too begins: 'Pourquoi ne commencerais-je pas par cette remarque que je comprends mal et qui m'étonne moi-même?' (*F* 255). The uncertainty is emphasized by a main verb in the conditional mode, couched in a negative, interrogative form. The twofold reflexivity of this opening, referring as it does to the act of beginning and to the ensuing sentence, contributes to this sense of hesitancy whilst at the same time marking a significant distinction from the hesitant openings of some of Laporte's earlier works. Both *La Veille* and *Une Voix de fin silence* opened with reference to a pre-textual agency, the enigmatic *lui* and the inspirational event respectively, although in each case it transpired that that agency could not be said to stand entirely outside of the work. The reflexivity of the opening of *Fugue*, on the other hand, does not invite us to suppose any pre-textual origin for the work, and the remainder of the first paragraph excludes one particular domain in which an origin of writing has traditionally been sought: the life of the writer.

Not only does the beginning of *Fugue* resist the notion of a pre-textual origin, it also erases itself as an origin through a process of originary delay. The first words of *Fugue* refer to the act of beginning, but then hesitantly defer that beginning to the words which follow. The remark thus posited, with such uncertainty, as the beginning participates in turn in the process of originary delay, as it concerns what the scriptor expects of 'l'ouvrage à écrire', so that what we are reading is still not yet the beginning of the work. That the moment of origin cannot be given a punctual assignation is underlined at the end of the first paragraph when, despite the deferrals of the first few lines of the text, we discover that a beginning has been made since the scriptor now imagines an alternative beginning, as he does again at the start of the second paragraph: 'J'aurais pu aborder cet ouvrage un peu autrement' (F 255). The process of originary delay continues, for the scriptor opens the second sequence of *Fugue* by signalling his uncertainty about 'l'ouvrage à écrire', and goes on to give an account of the difficulty of beginning: 'Le commencement n'est pas tant une ligne à franchir qu'une période à traverser, un espace dans lequel il faut s'insinuer, espace qui n'est pas impénétrable, mais dont les pistes multiples se perdent ou s'enchevêtrent si bien qu'au lieu d'être rejeté au-dehors comme un intrus, on se retrouve avant le commencement et pourtant avec un passé derrière soi' (F 257–8). Nothing in itself identifies a particular melodic line as the beginning of a fugue, but once that line has given rise to contrapuntal imitation the fugue *will have* begun. This future anterior is the temporality of beginning identified at the end of the passage cited above, there being no single identifiable origin of a writing which will none the less have begun, and it is also the temporality of *différance*, which has never been nor will ever be present but whose operation is always already underway.

The erasure of the beginning as an origin, along with the concomitant dissolution of the *telos* which we will explore later, denies the work its perfection as a totality so that it remains 'l'ouvrage à écrire' which has to be begun repetitively. The evidence we have already seen for this is underlined for example in the early part of the third sequence, when the scriptor wonders whether some instinct of self-preservation explains his reserve before the blank page and his tendency to 'différer le commencement' (F 263). In general, the breaks between sequences give rise to a reappraisal by the scriptor which in turn often suggests the need for a fresh start. The beginning of the seventh sequence is a particularly clear illustration of this, as the scriptor indicates that the preceding pages no longer provide a solid foundation for the continuation of his work; the work, he feels, has rather undergone an interruption 'pour faire place à un nouveau départ' (F 288). It transpires that this fresh start, like all the others, maintains a link with what has preceded it, as, in a process to which we shall return later, the scriptor proposes to survey the earlier sequences in order to salvage those parts to which he still feels close. The deferral of beginning is such that the end of *Fugue* returns us elliptically to a point still before the beginning, so that 'par la faveur d'un temps prophétique qui à rebours annonce le futur antérieur, la main, si jeune qu'elle n'a jamais tenu un style, est sur le point d'être touchée par la première lueur du soleil levant' (F 329). The ceaseless repetition of beginning means, then, that the work appears to erase itself, or to constitute itself as the interminable preface of a work to come. This is precisely the conclusion of the next volume, *Supplément*, in the closing lines of which the scriptor declares his failure to have instituted the new genre of *biographie*, the very same failure which had caused the bitter dissatisfaction with *Fugue* announced in the opening pages of *Supplément*. Hence the concluding remark of *Supplément*: 'Admettons que ce livre en constitue la préface' (FS 392). This analysis of the interminable repetition of beginning could be extended to *Fugue 3*, which also opens with a false start and concludes with a gesture of effacement, as does the *Codicille* appended to it, but before venturing too far down this path I should like to return to the early pages of *Fugue* to consider some particular difficulties of beginning identified there.

If writing as fugue implies the work's independence from any pre-textual origin, since the development of the work will derive from material generated within the work, then it might be expected that beginning such a work would pose particular problems, in so far as a certain creation *ex nihilo* seems to be involved. Immediately after his observation about the difficulty of beginning cited earlier, the scriptor of *Fugue* suggests precisely this: 'Dans un ouvrage comme celui-ci, les

pages les plus ingrates à écrire sont peut-être les premières: si je persiste dans mon entreprise, il me semble qu'à partir du moment où
j'aurai derrière moi un passé de quelque épaisseur, écrire deviendra
plus facile' (F 258). However, by this stage the scriptor has already
proposed a metaphor for the work he is setting out to write, which,
though appearing to offer support for the observation cited above,
will on closer inspection suggest that, as we have already noted, the
difficulty of beginning will be repeated throughout the work. This is
the metaphor of the work as *jeu*, the last of a series of metaphors
resulting from one of the deferred beginnings of *Fugue*, in which,
rather than attempting to answer directly the question 'Qu'est-ce
qu'écrire?', the scriptor adapts the guessing game known as 'le portrait
chinois'. All that the scriptor knows of the mystery object is its name,
'un livre', but he is able to offer answers to questions seeking the
object's identity by analogy. The resulting series of analogies displays
the reflexivity which is not only characteristic of fugal form, but
which we have seen to be a consistent concern of Laporte's ever since
the quest for self-coincidence in writing first revealed in *Souvenir de
Reims*; the work the scriptor wishes to write should be perfectly self-
contained by being the exact and only exemplification of its own
propositions, by being the theory of its own practice and vice versa.
Thus, in the first analogy proposed, if the work were a treatise on
physics, it would be Newton's gravitational formula such that it was
not simply a formula, 'mais elle-même, ou, mieux encore, elle seule
serait pesante: la pesanteur s'exercerait dans la formule, par la
formulation de la loi, et nulle part ailleurs' (F 256). In the last of this
brief series, the scriptor asks what the work would be if it were a
game: 'Il faudrait jouer et en même temps écrire le Traité de ce jeu,
ou, plus exactement, le jeu même consisterait à écrire le Traité du jeu.
Comment jouer? Je ne puis appliquer les règles d'un traité qui n'existe
pas encore! Une solution est possible: que l'élaboration du Traité fasse
partie intégrante de l'exécution' (F 256).

The scriptor's immediate solution to the dilemma arising from this
analogy is in keeping with his subsequent hope that the difficulty
experienced in beginning such a work will subside as the work pro-
gresses and is able to feed off itself: 'il faut, même à tâtons, commencer
par jouer, par provoquer et observer les mouvements, quitte, plus
tard, à reconstituer à partir des traces d'autres mouvements d'abord
inaperçus' (F 256). However, if this gives grounds for optimism on a
practical level, so to speak (inasmuch as it promises that the initial

difficulties experienced will subsequently be meliorated by the fact
that a beginning has at least been made and can be built upon), at the
same time it only serves to underline the originary delay which we
have already noted and to suggest that that delay will be perpetuated
throughout the work, since the beginning thus made proves to be
incomplete, therefore requiring the revision of another beginning
which will in turn be incomplete, and so on. This gives rise to the
process of re-reading and re-writing characteristic of the *Fugue* series,
to which we shall return later, which itself seems only to underline
the impossibility of the project of textual self-coincidence announced
in the early pages of *Fugue*, as the scriptor later observes: 'Je désirais
une simultanéité parfaite entre le discours et l'histoire, mais ce que je
dis du fonctionnement ne coïncidera jamais avec ce fonctionnement:
le discours commence toujours en retard, retard non rattrapable, car
en ce moment je lis la séquence précédente pendant que s'écrit un
autre texte que je pourrai commencer à lire seulement dans la
séquence suivante' (*F* 283).

The insuperable delay encountered by the scriptor in his quest for
perfect self-coincidence in writing may be explained in terms of the
philosophy of sentences (*phrases*) proposed by Jean-François Lyotard
in *Le Différend*.[49] In his own version of Cartesian hyperbolic doubt,
Lyotard maintains that what withstands the test of doubt is not the
cogito but the sentence, by which one should understand not the
meaning of a sentence or (in the terminology used in *Le Différend*) the
universe presented by a sentence, but the simple fact that there is a
sentence. Since we have been discussing the question of the origin in
writing, it is worth noting that, although the sentence is thus posited
as the ground of certainty, it cannot be regarded as a plenary origin;
there can be no first sentence, given that any sentence presupposes other
sentences which would, for example, define the terms used in it.[50] Even
to talk, as I have done, of the indubitability of 'the sentence' as an entity,
or of 'the fact' that there is a sentence, is potentially misleading, in so
far as such terms involve cognitive procedures which may be doubted;
what cannot be doubted is that there is a sentence, an absolutely unique
event which has not yet been conceptualized as an entity or category.
There is therefore a sort of division in the sentence between the universe
which it presents and the event of that presentation, such that these
two parts will never coincide: a sentence cannot present its own
presentation.[51] In similar vein, the scriptor of *Fugue*, commenting on
his project of instigating a new genre in which theory and practice

would be as one, a writing in which *dire* would be at the same time *faire*, eventually observes that 'entre le dire et le faire il n'y a jamais la plénitude d'un accord parfait: une page n'est jamais ni dite, ni faite une fois pour toutes, car, loin de coïncider avec elle-même, elle est toujours dédoublée au moment où elle est écrite' (*F* 277). In the essay 'Biographie' (*QV* 135–44), which first appeared as a review-article of Philippe Sollers's *Logiques*, Laporte discusses the project, shared by Sollers and other *Tel Quel* associates such as Jean-Louis Baudry, of a conjunction of textual theory and practice, reaching a similar conclusion about the possibility of such a project: 'on constate d'expérience qu'une parfaite coïncidence entre la pratique et le discours théorique est impossible, que l'après-coup est inévitable dans la mesure même où l'espacement est constitutif du langage' (*QV* 143). The invocation of the *espacement* at work in language reminds us that the impossibility of this project may also be explained in terms of Derridean *différance*.

The scriptor of *Fugue* cannot begin in the manner he would wish, and is consequently ensnared in an interminable originary delay, because his ideal of a writing in which theory and practice would coincide perfectly would require that an utterance be perfectly self-contained, a possibility precisely excluded by the working of *différance*. We have already suggested as much in noting that, in writing as fugue, the origin only belatedly becomes the origin in the light of what it is supposed to originate, and is therefore not complete in itself. This was apparent in the scriptor's response to the dilemma posed by the analogy of writing as perfect coincidence of 'le jeu' and 'le Traité du jeu', namely to begin by playing so that that beginning could subsequently be scrutinized in order to 'reconstituer à partir des traces d'autres mouvements d'abord inaperçus' (*F* 256). The beginning of the game is incomplete without a subsequent gloss, but that gloss only reveals what was already there but had passed unnoticed. The relationship of gloss to beginning instantiates what Derrida has described as the logic of the supplement, in so far as it stands as an addition to something which was already whole, but not wholly present to itself, making up for a lack in the beginning, but a lack which turns out to be a constitutive trace of that very beginning.[52]

The scriptor of *Fugue* is therefore obliged constantly to supplement a beginning which was already secretly constituted by the very lack which calls for a supplement. At the beginning of the third sequence, the scriptor makes another start by wondering whether he can now try to answer the question 'Qu'est-ce qu'écrire?', only to defer the answer because writing involves him in an operation which he feels he cannot define without first carrying it out. This operation can precisely be described as the composition of supplements, since 'le passé sur lequel je ferai fond, loin d'être constitué par les lignes que l'on a pu lire jusqu'à maintenant, appartient plutôt à une histoire différente, quoique liée à la première, histoire qui est en même temps derrière et devant moi' (*F* 262). Towards the end of the same sequence the scriptor notes that, in conservative moments, he tends simply to describe rather than write, but on other occasions his relationship with 'l'inconnu' is such that he is excluded not only from description but from his own writing, 'douleur sans voix qui se marque seulement par un cerne pauvre, excentré, si allusif que la sensibilité du lecteur doit suppléer à ce que l'écrivain n'aura pu dire' (*F* 268–9). The reader therefore supplements a silence at the very heart of the experience of writing. Since the supplement compensates a lack in what preceded it, but a lack which is already a constitutive trace, the supplement is in a sense prior to and a condition of that which it supplements. If the reader is a supplement and therefore already constitutive of the text, it is perhaps because, in a sense which will be fully explored later but has already been suggested by our discussion of *différance*, writing is constitutively dependent on a void or *espacement* which is the very possibility of reading.

Furthermore, if we accept the idea that *différance*, although nowhere present, is that which permits the operation of all signifying systems, then we must renounce any belief in the possibility of a full presence or plenitude which might arrest the sequence of supplements; whatever we take to be a presence will be revealed to be inhabited by absence, and whatever supplements this vitiated presence will in turn be constituted by traces of absence, and so on. This sequence of supplements underlines what we have already said about the deconstruction of the origin, since, as Derrida remarks, 'le supplément est toujours le supplément d'un supplément. On veut remonter *du supplément à la source*: on doit reconnaître qu'il y a *du supplément à la source*.'[53] We should also take care to note that the advent of the supplement is a necessity, as it is called for by a lack which turns out to be constitutive of that which is supplemented, but also by a lack which will not be eradicated: supplement will lead repeatedly to supplement. The logic of supplementarity therefore dictates not only the deconstruction of the origin, but also an interminable process of supplementary substitution.

The interminable composition of supplements in which the scriptor of *Fugue* finds himself involved may also be explained in the light of that other text we have recently employed to supplement Laporte's text, Lyotard's *Le Différend*. That there is a sentence is indubitable, but that does not mean that the sentence is an origin: there is no first sentence, since any sentence presupposes another one. There is necessarily therefore a series of sentences, and in that series, just as there is no first sentence, there can be no last sentence: 'Qu'il n'y ait pas de phrase est impossible, qu'il y ait: *Et une phrase* est nécessaire. Il faut enchaîner.'[54] The series of sentences will not be ended even by a silence, for a silence too is a sentence for Lyotard, as he explains near the beginning of *Le Différend* with particular reference to Faurisson's claim that there are no eye-witness accounts to attest to the existence of the Nazi gas-chambers.[55] Apart from the interminable series of sentences, which for Lyotard holds generally, the project announced in the early pages of *Fugue* gives rise to a particular interminable series in a way that we have already adumbrated. The coincidence sought by the scriptor of the *dire* and *faire* of writing would require that a sentence coincide with itself in the sense that its own event of presentation should be at the same time the universe it presents. But a sentence cannot present its own presentation, and here as always it would be necessary to 'enchaîner', to add another sentence presenting the former's event of presentation. This may be done, but what would be thus presented would no longer be the event of presentation as a unique occurrence, but merely the first presentation situated, for example, as referent in the universe presented by the second sentence: 'Une présentation en tant qu'elle est phrasable (pensable) est manquée comme occurrence.'[56] In the process, the event of presentation of the second sentence would also be missed, calling for another sentence, and so on.

The interminability of writing is evoked time and again in the *Fugue* series. At the beginning of the fifth sequence of *Fugue*, the scriptor notes this interminability, which is in keeping with the ateleological organization of his writing: 'Il n'appartient pas à l'aventure d'écrire, qui ne se dirige vers aucun but dernier, de s'achever d'elle-même' (*F* 274). The scriptor begins the third sequence of *Supplément* by suggesting that, if it were possible, this sequence would be the last, but adds: 'Cette nostalgie d'une limite, je n'entends pas la justifier, mais ce livre, commencé il y a plus de cinq ans, comment, sans effroi, envisager de l'écrire comme si seule la mort

pouvait mettre un terme arbitraire à une entreprise sans fin!' (*FS* 376).
At the end of the *Codicille* to *Fugue 3*, the scriptor differentiates
biographie from theoretical works on writing, since the theory of the
'processus scriptural'—the latter characterized here as a process of
'déchirure'—will itself be vitiated by that 'déchirure'. However, in
a remark which precisely reflects the process of supplementary
substitution that we have identified, he observes that one will no
longer be able to call it 'déchirure', 'car à ce terme on en substituera
un autre, puis un autre, et ainsi indéfiniment sans qu'aucun soit le
double d'une quelconque réalité' (*F3* 494).

The interminability of supplementary substitution is of course
further underlined by a series of works in which, for instance, *Fugue*
is followed by a *Supplément* whose opening paragraphs announce the
definitive closure of the former work and consequent expulsion of the
scriptor, but in the very act of so doing re-open the work by
beginning with a quotation from *Fugue* and pursuing a discussion of
its weaknesses. *Supplément* is followed in turn by *Fugue 3*, of which the
scriptor remarks near the beginning: 'Je me propose en effet
d'améliorer le fonctionnement et les résultats d'un processus
complexe, de remédier aux insuffisances de *Fugue* et du *Supplément* à
Fugue en écrivant un deuxième supplément' (*F3* 402). *Fugue 3* has its
supplement in the form of a *Codicille* which, like all supplements,
stands undecidably within and without the whole to which it is
added. This undecidability is emphasized by the publication history of
the *Codicille*, subsumed within *Fugue 3* on the latter's first publication
in 1976, but apparently accorded autonomy in the collected volume
Une Vie. Following the *Codicille*, Laporte made notes for what might
have been *Fugue 4*, published as 'Une œuvre mort-née' and effectively
disowned by Laporte in the special issue of *Digraphe* devoted to his
work.[57] The *Fugue* series appears therefore to be clearly demarcated
from the next volume *Suite*, as Laporte emphasizes in the *Digraphe*
interview, remarking for instance that *Suite* is not *Fugue 4*.[58]
Nevertheless, in its title and opening lines *Suite* in effect announces
itself as the supplement to the *Fugue* series, and it in turn is
supplemented by *Moriendo*, the relationship between the two last
works being further complicated by Laporte's references to both of
them constituting one work entitled *Moriendo* in his *Lettre à personne*
(see for example *LP* 21).

In 1972 (therefore before the publication of *Supplément*), Laporte
comments on the interminability of his enterprise in response to Jean

Ristat's question concerning the significance of the musical analogy in
Fugue's title and epigraph: '*Fugue* est inachevable. Ce n'est pas un
hasard si j'ai écrit un *Post-scriptum à Fugue*. Et peut-être y aura-t-il un
autre post-scriptum à celui-ci: une fugue, si elle est radicale, comment
pourrait-elle s'achever? De sorte que je passerai peut-être ma vie à
écrire indéfiniment des post-scriptum à *Fugue*'.[59] The freely imitative
counterpoint of fugal composition is open to limitless extension.
There is a parallel here with the status of the beginning of a fugue as
an origin, in that fugues do of course end, as do *Fugue* and indeed *Une
Vie*, but they are not organized teleologically. The difference from the
harmonic metaphors which dominated the earlier works is that the
latter obviously promised a resolution of sorts, however much the
texts themselves undermined such a promise. As Andrew Benjamin
remarks in his essay on Laporte: 'There can be no end to *Une Vie*, not
because the book cannot end, the book does end and in addition fugal
form posits not just an ending but its introduction within the stretto.
None the less, fugal form is open to an infinite repetition.'[60] In fact,
the stretto—the introduction of subject entries in close proximity—
underlines Benjamin's point in a way he appears not to recognize here.
The stretto does indeed often herald the ending of the piece in the
form which many, but not all, fugues take.[61] But it is important to
realize here that fugue is not a form in the sense, say, of sonata-form,
being variously described by musicologists as a procedure or, less
accurately but in keeping with our metaphorical use of the term, a
texture.[62] The relationship between the potentially limitless texture of
fugue and the finite forms, frequently including stretti, which actual
fugues take is analogous therefore with the relationship between the
interminability of writing as fugue and the finitude of the book.

The logic of supplementarity dictates that this interminability of
writing will also be an interminability of reading. If the reader, as the
scriptor of *Fugue* remarks (F 268–9), is called upon to supplement the
text then it is to compensate for a lack which was already a
constitutive *espacement* of the text and is the very possibility of reading.
The reader therefore participates in, or perhaps rather is an agency
inseparable from, the differential delay of writing. In *Fugue*, the
scriptor urges that the work he wishes to write should not be 'un
objet fini destiné à la consommation', from which a content could
be extracted without regard for the production of that content,
proposing instead of the work that 'écrit pour produire son mode
de production, cet ouvrage manifesterait le fonctionnement de la

machine d'écriture, ou plutôt édifierait cette machine faite de telle sorte qu'elle provoque le lecteur à l'écriture' (F 275). The void which the reader is called upon to fill is the *espacement* which permits reading but is never eradicated by it, never recuperated by reading as a 'theme' and always calling, therefore, for another supplementary reading. This is the inexhaustibility of the work, and its irreducibility to any summary, including, of course, this one: 'il sera toujours impossible de raconter cet ouvrage, de le condenser et sublimer en un "prière d'insérer" qui en donnerait l'intelligence, car aucune séquence, même pas l'ultime, ne peut être privilégiée: aucune connaissance ne pourra priver cet ouvrage de son avenir, de son incertitude; aucune compréhension ne sera capable d'interdire sa remise en jeu et par conséquent en chantier' (F 309).

The interminability of writing and the supplementarity of reading, which will always leave the future of the work an open question, appear to be at odds with what we have already described as the finitude of the book. The linearity of the book has so often served the literary end of exploiting, wittingly or not, the syllogism of *post hoc ergo propter hoc*, that the form of the book is already imbued with a teleology which, as we have seen, is alien to writing as fugue. Moreover, the confines of the book are suggestive of a totality in a way which Derrida has admirably described in *De la grammatologie*: 'L'idée du livre, c'est l'idée d'une totalité, finie ou infinie, du signifiant; cette totalité du signifiant ne peut être ce qu'elle est, une totalité, que si une totalité constituée du signifié lui préexiste, surveille son inscription et ses signes, en est indépendante dans son idéalité. L'idée du livre, qui renvoie toujours à une totalité naturelle, est profondément étrangère au sens de l'écriture.'[63] The scriptor of the *Fugue* series is frequently concerned that features of the book as a totality will be read in a way which falsifies the experience of writing. At a point in *Fugue 3*, for instance, in which the scriptor is contemplating the ruin of his work (a ruin which he feels might preclude its description as a *biographie*), he remarks that what appears on a book's cover, although often written last, is what is read first, and so, we might say, such paratextual[64] features—titles, generic designations, *prières d'insérer*—are read as signalling what Derrida calls the constituted totality of the signified which precedes the book. In this particular case, the eventual appearance of the word *biographie* on the book's cover places the reader in a privileged position of sorts which none the less may give rise to misconceptions: 'en cet instant, le lecteur connaît ce que j'ignore encore puisqu'il a vu si Biographie figure ou non sur la couverture de ce livre, si Biographie a donc ici supporté un effacement profond et pourtant passager, ou bien si "l'axe de tout l'ouvrage" a enfin été définitivement rompu' (*F3* 425). Although it is not spelt out on this occasion, a particular danger is clearly that the reader might be more inclined to read *biographie* as a product rather than a process, and consequently, according to the metaphysics of the book outlined by Derrida above, to read the book as a signifying totality which corresponds to a signified totality independent of the book, such as 'experience' or 'life': in other words, to make the very interpretative move which the first paragraph of *Fugue*, in its emphasis on the projected inextrication of life and writing, is at such pains to forestall.

In fact, the issue of reading the book as a totality is addressed as early as the second sequence of *Fugue*, at the beginning of which the scriptor, reflecting on his own uncertainty about 'l'ouvrage à écrire', wonders how to allow the reader to participate in the discontinuity of writing: 'Comment opérer de telle façon que le legato de la lecture soit brisé par les à-coups de l'écriture? Il faudrait arriver à écrire de telle sorte que le lecteur s'attende à une fin abrupte ou même soupçonne le volume de se prolonger artificieusement par de nombreuses pages blanches' (*F* 257). Later on, Laporte was to attempt to achieve a similar effect with the unusual manner of publication of *Suite*; before its eventual appearance in the form of a book, the first five sequences of this work were published individually *en feuilleton* by Editions Orange Export Ltd., so that the discontinuity of writing might be more readily transmitted to the reader approaching each sequence as it was published. It is important to understand what is meant by discontinuity here, for, as the imagined volume which continues with blank pages and the publication of *Suite en feuilleton* both imply, the discontinuity in question here is above all not the absolutely disjunctive interval implicit in the metaphysics of the book, which, through maintaining a rigorous division between what is inside and outside the totality of the book, allows the book to be read as signifying something entirely exterior to itself. The sense of discontinuity here is, on the contrary, such that the silence at the end of writing opens out onto an uncertain future; in the terms borrowed earlier from Lyotard, this would be a silence which, rather than marking the limit of the *enchaînement* of sentences, would itself be a sentence, marking the necessity of other sentences. It may also be understood in terms of that much misunderstood phrase of Derrida's: 'Il n'y a pas de hors-texte.'[65] This does not imply, as has often been supposed, that there is an unbridgeable chasm between the text and the real, for this would simply be a restatement of the division between inside and outside upheld by the idea of the book as a totality. Nor does it mean, as a more subtle misconception of the phrase would have it, that the relationship between the text and the real is one of seamless continuity, since both participate in an undifferentiated, homogeneous textuality. What it does mean is that there is a chiastic relationship between inside and outside, such that the borders between text and real, or text and text, are not absent, but neither are they entirely secure. The closure of the book fails to constitute the book as an independent totality, instead enclosing what was thought to be outside within, and inside without. The discontinuity at the end of writing—at the end of a sequence, of each sequence of *Suite* published *en feuilleton*, or of a volume—is therefore an articulating-disjunctive interval, a passage marked by *différance*.

The chiastic relationship between inside and outside at the border of the text means that this transgression of the border is repeated throughout the text, indeed this is nothing other than the effect which *différance* names. The meaning of what is given within the text to read is only made possible by what is absent, without the text: a text which was perfectly self-contained, whose interior was not also outside the text, would be unreadable, a private language. The textual inextrication of inside and outside is revealed in writing as fugue when the repetition of the theme discovers that theme to be different from itself, when writing reflects on itself to find itself other. This is why the scriptor of *Supplément* rejects the term self-referential for his writing, and why we would describe it as an Orphic rather than a Narcissistic text, 'car, s'il est exact qu'écrire ne renvoie ni à un réel qui lui serait extérieur, ni même à un texte qui lui serait immanent, il est faux d'affirmer qu'écrire est "sui-référentiel": comment écrire pourrait-il s'autodésigner puisqu'il ne possède rien en propre, nulle intériorité, aucun "soi-même"!' (*FS* 384). This aspect of Laporte's work is greatly illuminated by Andrew Benjamin, who talks of 'a writing that may involve imitation but cannot be said to involve mimesis'.[66] This apparently paradoxical statement is justified by the observation that, in the tradition deriving from Plato, mimesis involves a securely established distinction between inside and outside, between mimetic presentation within the work of art and the object

of mimesis outside of it. In fugal form, on the other hand, what is
imitated is generated within the form, but this imitation does not
reveal the inside to be identical to itself, giving rise in Laporte's work
to 'a writing that resists the opposition between the inside and the
outside and is therefore situated beyond the possibility of its own
incorporation into mimesis'.[67] Writing as fugue involves a repetition
which does not reinforce the identity of the same, but is instead
traversed by difference.

From a very early stage in *Fugue*, the difference of writing from
itself, which precludes textual self-coincidence, is given the name
of *contre-écriture*, a term which clearly owes something to the
countersubject of a fugue. The variety of fugal composition means
that any single definition of the term will admit exceptions, but most
commonly the countersubject is a continuation of the subject which
is heard against the subject when the latter is repeated in the form
of an answer.[68] The appropriateness of the analogy is apparent inasmuch as the countersubject is at once continuous with the subject
and contrapuntally differentiated from it. Furthermore, it is the
countersubject which marks the subject's difference from itself in
repetition, given that the subject repeated as first answer is no longer
the same because of the relationship in which it now stands with the
countersubject.

The scriptor first introduces the term *contre-écriture* in the second
sequence of *Fugue*:

S'opposant en effet à ce que provisoirement, et faute de mieux, j'appellerai
mon écriture, puisque posée noir sur blanc par celui qui dit 'je', il y a en effet
je ne sais quelle blancheur ennemie qui évide mon écriture, la disjoint d'elle-
même, un blanchiment qui efface par avance ce que j'aurais pu écrire, me
déloge sans cesse de ce que je ne suis donc pas en droit d'appeler mon
écriture: cette rayure, cette éclaircie, ce sillon, je l'appellerai contre-écriture,
tout en répétant que cette douleur est sans doute ma seule chance. (F 258)

The terms in which *contre-écriture* is described here, as what
disconnects writing from itself through the creation of blanks,
prohibiting the appropriation of writing through the disruption of
writing's own propriety, its presence to itself, cannot but recall the
operation of *différance*. At the same time as denying the possibility of
textual self-coincidence sought by the scriptor in his desire for a
writing which would be at once *dire* and *faire*, *contre-écriture* is the
scriptor's only hope inasmuch as it permits the continued play of the

text. It is the necessary supplement of writing, and therefore, of course, the supplement at the non-originary source of writing: 'le texte effectif est l'œuvre conjointe de l'écriture et de la contre-écriture [...]. [la contre-écriture] occupe le cœur sans cœur de l'écriture' (*F* 268). It is writing's other, the outside which has always already been contained within the work, and which in that chiastic moment has opened the work up to its uncertain future: 'Tout se passe donc comme si l'ouvrage était le lieu de l'affrontement entre un dedans et un dehors, entre l'écriture et la contre-écriture, adversaire qu'il serait pourtant injuste de considérer comme ennemi de l'ouvrage, puisque sans elle l'ouvrage se géométriserait, cristalliserait en un Traité qui, pour être parfait, n'en signifierait pas moins pour l'ouvrage, sublimé en l'Œuvre, une immobilité mortelle' (*F* 268). Clearly, then, the relationship between *écriture* and *contre-écriture* cannot be conceived in terms of a simple bipolarity. If *contre-écriture* is writing's other, it is the other which enters into the constitution of the same, an exterior which has always been at work in writing's interior, thereby always already blurring the boundary of inside and outside. Returning to the metaphor of writing as *jeu*, the scriptor observes that, although *écriture* and *contre-écriture* are, in one sense, more fundamentally opposed than the black and white squares on a chessboard, they are none the less inseparable, as one cannot say 'ici, à cette borne, finit l'écriture: au-delà commence la contre-écriture. Cette absence de frontière ne signifie pas qu'il y ait un joint ou une jonction, mais que la ligne de démarcation est perdue' (*F* 281).

In the self-generative form of writing as fugue, *contre-écriture* is what marks the difference in repetition—preventing the contrapuntal texture of writing from stabilizing in a false harmony—without being present in that writing. The scriptor insists, in a passage which again clearly recalls Derrida's *différance*, that *contre-écriture* is not itself an entity: 'La contre-écriture n'existe pas ou plutôt elle n'est rien d'autre que ce vide qui tôt ou tard efface toute œuvre ou même qui me retire par avance la page sur laquelle je me dispose à écrire, qui provoque ainsi la perte même du travail en faisant de l'écrivain un mort en sursis, et pourtant, de même qu'une roue ne peut tourner sans le vide du moyeu, de même il me faut faire l'hypothèse que sans passage à vide l'esprit ne pourrait travailler ni le texte se déplacer' (*F* 297). It is through the working of *contre-écriture* that the Orphic text returns on itself and finds, rather than the reflection which would confirm self-identity, an alterity which marks difference. It also separates the scriptor from his writing, condemning him to the *Noli me legere* described by Blanchot in *L'Espace littéraire*, the impossibility of reading which confronts the writer in the face of his/her own work, but which is not simply negative, as 'elle est plutôt la seule approche réelle que l'auteur puisse avoir de ce que nous appelons œuvre'.[69] The interval opened up in this way between the writer and the work is what compels the writer constantly to begin again, to compose interminable supplements. The impossibility of reading means for the writer 'pas d'autre possibilité que d'écrire toujours cette œuvre'.[70] So it is that, as we have already seen, the interval opened up by *contre-écriture* is what allows the scriptor to continue to write; it is precisely his sense of estrangement from *Fugue*, for instance, that provides the material which initiates its *Supplément*. In this process of constant revision, or fugal variation, the scriptor often quotes passages from earlier in the work, and this practice of self-quotation merits careful consideration.

iii. *Copies non conformes*: the other in the same

The process of revision and rewriting undertaken in Laporte's later works becomes apparent from quite an early stage in *Fugue*. In his interview with Jean Ristat, Laporte draws attention to the way in which individual sequences pick up on earlier ones, each sequence recalling earlier material 'tout en le contestant et en se différenciant des séquences précédentes',[71] thereby highlighting the *brisure* which both articulates and divides the individual sequences, and indeed volumes. It is a process frequently discussed in the texts themselves, as in this passage from *Fugue*, where the scriptor observes that successive pages cannot erase the preceding ones, 'mais le texte déjà fait constitue une matière première susceptible d'être indéfiniment œuvrée, c'est-à-dire transformée' (F 276). The clearest instance of this is when an earlier passage is actually quoted in a subsequent sequence or even volume, a practice which is particularly interesting, given the scriptor's ambition of textual self-coincidence. The fourth sequence of *Suite*, for example, opens with an assemblage of phrases already employed in the text, leading the scriptor to ask: 'En copiant cette dernière phrase sans faire la moindre correction, en mettant par conséquent mes pas dans mes pas, est-ce que je n'apporte pas moi-même la preuve que mon aventure est achevée?' (S 527). The image of retracing one's footsteps, which occurs a number of times in *Suite*, is itself a distant reworking of an image first encountered in *Une Migration*, and just as the narrator of that *récit* was unable to do this, so the scriptor of *Suite* subsequently dismisses the hope of self-coincidence through self-quotation out of hand.

On one level, it is not too difficult to see why he should do so. The passage extracted from an earlier sequence to be quoted in another one is no longer the same, in so far as the context has changed. The most celebrated literary model for the problems of quotation with which we are dealing here is Borges's 'Pierre Menard, Author of the *Quixote*', in which Menard's ultimate literary goal is said to have been 'to produce a few pages which would coincide—word for word and line by line—with those of Miguel de Cervantes'.[72] Menard completes two chapters and a fragment of a third, of which the narrator remarks, 'Cervantes's text and Menard's are verbally identical, but the second is almost infinitely richer.'[73] The principal reason for this has already been indicated in a letter from Menard to the narrator, which adduces the interval between Cervantes's text, composed at the beginning of the seventeenth century, and Menard's own attempt at the beginning of the twentieth: '"it is not in vain that three hundred years have gone by, filled with exceedingly complex events. Among them, to mention only one, is the *Quixote* itself."'[74] Similarly, in Laporte's use of self-quotation the intervening text and the very act of quotation transform the quoted passage, which may be verbally identical but is no longer the same.

In Laporte's practice, the quoted passage is frequently not even verbally identical, as the transformative effect of quotation is manifested in the text by his use of falsified self-quotation. The description of *contre-écriture* itself appropriately provides a good example of this; at one point the scriptor notes that the act of writing heals the rift between the manifest text and its hidden other, but at the same time, 'une opération silencieuse, sans temps ni lieu, détisse l'ouvrage qui se fait, provoque une divergence entre ce qui voulait se dire et ce qui pourra l'être, brisure cruelle mais sans laquelle la machine d'écriture cesserait de fonctionner' (*F* 277). This passage occurs in the fifth sequence, and is recalled in the ninth and final sequence of *Fugue*, where part of the earlier description is quoted verbatim but with a modification suggested: 'dans la cinquième séquence, désignant cet écartement, j'ai écrit qu'une "opération silencieuse, sans temps ni lieu, détisse l'ouvrage qui se fait": je peux reprendre cette formule, mais à la condition que soit récusé le terme d'opération' (*F* 314). The 'écartement' mentioned here refers to the textual divergence or rift, to which I alluded a moment ago; in this regard the scriptor has cited, just before the lines quoted here, a passage from the second sequence which suggests that this divergence, in the metaphor of text as weaving deployed frequently in *Fugue*, affects not only the woven text, but the act of weaving and the weaver-writer himself. It is a phenomenon beyond the control of the writer, hence the rejection of the term 'opération' as too connotative of an activity performed by someone. In the next paragraph the same passage is quoted again, but this time the proposed modification is actually incorporated in the quotation (which still retains its quotation marks) as the scriptor finds that even this is an inappropriate formulation for an event which does not actually take place, avowing that 'je ne saurais en effet justifier cette définition, pourtant corrigée, de l'écartement: "Une (non)-opération silencieuse, sans temps ni lieu, détisse l'ouvrage qui se fait"' (*F* 315). In this instance, the process by which the quotation is altered has been clearly laid out and is explicitly signalled—'pourtant corrigée'. Elsewhere, alterations of quotations often go unannounced, as at the end of this same paragraph where the working of *contre-écriture* is given its former designation as an 'opération silencieuse' in what is presented as quite a lengthy quotation, '"trait sans trace, déhiscence introuvable, opération silencieuse, [etc.]"' (*F* 316), which actually draws together phrases scattered throughout the preceding sequences; the parenthetical negation of the term 'opération' is no longer deemed necessary, presumably because all of these formulations are now grouped together as terms which a persona of the *je* named here as the 'mythographe' accords to an interval or *espacement* which, as the scriptor now insists, is never readable in the text anyway.

Laporte describes these falsified self-quotations as *copies non conformes*. He discusses their use and stresses the importance he attaches to them in the 1972 interview with Ristat, where he suggests that self-quotation and, more subtly, falsified self-quotation, is the best means of making manifest the discrepancy between the itinerary envisaged for writing and the actual path it takes, or between what one wrote and what one is now writing: 'Le lecteur n'a qu'à revenir en arrière, à comparer. Je fabrique des faux en écriture. Les grands blancs qui séparent les séquences sont les moments où il va y avoir une différence importante: ce qu'on écrivait n'était pas tenable, on devient étranger à soi-même. Expérience déroutante et bouleversante du

"Comment ai-je pu écrire cela".'[75] The account given here of *copies non conformes* in terms of the writer's estrangement from the constituted text, a discrepancy between the writing and the already written, is echoed in *Fugue* itself:

Il y aura toujours du jeu entre le trajet prévu et le tracé effectif. (*F* 267)

Lorsque je me relis en vue d'écrire, je ne vois pas le texte tel qu'il est, dans ce qu'il dit, mais j'essaie plutôt de repérer les éléments qui s'ouvrent sur un texte à écrire. (*F* 270)

The use of self-quotation underlines the Orphic movement in the text which we have already noted in respect of the effects of *contre-écriture*, giving rise to the *va-et-vient* so often noted by the scriptor of the *Fugue* series, as the return to earlier passages discovers a transformation which provides the impetus for the continuation of writing. Blanchot himself makes this point in his excellent short article on Laporte, '"Ne te retourne pas"': 'l'itinérant qui en principe avance (Orphée attirant le déjà passé, jamais présent, vers l'avenir du jour), marche à la façon de l'écrevisse, à reculons, copie et recopie scrupuleusement les pièces d'archive, copie conforme qui est aussitôt, de ce fait et même sans cette contestation, copie non conforme, redite qui est ce qu'il y a de plus inédit.'[76] What we might call the Orphic glance in the text is already transformative and precludes the writing from coinciding with itself. The sense of an unbridgeable interval or *écart* assumes increasing importance in Laporte's later work, particularly in *Suite* and *Moriendo*: 'l'écart, ne creusant pas deux fois le même sillon, m'interdit de copier ce que j'ai déjà écrit, et, en ce sens, je le dis sans rire, nul ne répète moins que moi: tel est mon drame ou du moins l'une des conséquences de cette épreuve dont l'écart est l'origine' (*S* 529). At this stage of our discussion, we need hardly add that if a divergence is an origin, it is one which collaborates in the deconstruction of the very notion. This passage from *Suite* underlines Blanchot's observations to the effect that self-quotation marks the impossibility of the copy, participating instead in a process of repetition which affirms difference, just as a fugal subject which comes to be repeated in the form of an answer is no longer the same because of the very act of repetition, and because of the changed context provided by the contrapuntal relationship in which it now stands with the countersubject.

But to say this is at the same time to raise the question why the falsification of self-quotation should be necessary. Given Blanchot's assertion that the *copie conforme*, 'de ce fait et même sans cette contestation', is already a *copie non conforme*, and Laporte's suggestion in interview that the reader has only to turn back to compare the *copie non conforme* with the original, it is tempting to conclude that, far from being more subtle, the use of falsified self-quotation is a rather crude prompt to the reader. To do full justice to the oxymoronic *copie non conforme*, we should consider more carefully the status of the copy in general.

Let us return first of all to Borges's 'Pierre Menard, Author of the *Quixote*'. The narrator makes some very interesting remarks about the nature of Menard's enterprise, defending him against those who claim that he was attempting to produce a copy of the *Quixote*: 'His admirable intention was to produce a few pages which would coincide—word for word and line by line—with those of Miguel de Cervantes.'[77] The goal of producing a perfect coincidence involved creating another original rather than a copy of the original. In one sense, Menard's project fails in an unexpected way, in that his fragment of the *Quixote* turns out to be richer than Cervantes's, in the narrator's reading, because of the changed historical context, so that what one would normally call the copy actually supplants the original. Implicit in Borges's story is a reconsideration of the relationship between copy and original which we can pursue with the help of Derrida.

In *De la grammatologie*, we find that the relationship of copy to original involves once again the logic of supplementarity. In his reading of Rousseau's *Essai sur l'origine des langues*, Derrida cites a passage in which Rousseau notes that, in their study of the Greek language, Roman copyists invented signs which were not present in the original Greek, which leads Derrida to observe that 'le moment de la copie est un moment dangereux, comme celui de l'écriture qui d'une certaine manière est déjà une transcription, l'imitation d'autres signes; reproduisant des signes, produisant des signes de signes, le copiste est toujours tenté d'ajouter des signes *supplémentaires* pour améliorer la restitution de l'original.'[78] The moment of the copy is dangerous because its supplementary amelioration of the original indicates, as we have already seen, that the original was never self-sufficient to start with; the lack which the copy supplements means that the original is, in a sense, dependent on the copy. We can gain further illumination of the relationship between the original and the copy from 'La Pharmacie de Platon', Derrida's reading of Plato on the subject of imitation, in which alphabetical writing is said to be a perfect imitation of the voice to the precise extent that it does not imitate it exactly: 'Une imitation parfaite n'est plus une imitation. En supprimant la petite différence qui, le séparant de l'imité, y renvoie par là même, on rend l'imitant absolument différent: un autre étant ne faisant plus référence à l'imité. L'imitation ne répond à son essence, n'est ce qu'elle est—imitation—qu'en étant en quelque point fautive ou plutôt en défaut.'[79] The copy, in this case the written imitation of the voice, must differ from the original in order to act as a copy. Furthermore, the choice of writing and the voice as an illustration is significant, as we recall the strategic inversion of the writing/speech hierarchy developed in *De la grammatologie*: what was taken to be the original—speech—reveals itself to be dependent on its divergent copy. The original requiring the advent of a copy in order to become an original, the copy comes to supplant that which it was supposedly imitating, as Derrida remarks in his essay 'La dissémination': 'le "réel", l'"originaire", le "vrai", le "présent" n'étant constitués qu'en retour à partir de la duplication en laquelle seule ils peuvent surgir'.[80]

The scriptor of the *Fugue* series is therefore caught in a double bind in his quest for self-coincidence in writing. In reproducing an earlier passage word for word, he finds, like Borges's Menard, that the same is already different, the *copie conforme* already *non conforme*. If, on the other hand, he seeks to neutralize that difference by incorporating it in a *copie non conforme*, to imitate perfectly through an imperfect imitation, the copy's improvement on the original reveals it to be the supplement without which the original was originally incomplete, that is to say, incomplete as an origin. What is discovered through the supplementary substitution of *copies non conformes* is the irrecuperable originary delay which will continue to frustrate the quest for textual self-coincidence.

The logic of supplementarity at work in the relationship between original and copy is often evoked in the *Fugue* series, as in the scriptor's description of the functioning of the text in *Supplément* as the 'stratification discordante du volume d'archives, composé des différentes fausses répliques d'aucun texte original' (*FS* 389), a description which itself is echoed in a sort of *copie non conforme* in *Fugue 3*: 'Pourquoi n'écrirai-je jamais qu'une suite divergente de copies non superposables d'aucun texte original?' (*F3* 439). The irrecuperable originary delay which, we have already suggested, provides part of the answer to this question, has already been signalled much earlier in *Fugue 3*, when the scriptor was analysing the relationship between this text and its predecessors: 'Je ne suis point parvenu à un point zéro à partir duquel tout pourrait commencer à nouveau, car le moment premier d'une séquence, voire d'un ouvrage, loin d'être inaugural, se fonde sur un certain rapport entre le scripteur et les archives' (*F3* 403). The beginning of a work is never truly inaugural, not only because of its relationship with previous works, but also because its status as a beginning is dependent on what we might call the trace of future archives, for, as the scriptor notes a few lines later: 'maintes pages seront nécessaires avant d'en venir au moment tardif où la première page de ce livre se détachera enfin de la dernière du livre précédent' (*F3* 404).

The paradox whereby the copy turns out to precede the original, which can no longer be understood as a self-present origin, may also be explained in terms of a generalized citationality at work in language. As Derrida points out in 'Signature événement contexte',[81] for any utterance to be meaningful it is necessary that it should be possible to understand it in a context other than that in which it was 'originally' uttered, indeed that this should be possible in a range of contexts that cannot be limited; in other words, the limitless possibility of its citation is a structural necessity. The possibility of citation, of repetition in unlimitable contexts, is equally a condition of the sign, which must at the same time be recognizable when it is repeated within an indeterminate range of difference—across varieties of handwriting, typeface, orthography, etc. This necessary possibility of differential repetition, of *copies non conformes* of no single original, is described by Derrida as iterability, a term which contains the notions of both repetition and alterity.

One of the interests for us of the notion of iterability, and one to which we shall return again in a moment, is the use to which Derrida puts it in this essay, namely to demonstrate that performative utterances are only possible on the very grounds of iterability— citation in a range of contexts, including such 'parasitic' ones as fiction or jokes—that J. L. Austin excludes from his speech act theory. This is not done, it should be said, in order to advance the absurd proposition that successful performatives are not possible, but rather to suggest, *pace* Austin, that such success depends on iterability and not on the event of the speech act as a singular contextualized occurrence: in other words, that possible failure is a structural necessity of successful performatives. This has obvious repercussions for a project such as that announced in *Fugue* of a perfect coincidence of *faire* and *dire*, of the performative and the constative. The effect of iterability excludes such a coincidence, not on the conventional grounds that the performative and the constative cannot coexist, but on the grounds of a necessary coexistence which none the less cannot become a perfect coincidence. The performative 'I hereby begin the work' necessarily harbours its possible constative re-citation, 'I wrote, "I hereby begin the work"', or 'I wrote in vain, "I hereby begin the work"', or even, with apologies to Laporte, 'I wrote, "I hereby fail to begin the work"'. Indeed, such possibilities already begin to sketch out the unlimitable context in which the meaning of the utterance, not simply present to itself, is deferred, and in which it becomes a necessary possibility that the utterance is already a citation. The utterance is caught in the fold of a citation, undecidably performative and constative without being the perfect coincidence of both which would saturate its own context and bring an end to such *différance*.

The fugal text, in which writing recites and reworks itself, gives rise to a form of self-reference in which, as the scriptor of *Supplément* has already reminded us, there is no 'self' for reference to designate. This process—imitation without mimesis as Andrew Benjamin puts it— reminds us of Derrida's reading, in 'La double séance', of Mallarmé's 'Mimique', a text whose self-referentiality, Derrida insists, does not produce a perfectly closed system: 'Telle écriture qui ne renvoie qu'à elle-même nous reporte *à la fois*, indéfiniment et systématiquement, à une autre écriture.'[82] Any signifying system must refer to itself in order to signify at all, but must at the same time refer outside of itself, otherwise it would be entirely closed and would cease to signify, becoming a text impenetrable to reading. As we have noted before, there is a chiastic relation between inside and outside which dictates that the self-reference which is the only possibility of language is also its impossibility. Thus, as Derrida remarks of another highly self-referential text, Philippe Sollers's *Nombres*, 'comme tout commence dans le pli de la citation [...], le dedans du texte aura toujours été hors de lui, dans ce qui semble servir de "moyens" à l'"œuvre"'.[83]

The interminable chain of simulacra, copies of no original produced by the folding of citation, leads the scriptor of *Suite* to ask, 'Si je pouvais affirmer: "En vérité je suis un simulateur", du même coup j'arracherais toute l'épaisseur de mes déguisements, mais serai-je enfin nu?' (*S* 507). The paradox of the affirmation, of the same type as the paradox of the Cretan liar, already yields an answer.[84] The strategies by which such self-referential paradoxes are generally resolved, such as the establishment of a hierarchy of types, or the distinction drawn between language and metalanguage, or between the use and the mention of terms, are excluded here by the absence of any ground from which to establish a priority amongst terms, by the impossibility of transcending the self-referential system which makes such paradoxes undecidable, 'car si l'on pouvait avoir sur un labyrinthe une perspective cavalière, on en serait déjà sorti' (*F3* 488). The scriptor of *Suite*, immediately after the passage cited a moment ago, recognizes the absence of any final presence which would arrest this chain of simulacra: 'Le masque s'ouvre sur un masque à peine différent, ou plutôt une figure succède à une autre figure, indéfiniment, mais jamais aucun visage dans sa nudité dernière' (*S* 507).

In this supplementary substitution of simulacra, there is no longer a simple disjunction between truth and simulation, but rather an interpenetration of the two terms. To understand this interpenetration, we might recall here Derrida's discussion of 'mimétologisme' in 'La double séance',[85] cited earlier in this chapter. If the self-referential text does not produce the mimetic truth of a perfect correspondence with an object wholly external to the text, neither is it an anti-referential closed system which, as a totality, would equally be grounded in some totality exterior to itself, falling now in the domain of truth as *aletheia*. We can take his argument a little further by remarking that, if within the self-referential text there is no moment of perfect self-coincidence which could also be conceived in terms of truth as *adaequatio*, self-reference producing instead a series of *copies non conformes* or simulacra, it should be stressed that neither is there absolute disparity between these simulacra such as would permit the dismissal of any notion of mimetic truth. The imperfect imitations produced by the fugal writing are irreducible to a simple opposition between pure simulation and mimetic truth, even as they dispel a notion of truth as correspondence to an original presence. What sort of conception of truth is in fact thus produced is a question we can explore in the light of Derrida's reading of another highly self-referential text, Francis Ponge's poem 'Fable', in his essay 'Psyché, Invention de l'autre'.[86]

Ponge's poem has become something of a paradigm of reflexivity; it begins thus: 'Par le mot *par* commence donc ce texte / Dont la première ligne dit la vérité'. Derrida notes that the self-reference of the opening line describes its own inaugural performance, is at once apparently constative and performative, and in referring to itself and nothing else, is at once language and metalanguage, and neither: 'tout dans cette première ligne [...] est à la fois langage premier et métalangage second—et rien ne l'est' (24). These simultaneities inscribe a division within the self-reference of the line: referring to itself, saying what it does, it refers to itself otherwise in the constatation of its own performance, articulated and divided, we might say, by the minimal *différance* which is the time of reading. This takes place within a fiction—'Fable'—but a fiction which, the second line tells us, begins by telling the truth: a fiction of truth, or the truth of/as fiction (more will be said about these undecidables in a moment). What takes place in 'Fable' is not therefore a perfect self-coincidence, but an instability: 'L'oscillation infiniment rapide entre performatif et constatif, langage et métalangage, fiction et non-fiction, auto- et hétéro-référence, etc., ne produit pas seulement une instabilité essentielle. Cette instabilité constitue l'événement même, disons l'œuvre, dont l'invention perturbe normalement, si on peut dire, les normes, les statuts et les règles' (25). Its performative reflexivity, or invention of itself, is at the same time an invention of the other, this invention constituting a 'normal' disruption of norms because, as Derrida will go on to argue, any invention is, in a sense, an invention of the other.

The performative and the constative in the opening line of 'Fable' correspond to two conceptions of *invention* identified by Derrida: 'le concept d'invention distribue ses deux valeurs essentielles entre les deux pôles du constatif (découvrir ou dévoiler, manifester ou dire ce qui est) et du performatif (produire, instituer, transformer)' (23). By this stage, Derrida has already suggested as exemplary types of these conceptions of *invention*, on the one hand, 'histoires' (fictional or 'fabuleux' narratives which invent without reference to a reality outside of them) and on the other, 'machines' (technical devices which, on the basis of materials already available, give rise to new possibilities). However, the instability of the performative and the constative in 'Fable', revealing what is there even as it produces it, indicates an undecidable complicity between these two conceptions, an iterability of invention. An invention can only come about from what is already there (lest it be a 'pure fiction'), but in order to be an invention it must transform it, repeat it otherwise. Furthermore, the 'invention' which is the result of an event of invention must, as an artefact, be susceptible to reproduction, repetition: 'Dès lors le "une fois" ou le "une première fois" de l'acte d'invention se trouve divisé ou multiplié en lui-même, d'avoir donné lieu à une itérabilité. Les deux types extrêmes des choses inventées, le dispositif machinique d'une part, la narration fictive ou poématique d'autre part, impliquent à la fois la première fois et toutes les fois, l'événement inaugural et l'itérabilité' (47). In situating itself between them, 'Fable' reveals the instability of the opposition between the two poles of invention. The poem's invention of itself without reference to anything outside it, its flickering oscillation of language and metalanguage, is only possible on the grounds of a language which precedes it and which it can redeploy, and this possibility also necessarily entails the possibility that the invented and inventive machine which is 'Fable' may also, as in Derrida's essay, be recited, repeated, reiterated.

'Fable' blurs the distinction between conceptions of invention through its reflection on its own linguistic performance, on the mirror of the word, that word which appears in its first line, 'Par le mot *par*': 'Entre les deux "par", le tain qui se dépose sous les deux lignes, entre l'une et l'autre, c'est le langage même' (31). The linguistic mirroring which will give rise to the instability of the performative and the constative begins here, in a reflection of the word 'par', a word which is repeated otherwise, but in the process reveals that iterability at work from the first: performance and constatation, 'par' used, then mentioned, but in that reflection, used *and* mentioned from its first appearance, cited originarily. It is in this reflection on reflection that the truth of 'Fable' resides, for the truth of poetic invention, we might say, is that impossibility which is the only possibility of language, including, for instance, scientific and philosophical discourses which must hold to that possibility to tell the truth, namely linguistic self-reference; the reflexivity of 'Fable', and of Laporte's texts, makes a virtue of that necessity, and an impossibility of that possibility. Such texts reflect on the conditions of language which are the only possibility of truth as *adaequatio* or *aletheia*, constatation or performance, but at the same time show that truth to be an invention or a fiction (which is not simply to say untrue). The text which, through self-reflection, invents itself, discovers the difference in its reduplication, the advent of the other in the repetition of the same: 'Le mouvement même de cette fabuleuse répétition peut, selon un croisement de chance et de nécessité, produire le nouveau d'un événement. Non seulement par l'invention singulière d'un performatif, car tout performatif suppose des conventions et des règles institutionnelles; mais en tournant ces règles dans le respect de ces règles mêmes afin de laisser l'autre venir ou s'annoncer dans l'ouverture de cette déhiscence' (58–9). The failure of self-coincidence in reflexivity necessarily opens such a text up to the chance of the future, the radically unpredictable event of the advent of the other. To this extent, the self-inventing text is, in a double genitive, the invention of the other, which, as Derrida remarks, is in turn an impossibility— 'l'autre n'est pas le possible' (59)—which is the only possibility of invention: without it, there could only be a circulation of the same.

The use of the *copie non conforme*—qualified by Blanchot, we may recall, as 'redite qui est ce qu'il y a de plus inédit'—is one of the strategies by which the self-invention of Laporte's texts can signal the invention of the other, the working of iterability which prevents the termination of the text's generation of itself in the resolution of a perfect harmony. The falsification of self-quotation can indicate the differential repetition at work in the text, but no constatation can ever exhaust the endlessly productive performance of this textual machine. Each *copie non conforme* does more than it can say, produces an excess which can only be recovered, but already repeated otherwise, in a subsequent copy, and so on. However, in exposing its own workings, the text produces the undecidable oscillation between performative and constative, language and metalanguage, practice and theory, which we have discussed in Ponge's 'Fable', and which the scriptor of *Fugue* describes in a passage worth quoting at length. Contrasting the visibility of the production of his own work with classical works which conceal their workings and theoretical works which seek to lay bare the workings of the former, he remarks that

quant au nouveau genre que je cherche, il n'est plus besoin de faire dans un autre livre la théorie de sa pratique, car celle-ci est elle-même une suite ordonnée d'opérations qui implique l'élaboration des concepts destinés à la commander. La constitution, non d'un Traité, mais de schèmes théoriques, fait partie du jeu littéraire: le texte ne pourrait fonctionner si la lecture de son fonctionnement ne s'y inscrivait en abîme, et pourtant, de même que cette séquence n'est point le double, mais une interprétation, une pratique neuve du texte déjà écrit, de même, du moins si l'ouvrage continue de fonctionner selon le mode qui jusqu'à maintenant a été le sien, il me sera plus tard possible, voire nécessaire, de revenir en arrière, de lire ces pages de telle sorte qu'elles deviendront la copie non conforme du texte qu'alors j'écrirai. (*F* 295)

The importance of exposing the 'travail' of the text underlined here is reiterated time and again by Laporte in the *Fugue* series, as well as in notebooks and interviews. It is a feature which invites a further parallel with Ponge, in view for example of the latter's publication of the drafts of the poem 'Le Pré' as *La Fabrique du pré*; this very parallel is drawn by Derrida in a note to the 'Hors livre' section of *La Dissémination*, where he writes of 'ces deux machines musicales que sont, aussi différemment qu'il est possible, *Le Pré* ou *la Fabrique du pré*, de Francis Ponge, *Fugue*, de Roger Laporte'.[87] We noted in Chapter 1 that, as early as 1954, Laporte had written of Ponge in his *Carnets*: 'Ce que j'aime dans ses œuvres: 1) (malgré lui) leur aspect *genèse* d'un poème' (*C* 35). On the other hand, in a later interview Laporte remarks: 'Je me suis rendu compte, surtout en lisant *La Fabrique du pré*, qu'en réalité, n'en déplaise à Ponge, le travail de création est invisible. Il se passe *entre* deux brouillons.'[88] We might recall here what we have gleaned from Derrida's reading of 'Fable', namely that, if the invention of the other is strictly impossible, it is none the less the only possibility of invention: the creative work of *différance* alone permits the movement of a text in which it will never be present. We should also bear this in mind when reading the scriptor's remarks about the *déchirure* which both disrupts and generates writing in *Fugue 3*: 'j'ai dû admettre que la déchirure n'a pas lieu parce que j'en parle, au moment où j'en parle: le travail practico-théorique n'est jamais assimilable à ce qu'on appelle en linguistique un discours performatif' (*F3* 463). At first reading, this seems to run counter to what we have said about Laporte's work, but we should underline that the practico-theoretical work of the reflexive text is not *simply* performative, but precisely gives rise to an oscillation of the performative and the constative, in which the unity of the performative event is originarily fractured, relayed outside of itself, by the necessary possibility of differential repetition, and it is in that iterability that the advent of the other, of writing's disruptive-generative other, may be read—or rather, we should say, allows reading without ever being actualized by reading, as the scriptor of *Fugue* has already suggested with the question: 'Pourquoi donc toute lecture de la contre-écriture comme telle est-elle impossible?' (*F* 283).

The writing of writing's other is as impossible as its reading, although the virtue of reflexive texts such as Laporte's and Ponge's is to demonstrate that this impossibility is paradoxically unavoidable. This strange obligation to write the impossible is noted in *Fugue*, in a passage following the likening of *écriture* and *contre-écriture* to the black and white squares of a chessboard:

L'écrivain ne peut en effet directement faire le jeu de la contre-écriture, car il est fonctionnellement du côté des noirs: dès qu'il écrit, il ne peut pas ne pas participer à l'activité combinatoire de l'écriture qui ne sait rien faire d'autre: il cherche la répartition la plus exacte, l'arrangement le plus cohérent, les définitions les plus arrêtées, mais ce souci même de justesse est le détour par lequel il mise sur la contre-écriture: il attend le moment imprévisible, qui pourtant jamais ne fait défaut, où le travail qu'il accomplit sera à son tour perturbé. (*F* 281–2)

The disruptive moment of *contre-écriture* is necessarily unpredictable, for the possibility of its anticipation in writing would entail the static repetition of the same, but the advent of writing's other is equally necessary for the same reason, namely to permit the movement of the text. Hence the passivity of the writer *vis-à-vis* this disruptive agency at the heart of writing suggested in this passage, and already made explicit in an earlier account of the relationship between the writer and *contre-écriture*: 'Tout écrivain se représente son métier sous la forme d'un frayage, et pourtant, dans son acte même, l'écriture est toujours aussi et en même temps d'une passivité foncière: l'acte d'écrire, en tant que surface réceptive, est donc toujours agi au cœur de son activité' (*F* 268). This passivity, as Derrida remarks in 'Psyché, Invention de l'autre', is not the resigned passivity which acquiesces in the circulation of the same, but an active passivity or 'passion' (to recall the term cited earlier in this chapter from Derrida's 'Ellipse'), whose provocation of an instability of performative and constative, language and metalanguage, constitutes a writing which is 'passible de l'autre, ouverte à l'autre et par lui, par elle travaillée, travaillant à ne pas se laisser enfermer ou dominer par cette économie du même en sa totalité' (61). If writing's other cannot itself be written, the use of *copies non conformes* and other strategies which we shall explore shortly reveals the interruption of identity in repetition, opening the text to the necessary but necessarily aleatory advent of the other which distances writing from itself: 'Donner sa chance à la chance de cette rencontre', in Geoffrey Bennington's phrase.[89]

Early in *Fugue*, the scriptor recognizes that the moment of the interruption of the text, the 'ajour' in its fabric, threatens to ruin his work, but at the same time gives a chance to the invention of the other: 'L'ajour est donc le moment de la chance: que se forme un texte aux figures toujours inattendues, mais aussi celui du plus grand risque, non seulement celui d'une interruption définitive, mais aussi, quant au livre, d'un ignoble gâchis' (F 261). In a feature which again suggests an element of continuity even with Laporte's earliest work, the scriptor of *Fugue* is therefore involved in a game of 'qui perd gagne', in which the moment of perhaps irreparable loss may also allow the scriptor to approach the perfection of his work, the moment of the *fête*. In the seventh sequence of *Fugue*, the scriptor describes the disruptions and deviations which his writing undergoes, but in doing so observes that he is once again implicitly evoking *contre-écriture*, which as a result comes to constitute a resistance to the very 'travail d'usure' he is undertaking, 'résistance qui risque d'être dangereusement supérieure à la force de mon esprit qui se dépense pour rien' (F 296). This is followed, in a new paragraph, by this observation: 'Ce que je cherchais ou plutôt ce que je ne cherchais pas, ce que je n'attendais point s'est à présent accompli: après avoir tant travaillé, j'ai connu pendant un instant le soulagement d'une pause et je connais encore la liberté, l'ivresse d'un jour de fête!' (F 296).

The articulation of an unproductive expenditure ('mon esprit qui se dépense pour rien') with the notion of 'un jour de fête' constitutes a clear echo of the writings of Bataille, an echo underscored in the eighth sequence by the scriptor's description of the 'partage du texte': 'Il y aurait trois domaines: celui du travail; celui de la perte, mais qui, par chance, peut s'ouvrir sur la fête; celui de la sauvagerie' (F 303). In very cursory terms, Bataille contrasts the profane world of utilitarian production and exchange with a sacred world of expenditure without recompense, exemplified by the practice of *potlatch* in certain tribal societies, and by other forms of ritual sacrifice: on the day of the *fête*, transgressions of the utilitarian code are sanctioned.[90] In texts like *La Part maudite*, Bataille argues that, underlying restricted economies which maintain themselves in a utilitarian equilibrium of gain and loss, there is an entropic general economy operating on a principle of dissipation and waste, whose paradigm is the sun's excessive and wasteful production of energy.[91] Roughly, then, we might say that the three domains of the text identified in *Fugue* correspond to the profane world of work, the limited transgression of the *fête* and the entropy of the general economy respectively.[92]

In fact, the limited transgression sanctioned by the *fête* may be said to be constitutive of, rather than opposed to, the profane world, inasmuch as it seeks to incorporate the entropic principle of absolute loss as a power of negation, contributing to the dialectic which maintains the equilibrium of the world of work.[93] Bataille may therefore be said to be proposing an economic model distributed between productive work and entropic play, accumulation and dispersal, in which the former is only made possible by a utilitarian domestication of a disseminatory force which will in the end always exceed it. In this light, it is interesting that a couple of pages after proposing a tripartite division of the text, the scriptor of *Fugue* offers this modification: 'je dis à présent que deux camps se partagent l'espace littéraire: la pensée joueuse et la pensée travailleuse séparées et unies par le vide d'un entre-deux' (*F* 305).[94]

The association of the literary space with wasteful expenditure is also suggested by Bataille's work, since literary creation is for him a sphere in which the attitude of *souveraineté* may be discovered.[95] In a form of Nietzschean *amor fati*, sovereignty is the acceptance of entropic play and irreparable loss, and is therefore opposed to the attitude of servility which is satisfied with the world of useful production.[96] But we should immediately add that sovereignty is not a possibility, being rather an impossible exigency.[97] The dialogue with Hegel in which Bataille is participating here is significant, since we may say that any attempt to assume sovereignty immediately transforms it into Hegelian mastery, which participates in a productive dialectic, and is therefore another means of utilitarian domestication: the attempt to embrace absolute loss fails precisely because it participates in a game of 'qui perd gagne'. As an instance of this, we may recall the discovery in *Fugue*, cited earlier, that an account of the disruptive and disseminatory forces in the text implicitly invokes *contre-écriture*, that is to say, preserves a textual figure which consequently ends up resisting the very 'travail d'usure' with which it is normally associated.

However, as has repeatedly been suggested in *Fugue*, *écriture* and *contre-écriture* do not entirely exclude one another, playful thought and working thought are separated *and* united by the 'vide d'un entre-deux': there is an ineluctable *glissement* from the restricted economy to the general economy.[98] We may recognize this *glissement* as the spacing which permits the sign to appear as a plenitude, whilst at the same time vitiating any such plenitude and instituting an interminable chain of supplementary substitution. The approach to unachievable sovereignty, giving a chance to this chance, may therefore involve the provocation of this *glissement*, the miming of its play; as Derrida remarks in his essay on Bataille: 'Pour courir ce risque dans le langage, pour sauver ce qui ne veut pas être sauvé—la possibilité du jeu et du risque absolus—il faut redoubler le langage, recourir aux ruses, aux stratagèmes, aux simulacres.'[99] We have already noted the excessive production of simulacra in the *Fugue* series in the form of *copies non conformes* which, in miming iterability, produce a remainder, a surplus over self-identity, which destabilizes the equilibrium of the textual economy.[100] In the rest of this chapter, we shall briefly consider some other strategies which promote the notion of the text as an entropic writing-machine.

We have already encountered one such strategy in observing the modifications in accounts of *contre-écriture* in the *Fugue* series. The terms proposed to account for the working of the text are destabilized by variations in their own repeated appearance in the text, and participate in a more general instability as the inadequacies discovered in one term lead it to be replaced by another, which in turn proves inadequate, and so on. So, for example, the description of *contre-écriture* which refers to it as an 'opération' is re-cited as a *copie non conforme* in which *contre-écriture* becomes a '(non-)opération'. Equally, as we have seen, *contre-écriture* is nowhere present in the text, but at the same time permits the very functioning of writing; at various points in the text, its secret inhabitation of writing and its radical alterity are alternately emphasized in a constant shuttling between perspectives which prevents it from becoming a stabilized concept. Furthermore, as we have just seen, the bipartite model of *écriture* and *contre-écriture*, which might, despite all the contrary indications, be regarded as a dialectical pair, gives way in *Fugue* to the tripartite model of the domains of *travail*, *perte/fête* and *sauvagerie*, which in turn gives way to the division of the literary space between 'la pensée joueuse et la pensée travailleuse séparées et unies par le vide d'un entre-deux'. *Contre-écriture* reappears early in *Supplément* (see *FS* 341–4), as the scriptor considers what might be salvaged from *Fugue*, but thereafter largely disappears from the lexicon of textual operation, although it does surface again, for example in the penultimate paragraph, in a reference to 'La différence en tant que procès, la contre-écriture "cœur sans cœur" d'écrire' (*FS* 342), a reference which clearly signals the proximity of the term to Derridean *différance*. By the time of *Fugue 3*, *contre-écriture* has been all but expunged from the scriptor's lexicon, although interestingly, on its one significant appearance, the scriptor suggests that a displacement rather than an eradication has taken place:

'la contre-écriture n'a aucune réalité propre, elle n'existe pas, elle n'est qu'un effet du jeu ou fonctionnement, et pourtant lorsque j'ai affirmé qu'au moment où je raye un passage devenu inadmissible "je répète et achève la rature effectuée par la fabrique textuelle", j'ai attribué à l'écriture le pouvoir qu'auparavant je reconnaissais à la contre-écriture. Singulier déplacement!' (*F3* 448). In this text, much greater use is made of the term *déchirure* to describe the interruption of writing, but the scriptor does in fact observe in the *Codicille* that this term too may be replaced in the interminable chain of supplementary substitution, in a passage we have already noted: 'car à ce terme on en substituera un autre, puis un autre, et ainsi indéfiniment sans qu'aucun soit le double d'une quelconque réalité' (*F3* 494).

This process of substitution produces a series of fluidly overlapping simulacra, not entirely set loose, so to speak, in an unlimited dispersal—the writing of absolute loss not being a possibility—but participating in a system which constantly destabilizes itself in a *glissement* which affirms entropic play; as Derrida remarks of Bataille's writing, '[la destruction du discours] multiplie les mots, les précipite les uns contre les autres, les engouffre aussi dans une substitution sans fin et sans fond dont la seule règle est l'affirmation souveraine du jeu hors-sens.'[101] In *Supplément*, the neologism *systase* is coined from the Greek *sustasis*, 'qui désigne non plus un état, mais une action: celle d'organiser, par exemple un arrangement de mots' (*FS* 388), to describe just such a shifting configuration, 'un assemblage sans unité qui ne constitue pas un système [...]. Une réunion qui laisserait prévoir la dispersion' (*FS* 388). The groundless instability of the simulacra in such a *systase* is, in Derrida's terms, the effect of dissemination rather than polysemy, since we may say of these shifting figures that they 'ne se laissent en aucun *point* épingler par le concept ou la teneur d'un signifié.'[102]

A similar process may be discovered in the series of metaphors employed to describe the scriptor's enterprise in the *Fugue* series.[103] We have already noted how the game of 'le portrait chinois' gives rise to metaphors for the work such, for example, as a treatise of physics which was its own unique exemplification, or a game whose only object was the elaboration of its own rules (*F* 256–7). As we have also seen, the metaphor of the game undergoes a complex series of modifications in the course of the *Fugue* series, as does another metaphor first introduced early in *Fugue*, that of the text as a woven fabric which, we are told on its first appearance, is 'enté d'ajours', this openwork being produced by 'un écartement qui n'atteint pas seulement le tissu et le tissage mais le tisserand lui-même' (*F* 261). The third sequence of *Fugue* sees the introduction of what is described as scarcely a metaphor: 'celle d'un mobile ou d'une machine, dotée d'une sorte de stylet sismographique, qui se déplacerait tout en marquant son mouvement, qui se décrirait par cette marche aussi essentielle et caractéristique que celle d'une pièce du jeu d'échecs' (*F* 262). This metaphor, which initiates another chain of metaphors around the notion of auto-inscription, receives its first modification immediately as the scriptor adds that 'il ne s'agit point d'un facile enregistrement' and that one should think instead of a 'mobile' which can only make its way by inscribing a trace: 'ce chemin lui-même, trace d'abord inaperçue mais telle qu'après-coup elle peut être décrite' (*F* 263). In the first version of this metaphor, we can note another principle of modification at work in the reference to 'une pièce du jeu d'échecs': these metaphors, which are themselves constantly shifting, interfere with one another. Here, the metaphor of 'le jeu' is grafted onto that of inscription; later, different senses of 'le jeu' will be exploited in other contexts, for example in the sense of 'give' or 'slack' in connection with metaphors of the work as construction or machine—'la machine n'est pas détraquée, mais elle ne fonctionne qu'en jouant' (*F* 278)—or in the sense of 'gambling' in economic models of the work: 'La réussite, et par conséquent l'échec, n'ont pas de sens là où, d'entrée de jeu, la maîtrise est exclue, mais il n'empêche que l'enjeu me paraît exorbitant: comment, humainement, ne pas désirer sauver la mise, mais, quant à l'ouvrage, comment ne pas comprendre aussitôt que ce geste serait absurde!' (*F* 260). Given what was said earlier about the interarticulation of 'la pensée joueuse' and 'la pensée travailleuse', it is worth noting here that the metaphor of work as production becomes contaminated by the give or slack of 'le jeu', releasing another sense of 'le travail' as a warping: 'Mieux vaut reconnaître que l'esprit alors ne travaille plus comme un ouvrier, mais au sens où on le dit d'une maçonnerie, d'un étai ou d'un navire: il fatigue dangereusement et connaît une guerre d'usure sans visage à laquelle il n'a presque aucune force à opposer' (*F* 310).

What we have sketched out here are simply the beginnings of one or two threads of the tangled play of metaphor in the *Fugue* series. The initial impetus of this play, the game of 'le portrait chinois', is eventually abandoned at the beginning of *Fugue*'s seventh sequence; an explanation for this, given in *Supplément*, is worth quoting at length:

J'ai dû renoncer même au jeu du portrait chinois dans la mesure où il suppose une réalité préexistant à la recherche, où par conséquent il implique un axe métonymique où s'inscriraient les métaphores successives, mais tout axe, aussi bien horizontal que vertical, est toujours rompu: à suivre, à ne pas pouvoir suivre, écrire à la trace, on ne trouvera jamais que l'irrectitude d'une ligne brisée, les sautes vertigineuses d'une arabesque lacunaire. (*FS* 381)

In the play of metaphor there is once again a *glissement* of overlapping simulacra, in the reflexive play of which everything is at once language and metalanguage, and neither; everything is metaphor, and nothing is:

Sans commencement ni fin, sans règles, sans unité, écrire, toujours dissident, n'est assimilable à aucun jeu codifié, mais c'est justement pourquoi parler du jeu insensé d'écrire n'est pas une métaphore. On peut même dire que le jeu est le seul élément non-métaphorique de mon lexique, mais que prenne garde celui qui en conséquence prétendrait saisir l'essence d'écrire! Ce serait seulement par un abus de langage que l'on attribuerait une réalité à ce qui excède l'opposition du métaphorique et du réel. (*FS* 385)

Writing discovers as its non-originary origin a recursive play of metaphoric substitution, in which the literal, the *propre* of writing, is always already inscribed. In his essay on Laporte, 'Ce qui reste à force de musique', Derrida writes of 'la productivité de métaphores qui sont essayées les unes après les autres, se substituent sans fin, de telle sorte que, dans ce *retrait* général de la métaphore, aucune bordure, aucun horizon de propriété ne vient garder contre l'extension à l'infini de suppléments métaphoriques'.[104] In this infinite extension, he goes on to remark, metaphor no longer comes up against any limit, so that 'ne s'appuyant plus sur rien, elle n'est même plus elle-même, proprement, métaphore'.[105] The outside of metaphor comes to be contained within it, so that one can no longer speak of a 'simple' metaphor, in the sense of a figure which might eventually be replaced by something outside the play of metaphor.

By such strategies, the *Fugue* series constructs itself as a machine which plays out the displacement of metaphor; producing and produced by the imperfectible simulacra of itself, it repeatedly invents itself otherwise. According to one such simulacrum, which is in turn modified by a series of supplements throughout these texts, it is a machine which 'ne fonctionne qu'en jouant, qu'en provoquant cet écart, ce déportement par lequel elle est elle-même entraînée, ne demeurant vivante qu'en se détruisant, en se construisant indéfiniment, machine inutile qui ne produit même pas une machine, mais qui a fonctionné et permis un déplacement effectif seulement parce qu'elle a exercé aussi contre elle-même son pouvoir de subversion' (*F* 278).[106] The instability of this writing-machine which always reinvents itself differently takes us back to Merleau-Ponty's autocritical hyperdialectic, to which we alluded near the outset of this chapter in respect of Laporte's project of a new genre, irreducible to literature or philosophy or, we might say, to 'pure' invention (fiction) or invention as discovery of what was already there (truth). In its reflection on itself, Laporte's writing discovers the necessary coexistence of the performative and the constative, language and metalanguage, practice and theory, invention of the other and invention of the same, literature and philosophy; but, in so doing, it discovers that necessary coexistence to be at the same time impossible as a perfect coincidence. In its reflexive performance of iterability, this writing-machine always produces an excess, a surplus over self-identity in repetition, always does more than it says: its own saturation or exhaustion of itself, of its own utterances and metaphors, in the 'travail d'usure' of its reworking of itself, does not in the end leave nothing.

It is in similar terms that Derrida concludes his discussion of Laporte in 'Ce qui reste à force de musique', in which we also find a suggestion of how it is, as we mentioned earlier, that this writing might be said to aspire to the condition of music. The remainder which subsists when the writing-machine has apparently played itself out, cancelled all its propositions, emptied all its metaphors,[107] is a writing as rhythm: a rhythm of analepsis and prolepsis, the scansion of the text, and a rhythm of iterability, differential repetition: 'On ne peut même pas dire que la musique est arrivée à quelqu'un (Laporte questionne et fait trembler quelque part le *me*, le *m'* réflexif ou auto-affectif, dans l'expression "*quelque chose m'est arrivé*") et pourtant le passé étrange et inquiétant du "*il y a eu écriture*" passe ici irréductiblement par du musical et du rythmique, et nous contraint— telle est aussi la force singulière de *Fugue*—à repenser, à réinventer ce que nous disposons sous ces mots: musique-rythme.'[108]

Notes to Chapter 3

1. Cf. the interview 'Lire Roger Laporte', 283.
2. 'Lire Roger Laporte', 285.
3. Cf. 'Entretien entre Roger Laporte et Serge Velay', 15.
4. It should be noted that, earlier in these notebooks, Laporte has already described

the individual volumes *Suite* and *Moriendo* as constituting the two parts of *Moriendo* (cf. *LP* 21). For other indications of the break between *Fugue 3* and *Suite/Moriendo*, see *LP* 30 and 47.

5. The assembling of the individual works from *La Veille* to *Moriendo* in this collected volume brings in itself another modification to the breaks between these works. For an interesting discussion of this and other issues, see Benjamin, 'The Redemption of Value: Laporte, Writing as *Abkürzung*'.

6. Jacques Derrida, *De la grammatologie* (Paris: Minuit, 1967), 96.

7. As regards the importance of their friendship and correspondence, Laporte remarks: 'Je ne saurais en effet distinguer ce que je dois à la lecture des ouvrages de Derrida de ce que je dois aux propos et aux lettres de l'ami' (*B* 67). The other pieces to which I have alluded are the brief '"Les 'blancs' assument l'importance"', *Les Lettres Françaises* 1429 (1972), 5, and the study 'Une double stratégie', in Lucette Finas, Sarah Kofman, Roger Laporte and Jean-Michel Ray, *Ecarts: quatre essais à propos de Jacques Derrida* (Paris: Fayard, 1973), 208–64.

8. Cf., for instance, the discussion of the trace of the ontological difference in 'The Anaximander Fragment' in Martin Heidegger, *Early Greek Thinking* (New York: Harper and Row, 1984), 50–1, and Levinas's article, cited in the previous chapter, 'La trace de l'autre'.

9. I have chosen to refer to the *je* of Laporte's later works by the term 'scriptor', translating the term 'scripteur' which Laporte himself often uses. Certainly, it no longer seems appropriate to talk of a 'narrator' in these works, though I shall continue to use that term in respect of the texts prior to *Fugue*. For a discussion of the identities of the *je*, see Ch. 4.

10. Philippe Lacoue-Labarthe *et al.*, 'Entretiens sur Roger Laporte', *Digraphe* 18/19 (1979), 175–203 (187).

11. Lacoue-Labarthe *et al.*, 'Entretiens sur Roger Laporte', 188.

12. Jean Ricardou first coined the expression in a discussion of the undermining of mimesis in the *nouveau roman* in *Problèmes du nouveau roman* (Paris: Seuil, 1967): 'Ainsi le roman est-il pour nous moins *l'écriture d'une aventure que l'aventure d'une écriture*' (111).

13. 'L'hyperdialectique' in *QV* 159–68, wherein a note indicates that the study originally arose from an invitation by the review *Textures*, which did not in the end publish it; the bibliography in *Digraphe* 18/19 dates it from 1972.

14. The original passage may be found in Jacques Derrida, *L'Ecriture et la différence* (Paris: Seuil, 1967, coll. 'Points' reprint), 317.

15. Cf. Derrida, *L'Ecriture et la différence*, 34: 'Notre discours appartient irréductiblement au système des oppositions métaphysiques. On ne peut annoncer la rupture de cette appartenance que par une *certaine* organisation, un certain aménagement *stratégique* qui, à l'intérieur du champ et de ses pouvoirs propres, retournant contre lui ses propres *stratagèmes*, produise une *force de dislocation* se propageant à travers tout le système, le fissurant dans tous les sens et le *dé-limitant* de part en part.'

16. The original is in Jacques Derrida, *La Dissémination* (Paris: Seuil, 1972), 235.

17. Derrida, *De la grammatologie*, 11–12.

18. Laporte, 'Une double stratégie', 229.

19. Laporte, '"Les 'blancs' assument l'importance"'.

20. Derrida, *De la grammatologie*, 89; cit. *B* 67, and 'Une double stratégie', 229.

21. Cit. Derrida, *De la grammatologie*, 84.

22. Derrida, *De la grammatologie*, 89.

23. Levinas, 'Roger Laporte et la voix de fin silence', 107.

24. In Bataille, *L'Expérience intérieure*, in *Œuvres complètes*, v. 76.

25. Cf. Levinas, 'La trace de l'autre', esp. 190–1.

26. Blanchot, *L'Entretien infini*, 66.

27. Libertson, *Proximity*, 258. I cannot do justice to these three writers' discussions of experience here, and instead refer the reader to Libertson's study, especially Ch. 5.

28. I take the term 'anoriginal' from Benjamin, *Art, Mimesis and the Avant-Garde*.

29. Cf. also the remarks on 'l'idée du livre' in Derrida, *De la grammatologie*, 30–1.

30. Derrida, *L'Ecriture et la différence*, 431.

31. Blanchot, *L'Espace littéraire*, 232.

32. Blanchot, *L'Amitié*, 251.

33. The sense of 'distancing' and 'sending' which Derrida finds in the *Ereignis* in a text such as 'Pas' (in *Parages* (Paris: Galilée, 1986), 19–116) marks a reorientation in relation to Derrida's earlier discussions of Heidegger, which focused on the latter's metaphorics of presence and proximity (cf. 'Ousia et grammè' in *Marges—de la philosophie* (Paris: Minuit, 1972), 31–78). A thorough discussion of this changing relationship, which also stresses the crucial mediation of Blanchot's work, may be found in Herman Rapaport, *Heidegger and Derrida: reflections on time and language* (Lincoln, Nebraska and London: University of Nebraska Press, 1989).

34. Derrida, *La Dissémination*, 204.

35. Derrida, *La Voix et le phénomène* (Paris: Presses Universitaires de France, 1967), 90.

36. Derrida, *La Voix et le phénomène*, 55.

37. Laporte, *Ecrire la musique* (Bordeaux: à Passage, 1986), 11. Some of the material in this and in the final section of Ch. 3 extends analyses sketched out in my '*Musique-rhythme*: Derrida and Roger Laporte'.

38. 'Harmony' and 'harmonics' are not, of course, synonymous; in fact, Laporte tends to favour metaphors of harmonics. However, in the context of the argument I am going to advance here, they are effectively synonymous in their reliance on the notion of a fundamental tone (even if that is regarded as absent); I shall use the term 'harmony' to cover the various forms of this type of metaphor.

39. 'Lire Roger Laporte', 286.

40. Cf. Alfred Mann, *The Study of Fugue* (London: Faber and Faber, 1958), 9.

41. Roger Bullivant, 'Counterpoint', in *The New Oxford Companion to Music*, ed. Denis Arnold (Oxford: Oxford University Press, 1983), i. 501–6 (501).

42. Edmund Rubbra, e.g. in his *Counterpoint: A Survey* (London: Hutchinson University Library, 1960), remarks of the broad development of counterpoint that 'it became progressively absorbed into harmonies, the expressive power of which continually increased as counterpoint became freer and more adventurous. These harmonies were then used for their own sake and became the bases for fresh developments of contrapuntal principles' (103).

43. Rubbra, *Counterpoint*, 15.

44. Lacoue-Labarthe *et al.*, 'Entretiens sur Roger Laporte', 191.

45. Lacoue-Labarthe *et al.*, 'Entretiens sur Roger Laporte', 191.
46. Igor Stravinsky, *Poetics of Music in the Form of Six Lessons*, bilingual edn. (Cambridge, Mass.: Harvard University Press, 1970), 98. My attention was drawn to this remark by Leonard Olschner's article 'Fugal provocation in Paul Celan's "Todesfuge" and "Engführung"', *German Life and Letters* 43:1 (1989), 79–89. Celan's two poems are perhaps the most obvious precursors for the application of fugal terminology to a literary work. Laporte has signalled his own admiration of Celan's work in 'Lectures de Paul Celan' (*E* 65–74).
47. Cf. e.g. Derrida, *L'Ecriture et la différence*, 410.
48. The notion of originary delay, and the associated logic of supplementarity, to which I return later, occur repeatedly in Derrida's work, particularly in his earliest texts. A particularly succinct account of originary delay, which underlines clearly what I am saying about the fugal subject as origin, can be found in Vincent Descombes, *Le Même et l'autre: quarante-cinq ans de philosophie française (1933–1978)* (Paris: Minuit, 1979), 170–1.
49. Jean-François Lyotard, *Le Différend* (Paris: Minuit, 1983); see esp. the section entitled 'La présentation', 93–129. For an excellent account of the aspect of Lyotard's argument to which I refer here, see Geoffrey Bennington, *Lyotard: Writing the Event* (Manchester: Manchester University Press, 1988), 123–34.
50. Cf. Lyotard, *Le Différend*, § 95 (93–4).
51. Lyotard, *Le Différend*, § 124 (118): 'La présentation comportée par une phrase est oubliée par elle, plongée dans le Lèthè [...]. Une autre phrase l'en retire, qui la présente, en oubliant la présentation qu'elle-même comporte. La mémoire se double d'oubli. La métaphysique lutte contre l'oubli, comment s'appelle ce qui lutte pour lui?'
52. The logic of the supplement is first outlined by Derrida in his discussion of the *parole/écriture* hierarchy in Rousseau's *Essai sur l'origine des langues*, where he observes that 'le concept de supplément [...] abrite en lui deux significations dont la cohabitation est aussi étrange que nécessaire. Le supplément s'ajoute, il est en surplus, une plénitude enrichissant une autre plénitude, le *comble* de la présence. [...] Mais le supplément supplée. Il ne s'ajoute que pour remplacer. Il intervient ou s'insinue *à-la-place-de*; s'il comble, c'est comme on comble un vide. S'il représente et fait image, c'est par le défaut antérieur d'une présence' (Derrida, *De la grammatologie*, 208).
53. Derrida, *De la grammatologie* , 429.
54. Lyotard, *Le Différend*, 103.
55. In the section entitled 'Le différend'; see esp. 26–7.
56. Lyotard, *Le Différend*, 115.
57. Mathieu Bénézet's liminary note begins by quoting Laporte: '"Publie cela sans moi; je n'en veux rien savoir"' (17). This remark is underscored in the interview with Laporte conducted by Bénézet and Ristat in the same volume, particularly at 125, 127, and 146–8.
58. 'Ce que vous avez là ['Une œuvre mort-née'], c'est le brouillon d'une œuvre qui n'a jamais existé et qui aurait été *Fugue 4*. Alors, il n'y a pas *Fugue 4*, il y a une *Suite* et ce n'est pas la même chose' ('Entretien entre Mathieu Bénézet, Roger Laporte et Jean Ristat', 148).
59. In 'Lire Roger Laporte', 286.
60. Benjamin, 'The Redemption of Value', 208.

61. Cf. Rubbra, *Counterpoint*, 57.

62. Cf. Roger Bullivant, *Fugue* (London: Hutchinson University Library, 1971), 28–9: 'One important fact has already emerged from the present preliminary discussion—the fact that the *fugue is not a form*. [...] It is of great importance to realize, however, that when we say "fugue is not a form" we do not mean "fugues do not have forms".'

63. Derrida, *De la grammatologie*, 30; cf. the scriptor's comments in a very similar vein, in *Fugue 3*, on the static totality of the book and the mobility of writing: *F3* 455–6.

64. I use the term in the sense introduced by Gérard Genette in his *Palimpsestes: la littérature au second degré* (Paris: Seuil, 1981) and exhaustively analysed in *Seuils* (Paris: Seuil, 1987). In the latter, Genette makes passing reference to paratextual features of Laporte's works at 93, 105 and 145.

65. Derrida, *De la grammatologie*, 227; different formulations of this notion can of course be found throughout Derrida's work.

66. Benjamin, 'The Redemption of Value', 201.

67. Benjamin, 'The Redemption of Value', 202.

68. For a full account, see Roger Bullivant, 'Counter-subject', in *The New Grove Dictionary of Music and Musicians*, ed. Stanley Sadie (London: Macmillan, 1980), iv. 852–4.

69. Blanchot, *L'Espace littéraire*, 13.

70. Blanchot, *L'Espace littéraire*, 13.

71. 'Lire Roger Laporte', 287.

72. Jorge Luis Borges, *Labyrinths*, ed. Donald Yates and James Irby (Harmondsworth: Penguin, 1981), 66. Borges's tale is mentioned in 'Lire Roger Laporte', 290.

73. Borges, *Labyrinths*, 69.

74. Borges, *Labyrinths*, 68.

75. 'Lire Roger Laporte', 287.

76. Blanchot, '"Ne te retourne pas"', *Digraphe* 18/19 (1979), 160–3 (161).

77. Borges, *Labyrinths*, 66.

78. Derrida, *De la grammatologie*, 323.

79. Derrida, *La Dissémination*, 159–60. A neat illustration of the perfection of imitation through imperfection is given in Descombes's *Le Même et l'autre*, in which a second title page is printed, bearing the following *avertissement*: 'Cette page reproduit la précédente. *Autre*, elle est la *même*. Mais pour éviter que le lecteur ne *compte pour rien* cette seconde première page, en l'attribuant par exemple à une erreur de reliure, j'ai dû y inscrire cet avertissement, qui ne figure pas sur la première première page. Pour être *même*, il faut qu'elle soit *autre*' (7).

80. Derrida, *La Dissémination*, 359.

81. Derrida, *Marges*, 365–93.

82. Derrida, *La Dissémination*, 229.

83. Derrida, *La Dissémination*, 351.

84. I cannot deal here with the philosophical debate surrounding such paradoxes which, fuelled earlier this century by the likes of Russell, F. P. Ramsey and Tarski, continues to flourish, often at a dauntingly technical level.

85. Cf. Derrida, *La Dissémination*, 234–6.

86. Jacques Derrida, *Psyché. Inventions de l'autre* (Paris: Galilée, 1987), 11–61; references immediately hereafter will be given in the text.

87. Derrida, *La Dissémination*, 14 n. 6.

88. 'Entretien avec Roger Laporte, recueilli et annoté par F.-Y. Jeannet', *Digraphe* 57 (1991), 71–6 (74). The reference to Ponge arises from a discussion of Laporte's own *brouillons*, which he has stipulated should never be published.

89. In Bennington and Derrida, *Jacques Derrida*, 18.

90. I give here and in the following lines a brief summary of notions which are developed throughout Bataille's work, particularly in *L'Erotisme* and *La Part maudite*. Steven Connor's *Theory and Cultural Value* (Oxford: Blackwell, 1992) includes a short section on 'Bataille and Absolute Expenditure' (71–80) which deals with a number of questions raised in my own discussion.

91. Cf. the 'Introduction théorique' of Bataille, *La Part maudite*, in *Œuvres complètes*, vii (Paris: Gallimard, 1976), 27–47; also, in the same volume, 'L'économie à la mesure de l'univers' (9–16).

92. The domain of *sauvagerie* also takes us back to the 'time of the absence of the gods', evoked in Ch. 2's discussion of *La Veille*.

93. 'Ainsi le déchaînement de la fête est-il en définitive, sinon enchaîné, borné du moins aux limites d'une réalité dont il est la négation. C'est dans la mesure où elle réserve les nécessités du monde profane que la fête est supportée' (Bataille, *Théorie de la religion*, in *Œuvres complètes*, vii. 313–14).

94. On these divisions of the text, cf. Michel Beaujour's 'Une poétique de l'autoportrait: *Fugue* (1970) de Roger Laporte', in *Miroirs d'encre: rhétorique de l'autoportrait* (Paris: Seuil, 1980), 224–36, esp. 233–6.

95. Laporte expresses his admiration for Bataille, and his particular interest in the *opération souveraine*, in 'Lire Roger Laporte', 292–3.

96. 'Faire œuvre littéraire ne peut être, je le crois, qu'une *opération souveraine*: c'est vrai dans le sens où l'œuvre demande à l'auteur de dépasser en lui la personne pauvre, qui n'est pas au niveau de ses moments souverains; l'auteur, autrement dit, doit chercher par et dans son œuvre ce qui, niant ses propres limites, ses faiblesses, ne participe pas de sa *servitude* profonde' (Georges Bataille, *La Littérature et le mal* (Paris: Gallimard, 1957, coll. 'Idées' reprint), 225).

97. Thus, in the same essay on Genet cited above, Bataille remarks that one cannot talk of a failed sovereignty in Genet, as if a real sovereignty existed: 'La souveraineté à laquelle l'homme n'a jamais cessé de prétendre, n'a jamais été même accessible, et nous n'avons pas lieu de penser qu'elle le deviendra' (228).

98. For Bataille's example of 'silence' as a 'mot glissant', see *L'Expérience intérieure*, in *Œuvres complètes*, v. 28–9.

99. Derrida, 'De l'économie restreinte à l'économie générale—un hégélianisme sans réserve', in *L'Ecriture et la différence*, 369–407 (386).

100. Cf. Mathieu Bénézet's remark in 'Où nous sommes défigurés' (in *Le Roman de la langue: des romans, 1960–1975* (Paris: Union Générale d'Editions, collection '10/18', 1977), 261–78): 'Roger Laporte, lui, fait du sur-place, c'est dans l'itération du même que peut se produire *un tremblement de langue*, l'hésitation du dire qui signe *la défaite* du discours du magister' (265).

101. Derrida, *L'Ecriture et la différence*, 403.

102. Derrida, *La Dissémination*, 32.

103. For another account of metaphors of writing and the writer in *Fugue*, see Dina Sherzer's chapter '*Fugue*: The Adventures of Metaphors' (in *Representation in Contemporary French Fiction*).

104. 'Ce qui reste à force de musique', *Psyché*, 98. Derrida's remarks on the 'retrait' of metaphor here are amplified in 'Le retrait de la métaphore', *Psyché*, 63–93; e.g.: '[Le retrait] *se* retire mais l'ipséité du *se* par laquelle il se rapporterait à lui-même d'un trait ne le précède pas et suppose déjà un trait supplémentaire pour se tracer, signer, retirer, retracer à son tour' (92). There are also some interesting remarks on the multiplication of metaphors in Laporte's 'Nietzsche: la métaphore et/ou le concept' (*QV* 185–204).

105. Derrida, *Psyché*, 99.

106. For other variations of this metaphor, see e.g. *F* 273, 275, 279, 280; *FS* 342; *F3* 407, 446, 454. In the last of these examples, the scriptor suggests that the source of the metaphor is Kafka's *In The Penal Colony*; the consequent associations of inscription on the body have a bearing on the psychoanalytic model explored in the next chapter.

107. 'L'écriture de *Fugue* évide les métaphores, elle les rend exsangues, elle fait de leur vide la condition de son œuvre; immense *désœuvrement* de *Fugue* qui ainsi ruine la figure romancière dans sa régence' (Bénézet, 'Où nous sommes défigurés', 271).

108. Derrida, *Psyché*, 103.

CHAPTER 4

Writing Bio-graphy:
A Matter of Life and Death

In the course of the previous chapter, we have already noted that the transition from the *Fugue* series to *Suite* constitutes another *brisure* in Laporte's work. The disjunctive element in this *brisure* is underlined by the abandonment of a projected *Fugue 4*, the working notes for which were published as 'Une œuvre mort-née'. The principal interest of the latter is the insight it affords into Laporte's compositional practice, a great deal of it, particularly in the early pages, consisting of extracts from Laporte's earlier works, above all *Fugue 3*, representing those parts of the previous work which might provide material for the generation of further writing. Indeed, the very excision and rearrangement of earlier passages already initiates the transformative process which we have seen to be so important in Laporte's work, as Mathieu Bénézet observes in a note which begins by indicating that almost the entirety of the preceding section is culled from *Fugue 3*: 'Mais ce qui est *inédit* c'est bien sûr la mise en rapport des citations, les prélèvements effectués dans des phrases, qui tentent à former un nouveau texte. Ou: comment travaille R.L.!'[1] The transformative process of self-quotation is soon brought to bear on this text itself, so that the manuscript, in Bénézet's words again, 'peu à peu devient lui-même objet à citations, incitation de texte (d'écriture)'.[2] In interview, however, Laporte has suggested that this abandoned work of salvage and transformation remained at the level of a commentary on the earlier text: a repetition which did not give rise to invention.[3]

We have also seen that, in interviews and in *Lettre à personne*, Laporte is at great pains to emphasize that *Suite* is not simply *Fugue 4*, marking instead another recommencement of the enterprise of *biographie*. To the remarks to this effect mentioned previously, we may add part of a later, published correspondence with Sylviane Agacinski, where Laporte outlines the interior margins of his work, concluding this summary of his literary enterprise with the following remark about the deferral of beginning in *Une Vie*: '*Une Vie* comprend 615 pages: la première page porte le numéro 495! Admettons que cette fois-ci je plaisante, mais si peu.'[4] In fact, a further delay in beginning had already been suggested in *Lettre à personne*, where Laporte suggests that *Suite* only really begins at the fourth paragraph of its fifth sequence, so that, as he remarks there, the first four sequences constitute another sort of *brisure* between the *Fugue* series and *Suite*: 'Ces quatre séquences assurent à la fois la jonction (elles sont liées au passé) et l'ouverture: elles me tournent à l'avenir' (*LP* 63–4). In both of the interviews published shortly after the appearance of *Suite*, Laporte stresses the difference in compositional technique between this work and its predecessors, suggesting that the work of revision of earlier material he carried out in drafts for the *Fugue* series meant that what eventually appeared on the final printed pages was becoming too 'programmé';[5] with *Suite*, the discontinuity of writing and the threat of an 'interruption définitive' was to be brought to the fore, an aspect of the work extended, as we have noted, to its initial manner of publication *en feuilleton*.[6] We may be inclined to think here that, as was the case to some extent in the transition from *Pourquoi?* to *Fugue*, the attempt to produce the instability which is essential to the project of *biographie* leads Laporte into a particularly severe reading of his earlier work. Given the argument of the preceding chapter, clearly I would want to insist that the work's repetitive invention of itself, in the *Fugue* series, at the same time signals an invention of the other, and thereby endeavours to give a chance to the chance of the future.

Of course, in describing it as a *brisure*, Laporte is also acknowledging the continuity that exists in the passage from the *Fugue* series to *Suite*, and this continuity may be seen to extend further than the first four sequences which Laporte described as necessary for *Suite* to separate itself from *Fugue 3*. The *Codicille* appended to the latter opens, for example, with the question of *biographie*, which the scriptor suggests he has long since had to renounce, but he goes on to ask, 'ce projet, n'est-il pas de longue date en cours de réalisation dans la mesure du moins où le "sujet" supporte une épreuve liée à l'écriture?' (*F3* 477). The project of *biographie*, the extent to which that project is connected with an *épreuve* undergone by the scriptor, and the reality of that *épreuve* are absolutely central to *Suite* and *Moriendo*, where they are explored in terms developed from the earlier writing, such as the concluding lines of the *Codicille* which amplify the scriptor's decision to retain the term *biographie*: 'Ecrire—une certaine modalité d'écrire—est en effet lié au cruel simulacre d'un supplice, à une crise qui n'est même pas réelle, mais dont à retardement, après ne pas l'avoir vécue, il est permis de dire à voix basse: "Il y a eu écriture", formule à coup sûr secrète, d'autant plus énigmatique qu'aussitôt on doit ajouter: perdre l'écriture ne serait-ce pas perdre la "vie"?' (*F3* 494).

The *brisure* which we are describing is further complicated by the articulation of *Suite* with some of Laporte's earliest works and projects. The title of *Suite* suggests not only a continuation of the previous writing, but also the 'pursuit' of the opening line of the work, which becomes a sort of refrain in *Suite* and *Moriendo*: 'Poursuivre.— Poursuivre, il le faut, mais pourquoi?' (*S* 503). As we have already noted, Laporte insists that it was of the utmost importance to him that this pursuit should be regarded as constantly threatened by a definitive interruption, so that, in another connotation of the title, the work should be *à suivre*, with its continuation always an open question. As early as 1954, we find Laporte recording a project for a novel in which the process of artistic creation would itself be laid bare, a project which would require that the work itself be incomplete in order to translate the open-endedness of creation: 'Le roman est bien essentiellement comme le disait Gide "pourrait être continué", et même "peut être continué", ou plutôt "doit être continué". Autrement dit: A SUIVRE' (*C* 41). In this respect, we may also recall Laporte's remark after *La Veille* had been completed: 'Ecrire doit toujours être une ouverture et non point un écran' (*C* 159). It was also in respect of *La Veille* that Blanchot, expanding on his observation that this work constituted an attempt to approach 'la pensée du neutre', wrote: 'Ecrire sous la pression du neutre: écrire comme en direction de l'inconnu.'[7] The connection between *Suite* and *La Veille* is further underscored by the renewed focus in the later work on the *épreuve* undergone by the writing-subject, with the distinction that this *épreuve* is now bound up with the project of *biographie*. Laporte has also acknowledged the connection between these two works, but in so doing stressed that this was a return to earlier terrain on a different level, another form of differential repetition, we might say: 'de nouveau j'étais soumis à une "épreuve" dont je m'étais longtemps écarté, et pourtant la boucle n'est pas bouclée, en particulier parce qu'il ne s'agit pas d'un cercle, mais d'une spirale sans fin.'[8]

It is also surely significant, in respect of this spiralling return, that *Suite* is the first of Laporte's works since *Une Migration* to be dedicated to Blanchot, and *Moriendo* the first since *Le Partenaire* to bear an epigraph by him. I would not wish this to be taken to suggest that Laporte had in any sense abandoned Blanchot in the intervening period, and I hope, in discussing the *Fugue* series, that I was able intermittently to suggest that this was not the case, even though the focus of my discussion necessarily shifted in response to Laporte's identification of the work of Derrida as decisive in the direction his writing took after *Pourquoi?*. In any case, to examine Laporte's writing in the light of Derrida's work is hardly to banish the figure of Blanchot, given the complex interrelations between the work of Blanchot and of Derrida, interrelations which have led Herman Rapaport to suggest that 'both Blanchot and Derrida enter into a transferential relationship with respect to one another's writing'.[9] Furthermore, Laporte's return to Blanchot is, in another sense, a return which does not simply close the circle. Blanchot's earlier writings still have a bearing on *Suite* and *Moriendo*, in terms, for example, of the discussion of writing, death and the Orphic myth in *L'Espace littéraire*, or of the phrase 'Toujours j'irai de ce côté, jamais d'un autre' which returns, in slightly varied form, as a refrain in *Suite* and *Moriendo* and which, as Laporte has attested, can be traced back to *Celui qui ne m'accompagnait pas*.[10] However, the exploration of writing, death, and the relationship of the writing-subject to an *épreuve*, which can never be said to be present, in *Suite* and *Moriendo*, also relates these texts to Blanchot's later, generically hybrid works, *Le Pas au-delà*, from which *Moriendo*'s epigraph is taken,[11] and *L'Ecriture du désastre*, published a year after *Suite*. To say this, however, is not to invoke a simple, unidirectional influence, since these late texts by Blanchot are already themselves networks in which there are traces not only of Blanchot's own earlier work, but also, more explicitly of course in the case of *L'Ecriture du désastre*, of the work of Derrida, Levinas, Bataille and others, including Laporte himself, to whose project of *biographie L'Ecriture du désastre* explicitly refers.[12] The relation to these texts is, then, a proximity to a practice of writing which not only probes the distinction between fictional and theoretical writing, but also disturbs the boundaries of the text and, with them, the conventional notion of authorial property which underpins the concept of influence.[13]

In my analysis of *Suite* and *Moriendo*, I propose to concentrate on two areas in particular: the notion of writing as *biographie*, which has of course been present in Laporte's writing since *Fugue* but which returns with particular force in these two texts, and about which I have said relatively little explicitly in the preceding chapter, although almost everything I *have* said about the *Fugue* series thus far relates to this question. This question is in turn intimately related to a second area, which assumes even greater importance in *Suite* and *Moriendo* than in the preceding texts, namely that of the writing-subject. So far, I have neglected the problem of the *je* in Laporte's works, designating it by the relatively neutral term of 'scriptor' which must now be subjected to scrutiny, given the importance in *Suite* and *Moriendo* of the distinction between the *biographe* and the *signataire* of these texts.

In pursuing these issues, I shall draw on a critical discourse inspired by psychoanalysis. I do so, first, because of the allusions to psycho-analytic models in Laporte's texts; secondly, with a view to the fact that Laporte's work has already occasioned a number of psychoanalytic readings which strike me as (in varying degrees) providing helpful insights while manifesting limitations in their approach which are themselves illuminating; thirdly, and most importantly, because the well-known linguistic and textual 'turns' in recent French work on psycho-analysis provide the theoretical framework best equipped to explore the restless economy of subjectivity in Laporte's work.

A psychoanalytic vocabulary is specifically exploited only on occasion in *Suite* and *Moriendo*, for example when writing's repeated dissolution of identifications of the writing-subject is described as 'un interminable procès suicidaire suscitant une terreur bien pire que celle de la castration' (*S* 505), or in references to a 'blessure narcissique' (e.g. *S* 529) already evoked in *Fugue 3* (e.g. *F3* 483–4), or in suggestions that representations of the predicament of the writing-subject are 'fantasmes' (e.g. *S* 557). Having said that, the language of psycho-analysis will clearly have a particular purchase on these texts, in which the project of *biographie* is always shadowed by *thanatographie*, and in which the *épreuve* of the writing-subject involves an uncertain relation with a 'chose en souffrance' and the approach to a 'crypte' which, near the beginning of *Moriendo* for instance, is said to conceal 'le secret d'une aventure qui me dépasse' (*M* 574).

A psychoanalytic vocabulary is exploited rather more frequently in the *Fugue* series, its first overt appearance coming in the eighth sequence of *Fugue*, where the scriptor suggests that, reading his own work 'par-dessus l'épaule de Freud' (*F* 308), the process of textual revision which gathers together disparate passages in his work can be likened to Eros (the life instincts), adding that writing is at the same time clearly linked 'si ce n'est à une pulsion, du moins à un principe de mort' but also seems to involve 'une très vivante pulsion de liberté qui, à la différence d'Eros, se joue de tout savoir, mais qui s'oppose aussi à Thanatos' (F 309); the invocation of Eros and Thanatos as forces in his work has obvious repercussions for a *biographie* shadowed by a *thanatographie*, and we shall return to these ideas later.[14] Eros is invoked again in *Supplément*, representing the scriptor's conscious work of textual organization (FS 344–5), and again contrasted with a destructive force, now represented by Dionysus; however, just as *écriture* and *contre-écriture* cannot be said simply to exclude one another, so the relationship between these forces is felt not to be entirely oppositional, and the position of the writing-subject in respect of these forces is also uncertain: 'Je est au service d'Eros, mais puis-je me contenter de dire qu'il s'oppose à Dionysos? Je se définit-il seulement en fonction d'Eros et de Dionysos, ou bien joue-t-il son propre jeu? Lequel?' (FS 347). Later, the scriptor announces the need for a new 'grille de lecture' in order to rework the text, and proposes a Freudian interpretation (FS 372) to replace the economic model which has dominated much of *Supplément* up to that point, and whose limitations may already be surmised from the problematics of gain and loss which we suggested from a Bataillian perspective in the previous chapter. A psychoanalytic perspective on the work continues to appear in *Fugue 3*, most remarkably in the *Codicille*, where the scriptor considers a formulation he has recently given to express the notion that he is not responsible for the dislocation of the text: '"Je ne suis point le père de cette fente"' (F3 482). This gives rise to an analysis of this phrase in Œdipal terms, which leads in turn to a consideration, still in a psychoanalytic framework, of the relationship between the *signataire* and the *biographe*, a relationship which is explored extensively in *Suite* and *Moriendo*, and which will be our concern later in this chapter.

   Laporte's notebooks and critical writings contain a number of references to psychoanalysis. I shall just cite two such references here, as they both concern the relation between psychoanalysis and textuality, with specific reference to Laporte's own writing. The first is from a short article entitled 'Freud et la question de l'art',[15] in which Laporte condemns that 'psychanalyse réductrice' which interprets a work of art in terms of the presumed psycho–biography of its author. In place of this, he advocates the approach taken by Sarah Kofman, for whom the work involves the production rather than the translation of fantasy, the mobile structuring of the latter, in the case of a literary work, being indissociable from the play of the text. In his conclusion, Laporte quotes a passage from Kofman which asserts that the concept of the 'texte-tissu' is unthinkable 'sans mettre un lien indissoluble entre la force et le sens, l'affect et la représentation, la combinatoire du symbolique et les transformations de l'économique'.[16] In a remark which clearly has a bearing on his own work, Laporte proposes the underlining of this bond between the psychoanalytic and the textual as a project for 'la littérature moderne' and offers a very brief indication as to how this project might be pursued: 'Empruntant à Francis Ponge le titre de son ouvrage *La Fabrique du pré*, affirmons donc que le sujet, l'objet, la matière du livre peuvent être constitués par la seule fabrique du texte.'[17] The relevance of this to Laporte's own practice of writing is clear enough, and the general import of Laporte's remarks here serves as a reminder, on the one hand, that a psychoanalytic reading of Laporte's texts need certainly not confine itself to those passages where a psychoanalytic model is explicitly proposed, and on the other hand, that psychoanalysis will not provide a hermeneutic tool with which we might extract a final, psycho-biographical signified from Laporte's writing.

The second reference comes from the *Carnets* in an entry dating from 1970, after the completion of *Fugue*. Here, a discussion of the genre of *biographie* leads to the observation that, at times, Laporte considers that 'la "Biographie" pourrait devenir un genre, un domaine nouveau, aussi vaste que la psychanalyse' (C 306). The parallel is underlined when Laporte goes on to state his conviction that there is an 'homologie' between *biographie* and psychoanalysis, adducing Freud's construction of models for the psychical apparatus in his metapsychological papers as analogous with the explorations of the 'machine d'écriture' initiated in *Fugue*, with the limitation that in his own work 'la réflexion théorique de et sur l'écriture' (C 307) is inseparable from the practice of writing.[18]

More specifically, the *Carnets* also reveal Laporte's interest in the work of Jacques Lacan. Notably, Lacan's *Ecrits* are cited in an entry dating from 1967, the year after their publication. The starting-point for Laporte's discussion is Lacan's 'stade du miroir',[19] a concept which is immediately related to Laporte's own work, as Laporte records that one reader of *Une Voix de fin silence* had written to him to the effect that 'il m'admirait dans la mesure même où il voyait dans mes écrits un modèle de narcissisme, type de compliment qui bien entendu m'a déplu' (*C* 245). Notwithstanding his aversion to such a reading, Laporte goes on to acknowledge that, without knowing the work of Lacan, he had wondered whether 'le sourire d'un éventuel partenaire n'était pas seulement *mon* sourire renvoyé par le miroir' (*C* 245), referring to an image which recurs throughout both volumes of *Une Voix de fin silence*. By the time of this entry in the *Carnets*, Laporte is inclined to see the smile of the elusive *partenaire* evoked in these texts as a sublimation of the identification with the specular image in the mirror phase, recalling as he does so Lacan's description of the 'assomption jubilatoire' of the image by the infant (*C* 246).[20]

If we wished to pursue the reading suggested here by Laporte, it would not be difficult to offer Lacanian accounts of features of Laporte's early work which we have already noted in Chapter 2 of this study.[21] This is particularly evident in respect of the vicissitudes of the first person in its quest for a self-coinciding identity, a repeatedly frustrated quest in which figures which seem to some extent to operate as 'doubles'—the anonymous visitor of *Le Partenaire* or the *il* of *La Veille*—turn out to depend on a conception of alterity which disrupts the parallelism of self and other, thereby preventing the identification of subject and double and instead propelling the subject on a perpetual errancy, an exile from self-identity. In Lacanian terms, this schema would correspond to the transition from the diadic relations which obtain in the Imaginary order to the triadic structure which marks the entry into the Symbolic order.[22]

Turning to the later texts which are our principal concern in the chapter, we once again discover a division of the writing-subject which appears explicable in Lacanian terms. At times, there appear to be two fundamental guises of the *je* in these texts: the *biographe* and the *signataire*. In fact, this distinction first appears in the *Codicille* of *Fugue 3*, where it is discussed in the context of perhaps the most extended passage of psychoanalytic speculation in the *Fugue* series, in which writing, and specifically the project of *biographie*, is analysed in terms of the castration complex, the elusive *épreuve* at the heart of writing being described as a 'blessure narcissique' (cf. *F3* 482–4). The interactive pair of impulses in the text, which have been approached in so many guises in the *Fugue* series—as *écriture* and *contre-écriture*, continuity and discontinuity, combination and dissemination, Eros and Thanatos—is now represented in the image of the 'pansement' of the narcissistic wound, of which it is observed that 'dans le couple de contraires pansement/blessure, si le second terme recevait une connotation purement négative, je n'agirais pas comme je le fais et d'abord je n'aurais pu reprendre à nouveaux frais mon projet biographique. Pourquoi l'accent négatif porte-t-il donc sur le premier terme? Parce que le biographe, à la différence du signataire, ne peut désirer la guérison, l'apaisement, l'oubli, mais pourquoi en est-il ainsi?' (*F3* 484). The temptation to answer this question in terms of Lacan's account of the splitting of the subject is only reinforced by the association of the impulse of the *biographe* with death, since for Lacan the entry into the Symbolic order is at the same time an entry into a pact with mortality.[23]

Laporte returns to the question of identity near the beginning of *Suite*, in an explicitly psychoanalytic perspective and in a context which underlines the connection with death: 'Ecrire—une certaine modalité d'écrire—, ruinant toute identification, entraîne la répétition, sans cesse plus nette, d'une exclamation longtemps tacite: "je ne suis pas cela", entretient un jeu de massacre dont jamais je ne peux me relever, un interminable procès suicidaire suscitant une terreur bien pire que celle de la castration: faute de visage, demeurer enseveli au-dessous de l'air libre' (*S* 505). Writing divides the subject from itself in a signifying chain which unsettles all imaginary identifications, and whose absent endpoint is death. This divergence from self, or *écart*, is given extensive treatment in *Suite* and *Moriendo*, and is connected with the guises of the *je* to which we alluded earlier: the *biographe* and the *signataire*. One might say, in an initial distinction, that the *signataire* is inclined towards the combination of the diverse elements of the work with a view to the completion of his project, and therefore the turning of loss to advantage by circumscribing the *écart*, whereas the *biographe* pursues the remorseless logic of writing towards dissemination and irreparable loss. However, these two faces of the *je*, and their respective impulses, prove not to be so readily distinguishable, inasmuch as the effort towards comprehension, achievement of the work and mastery is always undone by writing, so that the failure of the *signataire* turns out to be another form of 'qui perd gagne' to the benefit of the *biographe*. This is reflected in the following passage from *Suite*, in which, however, we find the figure of the *biographe* contrasted with that of the *écrivain*, with the *scripteur* apparently functioning as an intermediate term—these reconfigurations of the *je* are significant, and we shall return to them shortly:

Dans cette lutte qui m'oppose à l'écart, c'est-à-dire dans ce combat qui oppose le langage à l'"écriture', si je parvenais à définir l'écart, si par conséquent je réussissais en tant qu'écrivain, je me retrouverais du même coup sans emploi, je signerais par mon triomphe la perte du scripteur et en conséquence celle du biographe, mais je sais d'une expérience longue et amère, expérience dont il m'a bien fallu m'arranger, que le cercle ne se boucle pas sur lui-même, que l'écart a déjoué et 'par définition' déjouera toute définition. (*S* 528)

At the same time, however, the absent *rien*, or death, which propels, punctuates and is promised by writing, remains inaccessible: the subject cannot assume the loss which is its very condition. The *écart* excludes any collusion by the subject, even as it compels the latter to a descent which 'loin de dépendre de moi, exclut toute initiative et même [...] interdit que "je" prenne à mon compte un tel désir, et pourtant, parce qu'écrire ressemble à s'y méprendre à une interminable agonie, cette chute, tout à fait à mon insu, dans la mesure même où j'en étais inconscient, ne s'est-elle pas poursuivie? Je le crois, mais je ne saurai jamais ce qui s'est réellement passé—si quelque chose se passe—au-dessous, au-dehors de la zone que je surveille' (*S* 537).

Naturally, the association of writing and death has repercussions for the project of *biographie* as life in/of writing. In the sixth sequence of *Suite*, we find the return of a notion first encountered in *Supplément*: 'La Biographie ressemble, à s'y méprendre, et de plus en plus, à une thanatographie' (*S* 542). The tendency of the work towards a *thanatographie* is linked with the *écart* at the absent origin of the subject's itinerary, as well as with the enterprise of *biographie* as a whole, as is suggested in the same passage from *Suite*: 'Pour quelle raison, l'écart, à l'origine de la chute, est-il une chance, la chance sans laquelle la Biographie serait impossible?' (*S* 542). It becomes increasingly clear that *thanatographie* cannot simply be set up in opposition to *biographie*; of course, the very title of *Moriendo* implies as much, and this final volume in *Une Vie* is throughout concerned with the inextrication of death with the enterprise of *biographie*: 'j'ai accepté qu'écrire ressemble de plus en plus à une Thanatographie, mais, en dépit de l'écrasement, de l'asphyxie, j'ai toujours gardé la conviction, sans laquelle j'aurai tout abandonné, qu'à me dérober à l'épreuve je perdrais la "vie"' (*M* 574–5).

The treatment of death in *Suite* and *Moriendo* constitutes another point of contact with Laporte's earliest works. We saw, for example, in our discussion of *Une Migration*, in the light of Blanchot's critical writings, that the impossible quest for the origin of writing is linked to the impossibility of death. In similar vein, the subject repeatedly notes, in *Suite*, the impossibility of attaining the subterranean zone which haunts his work, exclaiming at one point: 'avoir toujours déjà perdu le mot juste qui m'aurait délivré et pourtant devoir me laisser arracher encore, sans fin, la formule que je n'ai jamais possédée, le mot de passe qui me ferait entrer au royaume des morts, est-il pire tourment?' (*S* 537). The consequence of this death as impossibility, which is the absent endpoint of writing—of the signifying chain in Lacanian terms—is that writing condemns the subject to an endless simulacrum of death: 'Je suis sans illusion: parce que la mise à mort n'a pas été réelle, son cruel simulacre sera interminable' (*S* 523).

However, in this respect an important shift takes place early in *Moriendo*, the first sequence of which ends with the subject noting that, after coming close to renouncing his entire project, he had known 'un semblant de sérénité' (*M* 576). The second sequence opens with the question: 'Si, contre toute attente, j'avais eu raison d'identifier écart et vie, pourquoi n'ai-je jamais été autant menacé qu'en écrivant la première séquence de ce texte?' (*M* 579). The subject goes on to add that 'la chute vers l'abîme s'est poursuivie et même brusquement accentuée: j'ai pénétré pour la première fois dans une zone interdite' (*M* 579). Shortly afterwards, the nature of this region is made explicit when the subject declares that, without understanding why, he must now follow a descending spiral, 'spirale probablement sans fin qui néanmoins m'avait fait pénétrer dans une région encore plus basse où mourir était enfin devenu possible' (*M* 580). This possibility is linked with the division of the writing-subject—a division which restores the distinction of *biographe* and *signataire*—since the subject has already pursued his first observation about reaching a forbidden zone with the remark that he now has the obscure conviction that 'le biographe et le signataire disparaîtraient, ou du moins pouvaient disparaître simultanément. En écrivant, rien qu'en écrivant, puis-je donc mourir de ma mort d'homme?' (*M* 580). The conclusion reached here is startlingly new, although the notion explored is one which had already been raised in *Suite*, as is indicated by the citation to which this obscure conviction is the response, the citation being a *copie non conforme* of passages in *Suite* (cf. *S* 557 and 563): '"Que j'écrive encore longtemps ou que je cesse d'écrire, l'issue toujours se dérobera, et c'est pourquoi le signataire de ces pages mourra sans que le biographe ait trouvé une juste fin"' (*M* 579–80). We should further note the provisional nature of the conclusion reached at this early stage of *Moriendo*. Later in the work, the subject asks whether he will only once have reached this zone in which the simultaneous disappearance of *biographe* and *signataire* had become possible, a zone in which, he adds, 'le pressentiment d'une fin prochaine n'a peut-être été qu'un moyen illusoire d'échapper pour un temps à un supplice sans fin et peut-être sans vérité' (*M* 588). In the fifth sequence, the issue is raised once more, with another significant variation: 'L'écrivain, le biographe et le signataire auraient pu disparaître simultanément, mais cette issue s'est dérobée; la mort du signataire—il m'est arrivé de la désirer—reste imprévisible; la sénilité de l'écrivain viendra-t-elle, de fait, mettre un terme dérisoire à une aventure inépuisable?' (*M* 599). The division of the subject has now reverted to a tripartite one with the reintroduction of the figure of the *écrivain*, but in a different configuration than that in which it appeared in the passage we cited earlier from *Suite*.

With the dramatic new perspective on death presented in these passages and the incessant shifts in the configuration of guises of the *je*, it would be well to abandon the essentially hermeneutic deployment of Lacanian psychoanalysis which we have been intermittently sketching out up to this point. This is not because of the incapacity of a Lacanian approach to deal with shifting configurations of the subject—on the contrary, such is precisely the privileged domain of psychoanalysis—but rather because both the new perspective on death and the changing faces of the *je* bring into play the question of the literary frame, a question which, as Derrida suggests in 'Le facteur de la vérité', poses a challenge to any psychoanalytic reading with hermeneutic ambitions.[24]

The question of the literary frame is brought to the fore in these texts by transgressions of the frame which, without simply dissolving it, make of it a chiastic border. We have already encountered the chiasmus of textual borders in the previous chapter, but in *Suite* and *Moriendo*, the challenge to reading is intensified by a proliferation of chiastic relations (although we should also recall that the chiasmus, opening the text to its 'outside', is the very possibility of reading). The project of *biographie* reveals the encroachments of its 'other', *thanatographie*. Furthermore, *biographie*, which had at the outset of *Fugue* been distinguished from autobiography by the systematic exclusion of the *autos* (the 'vie d'homme' of the writer), increasingly incorporates references to this apparently extra-textual dimension. This in turn is reflected in the guises of the *je* (*écrivain, signataire, scripteur, biographe*), but in such a way as to remind us that the *écrivain*, for example, is also a textual figure, inscribed and constantly reworked in reconfigurations of the first person. If *biographie* is revealed at the same time to be *auto-biographie* (but also *allo-graphie*, writing of the other), *thanatographie* as death in/of writing is equally revealed to be chiastically related to the death of the writer: 'En écrivant, rien qu'en écrivant, puis-je donc mourir de ma mort d'homme?' (*M* 580). As for psychoanalysis, it finds its manoeuvres already inscribed within the 'analysand-text', which has repeated recourse to psychoanalytic models and which, in the case of *Moriendo*, greets psychoanalysis at its very threshold with this epigraph: 'Ces singularités, distribuées le long d'une droite perverse, mourir, devenir-fou, écrire' (*M* 569). I am not proposing that psychoanalysis is simply rendered redundant because it encounters its own categories in texts like Laporte's, but the fold thus engendered does pose a problem for a psychoanalytic (or any other) hermeneutics. For hermeneutics, in its quest to extract meaning, is in the end obliged to maintain the borders of the text and cannot tolerate the chiasmus, and it is Derrida's argument in 'Le facteur de la vérité' that Lacanian analysis is a hermeneutics which, wherever it looks, finds itself.[25]

It is the hermeneutic orientation of psychoanalysis which constitutes the limitation of the Lacanian readings of Laporte which I noted earlier. The hermeneutic circumscription of the text is a risk which, for example, Catherine Clément seems to me to run in her ingenious Lacanian readings of Laporte's work, as evidenced by her claim, following her interpretation of part of *Supplément* in terms of a refusal of the passage of birth and an attempt to remain at a point where Imaginary and Symbolic are united, that 'les difficultés de l'événement, les entours de l'acte, *deviennent compréhensibles*'.[26] We cannot simply avoid hermeneutics; none of the present study could have been written, nor indeed any reading ever undertaken, without taking up interpretative positions which, however provisionally, re-establish the borders of the text. But, in the case of texts such as Laporte's, it is urgent to attend to what escapes, but makes possible, hermeneutics. I am not going to abandon psychoanalysis at this point, then, but will instead endeavour to move towards a psychoanalytic poetics. In order to do so, I shall draw on some of Derrida's work on psychoanalysis.

Derrida's first essay on Freud, 'Freud et la scène de l'écriture',[27] is one to which Laporte often refers in his writings on Derrida, and in which the interrelations between textuality, life and death are to the fore. In this essay, Derrida takes as his starting-point Freud's 'Note upon the "Mystic Writing-Pad"',[28] which proposes the model of the child's toy writing-board, the writing on which can be erased with a cursor, still leaving traces on the wax block underneath, as an analogy for the phenomenon whereby memories become inscribed in the unconscious without ever having been present to consciousness. For Derrida, Freud's choice of this model as well as his consistent experimentation with models involving an element of inscription may be read as indicative that the non-present, dynamic structure of the unconscious can only be conceived in terms of writing, traces, *différance*:

Le texte inconscient est déjà tissé de traces pures, de différences où s'unissent le sens et la force, le texte nulle part présent, constitué d'archives qui sont *toujours déjà* des transcriptions. Des estampes originaires. Tout commence par la reproduction. Toujours déjà, c'est-à-dire dépôts d'un sens qui n'a jamais été présent, dont le présent signifié est toujours reconstitué à retardement, *nachträglich*, après coup, *supplémentairement*: *nachträglich* veut dire aussi *supplémentaire*.[29]

The priority of representation, which we have seen in Chapter 3 to be dictated by the logic of supplementarity, is posited here in terms of originary traces of what are, for consciousness, non-events. To consider why the prior moment of representation should be identified by Derrida with death, we should look more carefully at the principles of Eros and Thanatos, which we have already encountered in Laporte's work.

In *Beyond the Pleasure Principle*,[30] Freud undertakes a recasting of the psychical economy, initially in an attempt to explain the frequently observed symptom of a compulsion to repeat, the repetition often concerning clearly unpleasant experiences and therefore not readily explicable by the operation of the pleasure principle modified by the reality principle. Freud speculates that this repetition compulsion is a manifestation of an instinct of all organisms to return to an earlier state, ultimately to the state of organic stability from which they are supposed to have developed. In Freud's new formulation of the psychical economy, these retrogressive and disseminatory death instincts are set against the combinative life instincts or Eros. Freud suggests that the interplay of these opposing sets of instincts can be seen as producing a life-shaping equilibrium which seeks to ensure that the process is not short-circuited and that the teleological coherence of life is assured by the organism's attainment of a 'proper' death: 'what we are left with is the fact that the organism wishes to die only in its own fashion.'[31] This convenient view of the role of the death instincts has subsequently been questioned, and is indeed cast into doubt within *Beyond the Pleasure Principle* itself, as Freud concedes that his theory may only constitute another reassuring illusion in the face of inevitable death.

From our point of view, the crucial ambiguities in the relationship between Eros and the death instincts are the ambivalent role of the pleasure principle and the decision as to whether the psychical apparatus is governed by the constancy principle or by the zero (or Nirvana) principle; it will be seen from the following passage from *Beyond the Pleasure Principle* that these two factors are entirely interdependent: 'The facts which have caused us to believe in the dominance of the pleasure principle in mental life also find expression in the hypothesis that the mental apparatus endeavours to keep the quantity of excitation present in it *as low as possible or at least to keep it constant.*'[32] Since increases in excitation are felt as unpleasurable, this is effectively a restatement of the pleasure principle. However, the choice between the constancy principle and the zero principle, quickly passed over in this passage, is decisive as regards our view of the pleasure principle and of the psychical economy in general. To put it briefly, the hypothesis of the constancy principle is dictated by the voice of reason, the secondary process, whereby the pleasure principle negotiates with the reality principle; the hypothesis of the zero principle, on the other hand, is cognate with absolute discharge, the primary process, the pleasure principle in the service of the death instincts. In *Vie et mort en psychanalyse*, Jean Laplanche poses the alternative in these terms: 'le principe de plaisir, en tant qu'il est, tout au long de ce texte, énoncé d'une seule traite avec "sa modification" en principe de réalité, est situé désormais du côté de la constance. C'est "sa forme la plus radicale" ou son "*au-delà*" qui, comme principe de Nirvâna, réaffirme la priorité de la tendance au zéro absolu, ou "pulsion de mort".'[33]

Alternatively, one can ascribe the vacillation between constancy and zero principles to a non-oppositional differential structure within the pleasure principle itself, in the analeptic and proleptic commutation between libidinal binding and unbinding which would never be resolved into the ultimate stasis of absolute binding or unbinding, but in which is inscribed, though nowhere simply *present*, the 'theoretical fiction' of the primary process, zero-point, death. Derrida argues along these lines in 'Spéculer—sur "Freud"',[34] in which he also suggests that

Les trois termes [pleasure principle, reality principle, *différance*]—deux principes plus ou moins la différance—n'en font qu'un, le même divisé, puisque le second principe (de réalité) et la différance ne sont que des 'effets' du principe de plaisir modifiable.

Mais par quelque *bout* que l'on prenne cette structure à un-deux-trois termes, c'est la mort. *Au bout*, et cette mort n'est pas opposable, elle n'est pas différente, dans le sens de l'opposition, des deux principes et de leur différance. Elle est inscrite, quoique non inscriptible, dans le procès de cette structure—nous dirons plus loin stricture. Si la mort n'est pas opposable, elle est, déjà, *la vie la mort*.[35]

In this conception, death precedes, inhabits and exceeds life, not in the sense of a presence or in the temporal framework of a linear constitution of present moments, but rather as originary delay or *différance* which is unrepresentable but is the very condition of representation, bringing us back to Derrida's earlier essay on Freud: 'Il faut penser la vie comme trace avant de déterminer l'être comme présence. C'est la seule condition pour pouvoir dire que la vie *est* la mort, que la répétition et l'au-delà du principe de plaisir sont originaires et congénitaux à cela même qu'ils transgressent.'[36]

Returning to Laporte, we may say then that the project of *biographie* was from the outset shadowed by *thanatographie*, for, in a form of the chiastic relation between inside and outside which we have already explored, the possibility of *biographie* as life in/of writing is conditional upon death in/of writing, to the extent that death is the non-originary source of that syncopation or rhythm of the text with which we were concerned at the end of Chapter 3. This death as *différance* is at the same time what divides the subject from itself even in its own inscription of itself: 'Tout être-ensemble [...] commence par *se-lier*, par un se-lier dans un rapport différantiel à soi. Il s'envoie et se poste ainsi. Il se destine. Ce qui ne veut pas dire: il arrive.'[37] These messages to the self may be described as *arrêts de mort*, a term Derrida uses in 'Spéculer—sur "Freud"' and elaborates, with reference to Blanchot's *récit* of that title, in 'Survivre', punning on the two senses of *arrêts de mort*, the normal meaning of the phrase ('death sentences'), and 'suspensions of death' or 'stays of execution'.[38] These *arrêts de mort*, as stays of execution, are the constitutive forces which allow the survival of any structure or subject, but at the same time they are death sentences, inscribed with another destination. Their former, constitutive property leads Derrida, in 'Spéculer—sur "Freud"', to employ the term *pulsion du propre*, with the crucial proviso that the operation of *différance* will always interrupt the self-identity of the *propre*: 'Le propre n'est pas le propre et s'il s'approprie c'est qu'il se désapproprie—proprement, improprement. La vie la mort ne s'opposent plus en lui.'[39]

The subject of *Suite* and *Moriendo* therefore discovers that the life in/of writing is always already constituted by a death which never arrives, and which, as the detour of *différance*, is the only possibility of self-identity, but at the same time its impossibility, the other in the differential repetition of the same. In *Moriendo*, the subject declares: 'J'ai franchi un pas infime, décisif, le jour où j'ai admis que je suis un otage, que je dois souffrir à la place d'un autre, que mon épreuve, pourtant bien réelle, n'est que le simulacre, l'impossible répétition d'une souffrance sans commencement ni fin' (*M* 575). But the step towards recognizing the alterity in subjectivity, the death in life, is the Blanchotian *pas* explored by Derrida in 'Pas',[40] and by Laporte in 'L'ancien, l'effroyablement ancien', where he notes that: '"Pas" a ou doit avoir simultanément au moins quatre sens: le pas entendu comme marche; le pas en tant que "ne pas" ou "ne pas encore"; le pas du passif (de la "passion", de la patience); le pas du passé, quatre acceptations donc, mais qui communiquent dans et par l'écriture' (*E* 33). It is a step forward which is also a step back to an irretrievable origin, the turning of Orpheus to Eurydice, a step which cannot be made ('ne pas') towards that with which the only relation is, in a phrase Laporte cites from Levinas, 'une passivité plus passive que toute passivité' (*E* 32).

It is this *pas* (not/step) which the subject takes forward, and which takes the subject back, as if to cross the threshold which cannot be crossed, into—but never yet quite into—the crypt: 'Quelle est donc cette pensée dont je me défends, avec laquelle je ruse en la ravalant au niveau d'une fiction? Les portes de la mort ont été franchies, le tombeau est vide, mais la délivrance a été éphémère et la fête irréelle puisqu'en même temps—en même temps!—quelqu'un est en agonie jusqu'à la fin des âges' (*M* 607). If death is already at work in the life of the text, an outside which is already inside and therefore no longer opposable, then writing death is at once inevitable and impossible, death as *différance* being the unrepresentable condition of representation. But if this is the case for writing in general, what then of a writing which reflects on the 'agonie interminable' of writing, on the turning of *biographie* to *thanatographie*, a writing in which the subject seeks to respond to the injunction never to abandon 'cette "chose" sans nom' (*S* 563), and always to go in the direction of an inaccessible crypt? The exploration of this question will require another brief detour via Freud and Derrida on mourning and crypts.

In the normal process of mourning following the loss of a loved object, as described by Freud in *Mourning and Melancholia*,[41] the work of mourning enables libidinal detachment from the lost object. In melancholia, on the other hand, this libidinal detachment is not achieved, so that the relationship of the subject to the lost object remains at the level of narcissistic identification which is normally an initial stage of the work of mourning. In *Le Verbier de l'homme aux loups*, Nicolas Abraham and Maria Torok propose a distinction based on the terms of introjection and incorporation used by Freud. The process of introjection is one of assimilation which seeks to neutralize the alterity of the object; it is therefore a stage in the normal work of mourning prior to hypercathexis and eventual libidinal detachment. In the case of incorporation, on the other hand, there is an attempt to internalize the other in its alterity, to 'swallow' the other: we may already be reminded of the dreadful thought, in the passage cited recently from *Moriendo*, with which the subject ruses 'en la ravalant' in the fiction of a crypt. Taking the lead from Abraham and Torok in his introduction to their work, Derrida describes the paradoxical *topos* of the crypt, the 'place' of incorporation, as 'une sorte de "faux inconscient", un inconscient "artificiel" *logé* comme une prothèse, greffe au cœur d'un organe, dans le *moi clivé*. Lieu très particulier, fort circonscrit, auquel on ne pourra toutefois accéder que par les voies d'une autre topique.'[42] Indeed, it is a-topic in that it seeks to include that which cannot be included—the other, death—to include it in exclusion, the crypt being constructed as an interior which is at the same time external to the interior. Incorporation mimes an impossible introjection, and, to perfect this simulation of introjection, the hiding-place and the act of hiding involved are themselves hidden, and hidden from themselves, encrypted: 'Une crypte ne se présente pas. Une certaine disposition des lieux est aménagée pour dissimuler:

quelque chose, toujours un corps de quelque façon. Mais pour dissimuler aussi la dissimulation: la crypte qui d'elle-même se cèle tout autant qu'elle recèle.'[43] Cryptic incorporation, as Derrida goes on to remark, always signals 'un effet de deuil impossible ou refusé',[44] the effect of a mourning with which one will never have done, for an other neither simply within nor without the subject, in respect of a death which is no longer opposable to life, an exteriority which disturbs the threshold of the interior, for the 'chose' which, Derrida here writes, may be thought of as an 'effet de crypte',[45] and which, he writes in 'Survivre', has always designated, in philosophy, 'ce qui n'arrive pas':[46]

Tout se passe comme si je devais indéfiniment m'approcher d'une région inférieure, d'une crypte étouffante, si opaque qu'elle exclut toute éclaircie, où je ne sais qui ou quoi—le 'sujet' entendu comme 'subjectum'? le ci-gît?— subit depuis toujours un inimaginable tourment.
[...]
Cette 'chose', qui suscite la fascination, constitue-t-elle, au fond du labyrinthe, le but ultime, ou bien est-elle un leurre qui, masquant l'abîme, me détourne d'une tout autre épreuve? [...] Cette 'chose' muette, dont me sépare une distance infime, infinie, si j'avais été capable de l'aimer, de prendre sur moi sa détresse, de dire sa passion, n'aurai-je pas du même coup trouvé l'issue du labyrinthe? (S 557–8)

The effect of the crypt is to mark the impossibility of ever having done with this *chose*, this death which haunts the life in/of writing, but which will never finally arrive, only ever repetitively returning: a *revenant*. Through a circuitous route, we are rejoining, repeating differently, the invention of the other explored at the end of the last chapter. The text which reflects on itself produces an instability, does more than it says, in an impossible invention of the other which is the only possibility of invention. In *Suite* and *Moriendo*, we discover the impossibility of mourning or of having done with the mourning of the other, of including or excluding once and for all the other in the same, the death in life. The project of *biographie* can neither embrace nor expel *thanatographie* (in *Suite* and *Moriendo*, the subject repeatedly asks whether the *biographie* has given way to *thanatographie*: it is not a question which is finally answered), but in the chiasmus of its imperfect folding on itself, the unstable reflexivity of these texts discovers the death encrypted in the life in/of writing.

Moreover, a project which began by announcing the exclusion of the 'vie d'homme' and by asserting that 'il n'est point question d'écrire une autobiographie' (F 255) ends up revealing that the subject always finds itself in what Derrida describes at one point as 'une scène d'écriture auto-bio-thanato-hétéro--graphique'.[47] This is, above all, not just to say that Laporte has written an autobiography, but rather to suggest that writing as *biographie* reveals the simultaneous inevitability and impossibility of writing autobiography, revealing writing as constitutive of subjectivity but of a subjectivity in which the self is traversed by the other. In the *Codicille* of *Fugue 3*, there is a renewed commitment to avoid autobiography, but with a quali-fication: 'Je ne renonce pas à différencier la Biographie de l'autobiographie, mais j'ai eu raison, encore plus que je ne le croyais, d'affirmer que la marionnette est, au moins par un fil, à jamais liée au signataire: dans la mesure, dans la seule mesure où la question "Qu'est-ce qu'écrire?" signifie: "Pourquoi Roger Laporte écrit-il?", c'est-à-dire "Comment est-il devenu écrivain?", la réponse est d'ordre analytique' (*F3* 482). The text therefore comes to be marked by the signature of Roger Laporte, the *signataire* who assumes an increasingly important role in *Suite* and *Moriendo*, a signature in the uncertain margins of the *biographie* which may also perhaps be read in some other unstable thresholds: 'les portes de la vie, les portes de la mort'. But I do not mean by this to pursue the questions explicitly raised in the quotation from *Fugue 3*, and thereby to reduce Laporte's writing to an extra-textual signified, psychoanalytic, autobiographical or other. I am concerned rather with the effect of the signature.

One lays claim to an invention, for example, by dint of a signature, the mark of propriety (the invention may properly be said to be my own work) and of property (I lay claim to the invention), the mark of the *propre*. But in order to be effective, the signature must submit to the logic of iterability: it must be repeatable across an indefinite range of difference, falsifiable even.[48] Like the proper name—the *nom-du-père*, in fact—the signature is a mark of identity and alterity, what is most proper to me, but also disappropriates me from myself, a living authentification which is necessarily effective after my death, already inscribed by death. However, unlike the proper name (and this is what links it to a certain conception of the literary for Derrida) the signature is structured *en abyme*, like the reflexive text whose instability we have explored. It seeks to restore the propriety of the *propre* by distinctively recording its own singular performance. But in so doing, it requires that that singular performance be iterable, repeatable—recognizable and even reproducible by an other. The signature requires recognition, it necessarily calls for, is already marked by, the countersignature of the other—just as the singularity of the reflexive text is already inscribed by the countersignature of reading, for it is the possibility of reading which dictates its imperfect closure, its difference from itself, its iterability or *différance*. As Bennington remarks: 'On doit alors repenser la lecture comme un rapport de signature et de contre-signature, ce qui permet de penser ce en quoi un texte reste *essentiellement* ouvert à l'autre (à la lecture). La signature du texte appelle la contresignature du lecteur, comme c'est le cas de toute signature'.[49] The countersignature of reading will, in part, be our concern in the final chapter.

Notes to Chapter 4

1. Laporte, 'Une œuvre mort-née', *Digraphe* 18/19, 'Roger Laporte' (1979), 17–76 (22 n. 9).
2. Laporte, 'Une œuvre mort-née', 45 n. 37.
3. Cf. 'Entretien avec Mathieu Bénézet, Roger Laporte et Jean Ristat', where Laporte remarks, e.g., that 'au lieu de préparer une autre œuvre, c'est devenu simplement un commentaire de l'œuvre passée [...] c'était une répétition sur un plan disons intellectuel de ce qui avait été déjà fait dans l'entreprise *Fugue* donc que c'était mort-né' (146). In a slightly later interview, Laporte suggests that the *impasse* represented by 'Une œuvre mort-née' is explicable in terms of a certain conservatism resulting from the compositional practice of the *Fugue* series: cf. 'Entretien entre Roger Laporte et Serge Velay (janvier 1980)', esp. 15.
4. 'Correspondance avec Sylviane Agacinski', Digraphe 57 (1991), 77–94 (87); p. 495 of *Une Vie* is of course the title-page of *Suite*.
5. Cf. 'Entretien entre Mathieu Bénézet, Roger Laporte et Jean Ristat', 146–7, and 'Entretien entre Roger Laporte et Serge Velay', 15.
6. Cf. 'Entretien entre Mathieu Bénézet, Roger Laporte et Jean Ristat', 147: 'la lecture de *Suite*, en tout cas, doit être plus abrupte, plus discontinue que la lecture de *Fugue*, dans la mesure même où pour moi-même, je ne sais pas jusqu'où ça ira, étant donné que je ne fais plus de travail préparatoire; j'essaie directement d'écrire le texte.' However, from the remarks which follow this, and from Laporte's references to the thousands of pages of *brouillons* for *Suite* and *Moriendo* in the 'Entretien avec Roger Laporte, recueilli et annoté par Frédéric-Yves Jeannet', it is clear that Laporte means he eschewed the particular form of preparatory work undertaken for the *Fugue* series.
7. Blanchot, *L'Amitié*, 251.
8. 'Entretien entre Roger Laporte et Serge Velay', 16.
9. Rapaport, *Heidegger and Derrida*, 129.
10. This is noted in Laporte's study of Blanchot, 'L'ancien, l'effroyablement ancien' (*E* 43–4), where Pierre Madaule is credited with reminding Laporte of this echo. The passages cited there concern the exigency imposed on the narrator of *Celui qui ne m'accompagnait pas*, which he describes, having reached the point he has,

as 'aller plus loin, plus loin de ce côté, jamais d'un autre' (121), recalled a little later as 'l'affirmation qui persiste: j'irai de ce côté, jamais d'un autre' (145).

11. 'Ces singularités, distribuées le long d'une droite perverse, mourir, devenir-fou, écrire', Maurice Blanchot, *Le Pas au-delà* (Paris: Gallimard, 1973), 144.

12. Cf. Maurice Blanchot, *L'Ecriture du désastre* (Paris: Gallimard, 1980), 156–7.

13. Derrida's writings on Blanchot have repeatedly explored these questions of borders—between genres, between texts, between text and commentary—as, for instance, in 'Survivre' where he refers to the notion of the text 'qui ne serait plus, dès lors, un corpus fini d'écriture, un contenu cadré dans un livre ou dans ses marges mais un réseau différentiel, un tissu de traces renvoyant indéfiniment à de l'autre, référées à d'autres traces différentielles' (*Parages*, 127).

14. On Eros and the death instincts, see e.g. the chapter 'The Two Classes of Instincts' in *The Ego and the Id*, in the *Pelican Freud Library* xi (Harmondsworth: Penguin, 1984), 380–8.

15. The piece is effectively a review-article of Sarah Kofman, *L'Enfance de l'art: une interprétation de l'esthétique freudienne* (Paris: Payot, 1970).

16. Laporte, 'Freud et la question de l'art', *Europe* 539, 'Freud' (1974), 185–9 (189).

17. Laporte, 'Freud et la question de l'art', 189.

18. It is also significant that, besides the names of Lacan and Leclaire which he cites, Laporte refers here to Derrida's essay 'Freud et la scène de l'écriture'.

19. Cf. 'Le stade du miroir comme formateur de la fonction du Je', in Lacan, *Ecrits I* (Paris: Seuil, coll. 'Points', 1970), 89–97. Lacan's mirror phase is effectively a reworking of Freud's primary narcissism. For these and other psychoanalytic terms, J. Laplanche and J.-B. Pontalis, *Vocabulaire de la psychanalyse* (Paris: Presses Universitaires de France, 1967), remains an indispensable guide. My understanding of Lacan is also indebted to the works by Bowie, Forrester, Lemaire and Wilden listed in the Bibliography.

20. Cf. Lacan, *Ecrits I*, 90.

21. Indeed, I did so in some detail in the doctoral thesis on which the present study is based, although not without indicating the problems in such an approach. However, I am grateful to the examiners of that thesis, Leslie Hill and Michael Holland, for encouraging me to give further consideration to the status of my Lacanian readings of Laporte.

22. The detail of the transition from the Imaginary to the Symbolic order is too complex to elaborate here, and in any case has been outlined by many commentators. Of the texts collected in the *Ecrits*, 'D'une question préliminaire à tout traitement possible de la psychose' and 'La signification du phallus' in Lacan, *Ecrits II* (Paris: Seuil, coll. 'Points', 1971), 43–102 and 103–15, contain discussions of the infant–mother relationship, the Œdipal complex, castration, the phallus, etc. A clear summary of this aspect of Lacan's work may be found in Anika Lemaire, *Jacques Lacan*, rev. edn., trans. David Macey (London: Routledge and Kegan Paul, 1977), 78–92.

23. See e.g. the closing pages of 'Fonction et champ de la parole et du langage en psychanalyse', where Lacan, with a familiar Hegelian allusion, remarks that 'le symbole se manifeste d'abord comme meurtre de la chose, et cette mort constitue dans le sujet l'éternisation de son désir' (*Ecrits I*, 204). The accession to language submits the subject to the law of the signifier which structures the subject's desire around a void or absence, the death which is the origin and end

of subjectivity, as Lacan goes on to affirm: 'Aussi quand nous voulons atteindre dans le sujet ce qui était avant les jeux sériels de la parole, et ce qui est primordial à la naissance des symboles, nous le trouvons dans la mort, d'où son existence prend tout ce qu'elle a de sens' (205).

24. 'Le facteur de la vérité' is collected in Jacques Derrida, *La Carte postale: de Socrate à Freud et au-delà* (Paris: Aubier-Flammarion, 1980), 439–524. See e.g. Derrida's remarks on the consequences of Lacan's neglect, in his 'Séminaire sur "La Lettre volée"', of Poe's framing narrative in 'The Purloined Letter' (459–61 and *passim*).

25. This is an issue raised by Derrida throughout this essay, right from its opening pun: 'La psychanalyse, à supposer, se trouve' (441). The challenge posed to hermeneutics by the chiasmus is raised, at least by implication, in this essay and in many other texts by Derrida (the essay 'La loi du genre' in *Parages*, 249–87, provides a good example); for a lucid secondary account of Derrida's treatment of this question, see the chapter 'Borderline aesthetics' in David Carroll's *Paraesthetics: Foucault, Lyotard, Derrida* (New York and London: Methuen, 1987), 131–54.

26. Catherine Clément, 'Le Shamanisme de l'écriture', *Sud* 10 (1973), 75; my emphasis. For other examples of Lacanian readings, see the same author (under the name Catherine Backès-Clément), 'Histoire d'un sourire', *Critique* 276 (1970), 413–37; Charles Bouazis, 'Rets', *Critique* 323 (1974), 335–53; and an excellent study which makes some use of Lacanian analysis, Michel Beaujour, 'Une poétique de l'autoportrait: *Fugue* (1970) de Roger Laporte'.

27. In Derrida, *L'Ecriture et la différence*, 293–340; some of the discussion of Freud and Derrida in the concluding part of this chapter is a reworking of material which appeared in a different context in my article 'Playing dead: Edmond Jabès's *Livre des questions*', *Paragraph* 13:1 (1990), 30–43. For an account of the conceptions of death and mourning at issue in the following pages, see the chapter *'bio'* in Robert Smith's *Derrida and Autobiography* (Cambridge: Cambridge University Press), 129–71.

28. Collected in the *Pelican Freud Library*, xi. 429–34.

29. Derrida, *L'Ecriture et la différence*, 314.

30. Collected in the *Pelican Freud Library*, xi. 275–338.

31. *Pelican Freud Library*, xi. 312.

32. *Pelican Freud Library*, xi. 277; my emphasis.

33. Jean Laplanche, *Vie et mort en psychanalyse* (Paris: Flammarion, coll. 'Champs', 1970), 177.

34. In Derrida, *La Carte postale*, 275–437. Lyotard discusses the hesitation between constancy and zero principles in comparable terms in his *Discours, figure* (Paris: Klincksieck, 1971), 351–4.

35. Derrida, *La Carte postale*, 304–5.

36. Derrida, *L'Ecriture et la différence*, 302.

37. Derrida, *La Carte postale*, 429.

38. In 'Spéculer—sur "Freud"', Derrida writes of 'cet *arrêt de mort*, qui arrête la mort en deux sens différants (sentence condamnant à mort et interruption suspendant la mort)' (*La Carte postale*, 305). 'Survivre' is in *Parages*, 117–218; on the *arrêt de mort*, see e.g. 154–5 and 159–60.

39. Derrida, *La Carte postale*, 379.

40. In Derrida, *Parages*, 19–116.

41. In the *Pelican Freud Library*, xi. 251–68. The concepts raised in this paragraph can again be pursued through the relevant entries in Laplanche and Pontalis's *Vocabulaire de la psychanalyse*, although, of course, their work is not able to take account of the theories of Nicolas Abraham and Maria Torok which I go on to cite.

42. Jacques Derrida, 'Fors: les mots anglés de Nicolas Abraham et Maria Torok', in Nicolas Abraham and Maria Torok, *Cryptonymie: Le Verbier de l'homme aux loups* (Paris: Aubier-Flammarion, 1976), 7–73 (11).

43. Derrida, 'Fors', 12. A very brief, but clear outline of mourning and the crypt is given in Bennington and Derrida, *Jacques Derrida*, 138–9. The chapter 'Cryptaesthesia: the Case of *Wuthering Heights*' in Nicholas Royle's fascinating *Telepathy and Literature: essays on the reading mind* (Oxford: Blackwell, 1991), 28–62, deals with these matters in more detail, as well as offering a 'cryptonymic' reading of *Wuthering Heights* which, in its exploration of doors, gates and thresholds, also has a bearing on the *pas*, the step (not) taken in *Suite* and *Moriendo*.

44. Derrida, 'Fors', 25.

45. Derrida, 'Fors', 10.

46. Derrida, *Parages*, 178.

47. Derrida, *La Carte postale*, 357.

48. Derrida has discussed the proper name and the signature in too many texts to list here; however, the signature and its relation to the literary is the chief concern of *Signéponge* (Paris: Seuil, 1988). Helpful accounts may be found in Bennington and Derrida, *Jacques Derrida*, 140–56, and Timothy Clark, *Derrida, Heidegger, Blanchot*, 150–80.

49. Bennington and Derrida, *Jacques Derrida*, 153.

CHAPTER 5

Giving Reading

What is the distinctive opening to reading effected by Laporte's work? To seek this distinction is not to seek an absolute singularity, which would definitionally not be open to reading, but to ask about the iterable signature of 'Roger Laporte'. In particular, it might be wondered what is so distinctive about a body of work, many of whose characteristics—reflexivity, generic transgression, self-quotation, a *scriptible* openness to reading, the dislocation of unified subjectivity by alterity, etc.—seem to be the very passwords of our literary post-modernity, as innumerable commentators have attested.[1] In briefly distinguishing Laporte's work from a particular current of literary postmodernism in France, to which it bears a limited resemblance, I will at the same time be signalling the proximity of Laporte to certain other writers in the sort of community described by Laporte in *Entre deux mondes*, in which, having cited Bataille's phrase, 'une communauté de chercheurs', he remarks that his own work has become 'un point, un seul point, d'un réseau qui ne comporte ni bords, ni centre, singulier espace—un texte?—toujours en train de se défaire, parfois de se déchirer, mais aussi de se réinventer' (*EDM* 54). It is in fact a sort of community inseparable from a certain practice of writing, a community of works, for example, in which the idiosyncrasy of the signature at once questions that idiosyncrasy, is already marked by the other, and at the same time resists absorption into an undifferentiated fusion. It is the heteronomous community described in Blanchot's *La Communauté inavouable*, to which Laporte alludes, in which Blanchot, drawing on the work of Bataille and on Jean-Luc Nancy's *La Communauté désœuvrée*, writes of a community inextricably linked with 'une certaine sorte d'écriture, celle qui n'a rien d'autre à chercher que les mots derniers: "Viens, viens, venez, vous ou toi auquel ne saurait convenir l'injonction, la prière, l'attente."'[2]

The crucial place of Blanchot in this community will, I hope, already have been suggested in the foregoing pages. To the particular points of contact outlined earlier, I would simply add here that Laporte's attempt to inaugurate a new genre of *biographie*, neither simply literature nor philosophy, in order to pursue an essential element of the literary which also haunts philosophy as its repressed other, mirrors what has been the central concern of Blanchot's work, from the fiction of the 1940s and 1950s in which narrative strategies are adopted which seek, in Michael Holland's words, 'to turn the standpoint of narrative into the conscious expression of that moment of eclipse when, in *my* consciousness, I am *no-one*',[3] to the fragmentary and generically hybrid works of the 1960s onwards which seek to stage an encounter between the literary and the theoretical or philosophical.

It is a community in which, for example, one would place the figure of Edmond Jabès, whose work presents a great many parallels with that of Laporte,[4] some of which I will rapidly enumerate:[5] the ambivalent *brisures* which exist between individual volumes in the series into which Jabès grouped his works, and between those series, these *brisures* being effected, for example, by structuring devices which problematize the frame of the text and by self-quotation;[6] a reworking of the notion of the origin in respect of writing, so that, as Seán Hand remarks of *Yaël*, we discover that 'digression lies already in the source, indeed, that the source of this work is the sense of digression';[7] the disruption of the self-identity of the subject through its inscription in the text—'Tu es celui qui écrit et qui est écrit'[8]— which in turn gives rise to a notion of the life in/of writing as inseparable from death—'Vivre, écrire, c'est permettre à la mort de se mouvoir, telle la plume dans la main, telle la sève dans la tige';[9] the invocation of the reader as an active collaborator in the life of writing, rather than a mere recipient of the work—'Si une phrase, un vers survivent à l'œuvre, ce n'est pas l'auteur qui leur a donné cette chance particulière aux dépens des autres, c'est le lecteur'[10]—but in a conception of reading which is also inseparable from death, as Jabès suggests in an essay on Michel Leiris—'Sentence. Le texte n'est autre que cette sentence implacable à laquelle nul n'échappe./ Ecrivain et lecteur se perdent dans les mêmes vocables.'[11]

A number of figures associated primarily with the philosophical domain would also participate in Laporte's heteronomous *réseau*, some of whom have already been discussed here in relation to Laporte's work, such as Levinas and Derrida, whilst others have been passed over, including for example Jean-Luc Nancy, mentioned a moment ago, and Philippe Lacoue-Labarthe. The work of Lacoue-Labarthe, one of the dedicatees of *Fugue 3*, whose presence in this network has frequently been signalled by Laporte, offers a number of illuminations of Laporte's enterprise; his exploration of *(auto)biographie, thanato-graphie*, music and rhythm in 'L'écho du sujet', in which he cites *Fugue* as an instance of the rapport between 'compulsion autobiographique et hantise musicale' with which he is concerned, would shed further light on my argument in Chapters 3 and 4, for example.[12]

The current of French writing with which I want briefly to contrast Laporte's work is that associated with the journal *Tel Quel*. The parallel between Laporte's work and the *Tel Quel* programme is at its most apparent at the time of the *Fugue* series, in the metaphorics of the writing-machine and of the *jeu*, for example, and more generally in the conception of *écriture* and of the text as *tissu*. It is in this last regard that Laporte, in his 1972 interview with Jean Ristat, indicates the importance for him of *Tel Quel*, and specifically of that journal's *Théorie d'ensemble* of 1968: 'Il m'a beaucoup apporté et permis de reprendre de très anciens projets que je n'avais pas été capable de mener à bien.'[13] Once again, one can readily enumerate some of the common denominators of Laporte's enterprise and the work of the *Tel Quel* group: a shared literary inheritance, headed by Mallarmé, and including such figures as Valéry, Ponge, Artaud and Bataille; a conception of writing as intransitive and as fundamentally transgressive; a concern to lay bare the workings of the text, about which Laporte remarks: 'Je suis, *et pour des raisons également politiques*, très sensible à cette malhonnêteté qui consiste à effacer le travail en parlant d'inspiration, de grâce';[14] and the dislocation of the unified subject effected by writing.

More specifically, there are certainly strong resemblances between Laporte's work and the fiction of Philippe Sollers, particularly in the texts of what one might call Sollers's second period, *Drame* and *Nombres*.[15] We already find, for example, the metaphor of the chess-board, pursued in *Fugue*, in the 'échiquier mobile' of *Drame*, a metaphor which, as in *Fugue*, immediately raises the question of the place of the writing-subject in this game—'Prisonnier du jeu?'—and which finds the subject in a quest to write the unknown: '"Dans le jeu, sur cet échiquier invisible (et sans attendre, sans chercher plus loin l'instant), je décris celui que j'ignore [...]"'. It is also a game in which an originary delay prohibits the self-coincidence of the subject, whilst at the same time allowing the perpetuation of the game: '"Je suis donc perpétuellement en retard par rapport à moi—mais aussi perpétuellement libre de susciter l'aventure[...]"'.[16] Laporte's work does not, of course, share the alternation between first and third persons utilized in *Drame*, let alone the quadripartite division of sections which we find in *Nombres*. However, one only has to read Derrida's essay on *Nombres*, 'La Dissémination',[17] to recognize the extent to which the consequences of this and other features of Sollers's text, in respect of the deconstruction of the origin, the instability of reflexivity, the *pli* of citation, the dissemination of the subject, are reflected in Laporte's work.

The specific affinity with Sollers is signalled by Laporte in 'Bio-graphie', his enthusiastic review-article on Sollers's collection of theoretical writings, *Logiques*.[18] That affinity is immediately apparent in the title of the piece, which is amplified by a quotation from Sollers who, in turn citing Baudelaire, ponders what a true *biographie* might be, 'bio-graphie, *écriture vivante* et multiple, fiction logique' (cited in *QV* 135); Laporte records his belief that *Logiques* may be the realization of such a dream 'ou du moins sa scansion abstraite' (*QV* 135). The parallel is underscored when Laporte goes on to cite Sollers to the effect that the experience of this *écriture vivante* is, in a sense, a debilitating one and that, leading us even into the domain of death, it is a *thanatographie* (*QV* 139). The article suggests a number of other points of contact between Laporte's and Sollers's work, but I want to pass over these to reach a point near the end of the piece, where Laporte expresses a disagreement with Sollers's viewpoint, as this takes us to a critical divergence between Laporte and Sollers.

Laporte quotes a passage from the essay 'La science de Lautréamont', in which Sollers talks of a writing which becomes contemporary with itself, 'déployant toute représentation à partir de son tracé producteur' (cited in *QV* 142). Given what we noted time and again about the impossibility of a perfect self-coincidence in writing in Laporte's work, it is no surprise that he differs on this point. The disagreement comes to encompass more than just this part of Sollers's essay when Laporte quotes from Jean-Louis Baudry's 'Linguistique et production textuelle', collected in *Théorie d'ensemble*: 'une théorie du texte ne pourra se constituer qu'en étant liée à la pratique scripturale elle-même' (cited in *QV* 142). Laporte's response, which we have already had occasion to cite in Chapter 3, is that, even when theory and practice may be said to co-exist in a work, 'une parfaite coïncidence entre la pratique et le discours théorique est impossible, que l'après-coup est inévitable dans la mesure même où l'espacement est constitutif du langage' (QV 143).

The importance of this divergence should not be underestimated, for it is this impossibility of self-coincidence in writing that would prevent Laporte from subscribing to the notion of textual materialism promulgated by Tel Quel,[19] a notion whose untenability is demonstrated by Derrida's analysis of the sign, which deconstructs the materialism/idealism opposition.[20] That the doctrine of textual materialism and the notion of a perfect self-coincidence in practico-theoretical écriture go hand in hand is repeatedly illustrated in the writings of Jean Ricardou, sometime member of the Tel Quel editorial board, whose work did so much to set the agenda for avant-garde writing in the late 1960s and early 1970s. The short section on 'Le matérialisme textuel' in Nouveaux Problèmes du roman, for example, suggests that the referentiality of fiction is attributable to 'une curieuse symétrie' between the material reflexivity of the written text on the one hand, and the constituent material of the world on the other.[21]

The notion of a perfect reflexivity of the text ineluctably leads to a simple refusal of the notion of mimesis, amounting to the claim to escape 'le mimétologisme' which Derrida, in a passage from 'La double séance' to which we have already alluded, insists can only lead to entrenchment in the system one had thought to escape: 'on supprime le double ou on le dialectise et on retrouve la perception de la chose même, la production de sa présence, sa vérité, comme idée, forme ou matière.'[22] To make such observations is not to deny the importance of the critical work carried out under the auspices of Tel Quel, in terms of both a theory and a practice of writing, which was crucial in forcing the interrogation of received ideas about language, mimesis, the relation of the literary text to the social text, and so on. However, the notion of the text advanced in that cause becomes too easily indistinguishable from the facile exploitation of the ludic dimension of the text and the gratuitous manipulation of the possibilities of literary mise en abyme which characterize so much contemporary writing, and which amount to a jeu without enjeu. In 'Ce qui reste à force de musique', drawing a clear distinction with the function of mise en abyme in Fugue and Supplément, Derrida mounts a fierce attack on this exploitation of reflexivity in which one can detect 'cette auto-défense du texte qui, à s'expliquer, à s'enseigner, à se poser lui-même, à s'installer complaisamment dans son auto-telisme ou son auto-thétisme, dans la représentation de soi à l'infini, se garde précisément contre l'abîme dont il se contente alors de parler, dont il a la bouche pleine après avoir fait le plein d'abîme'.[23] The textual materialism of the *Tel Quel* programme can give rise to a liberated play of signifiers which, one can say perhaps a little too easily with hindsight, may indifferently signify an advocacy of Althusserian Marxism, Maoism or a politics of dissidence.[24]

The distinction between notions of reflexivity which we are pursuing here becomes an ethical question, in so far as it concerns openness to reading, communication and the relation to the other. Once again, one cannot deny the part played by *Tel Quel* in effecting a reorientation of notions and practices of reading, but it is none the less the case that the achievement of the perfect reflexivity evoked by some of those involved in elaborating the *Tel Quel* programme would foreclose reading. It is only through the impossibility of absolute reflexivity that the possibility of communication is opened, and it is this possibility which is addressed by the unstable, imperfect reflexivity of Laporte's works, without falling back on the notion of the text as the communicative vehicle for a self-present intention which precedes it and which might safely be conveyed to the reader.[25]

In this regard, we should not overlook the obvious: the simplicity of Laporte's writing, the persistence with the use of the first person and of the present tense (see *FS* 382–3) and the eschewal of fragmentary form (see *F* 302), for example, notwithstanding the aporia to which this gives rise: 'nécessairement j'échouerais si je pouvais, contredisant mon propos, tenir un discours continu sur la discontinuité' (*F* 319). It is a feature which distinguishes Laporte not only from the writers associated with *Tel Quel*, but also from Blanchot and Jabès, and is constant throughout his writing. In Chapter 2 we observed the importance which he accorded to linguistic sobriety from an early stage, and in the closing pages of *Suite*, we read: 'en répondant, en cherchant à répondre à la nécessité, toujours impensée, de dire l'épreuve, je compte parvenir jusqu'aux confins du langage; en luttant pour la clarté—je ne puis faire autrement, et sans doute ne dois-je rien faire d'autre—, j'espère en venir à cette désappropriation sur laquelle je suis sans pouvoir, mais sans laquelle l'épreuve serait révolue, l'épreuve—ma seule chance' (*S* 562). The next paragraph proceeds to reiterate the impossibility of this quest, but the resolute pursuit of this impossibility, the attempt to go 'toujours de ce côté, jamais d'un autre' without recouping the loss this provokes is a key part of the opening to reading effected by Laporte's work.

Writing the loss, the *désœuvrement*, in writing *as* loss, losing the game of *qui perd gagne*, is impossible. Writing always turns the loss to profit, survives the death inscribed in it: 'L'écriture est triomphe [...], assurance maniaque de sur-vie. C'est ce qui la rend insupportable.' And this is no less the case when one writes about this impossibility: 'Parler de l'écriture, du triomphe, et d'écrire comme *survivre*, c'est énoncer ou dénoncer le phantasme maniaque. Non sans le réitérer, cela va sans dire.'[26] But, at the same time, we have already seen that writing loss, writing death in the life in/of writing, is as inevitable as it is impossible. We also saw, at the end of Chapter 3, that the instability of reflexivity signals the impossible invention of the other as the only possibility of invention, the only possibility of communication as irrecuperable loss in the movement towards the other which does not immediately return to the circulation of the same. What, in a Blanchotian inspiration, we have called the Orphic text returns on itself in search of an origin which is always already reinscribed in the movement of the writing it was supposed to originate. However, that recursive movement which discovers the failure of self-coincidence, the loss of the work's integrity, by the same token constitutes a writing which always does more than it can say, or whose saying (*le dire*) always exceeds the capacity of the said (*le dit*).[27]

The instability of reflexivity is the opening which awaits (without anticipating) the radical unpredictability of reading, the reading whose silent scansion is the necessary precondition of the text but which constitutes a destination that the text can never assure. In the 'Postscriptum' of *Moriendo*, the suspended termination of the work, its final but penultimate sequence ('cette séquence ultime jamais je ne pourrai l'écrire', *M* 614), the implacable injunction 'Poursuivre' is again recalled, but there soon follows this remark: 'Si, à bout de course, j'ai transmis le message, ne puis-je être tenu pour quitte? Poursuivre. Poursuivre: silencieuse injonction à laquelle plus tard d'autres répondront' (*M* 612). The termination of the interminable opens out onto a future, to which the only relation is in the modality of hope indicated in the penultimate line of the work: 'Ai-je ainsi satisfait à l'appel du lointain comme lointain? Je peux seulement l'espérer' (*M* 614).

The impossible but necessary movement towards the other signalled by *Une Vie* is also the movement of the gift, of a donation without recompense.[28] I raise this idea briefly to introduce, as a manner of conclusion, the difficulty of writing on Laporte, for that difficulty does not principally reside, as might be thought, in the autocritical dimension of Laporte's work; as Blanchot remarks in respect of *Don Quixote* and *The Castle*: 'Plus une œuvre se commente, plus elle appelle de commentaires; plus elle entretient avec son centre de rapports de "réflexion" (de redoublement), plus à cause de cette dualité elle se rend énigmatique.'[29] Rather, the difficulty lies in avoiding the return of the gift, the reduction of the ethical saying of the work to the thematization of the said.

This difficulty is insurmountable, the gift cannot be preserved: no sooner have I recognized it as a gift than I have returned the gift by that recognition, *reconnaissance*, gratitude. Yet the gift of *Une Vie* at the same time cannot but be preserved, cannot but persist. For there to be a gift, Derrida argues, the gift can never be present if it is not to be annulled in an economy of exchange: '*A la limite, le don comme don devrait ne pas apparaître comme don: ni au donataire, ni au donateur. Il ne peut être don comme don qu'en n'étant pas présent comme don.*' The gift is impossible, but it is the very condition of the economy of exchange, which could not come to be without donation—the gift is that movement of deferral, of *différance*, without which such an economy would be no longer an economy but immediate restitution, paralysis in fact. What is given, then, is time: 'le don n'est un don, il ne donne que dans la mesure où il *donne le temps*. La différence entre un don et toute autre opération d'échange pur et simple, c'est que le don donne le temps. *Là où il y a le don, il y a le temps.*' Writing and reading take time. In Laporte's work, with the differantial repetition, the invention of the other which has often been our concern in this study, the time of writing becomes re-marked, opening the work to the chance of the future, in a giving which is never accomplished. 'Ce que ça donne, le don, c'est le temps, mais ce don du temps est aussi une demande de temps.'[30] *Une Vie*, in never ceasing to give, never ceases to indebt us, to demand that we take time: 'Poursuivre: silencieuse injonction à laquelle plus tard d'autres répondront' (*M* 612).

Notes to Chapter 5

1. Rather than offer a proliferation of references here, I would simply point to the distinctions drawn by Ihab Hassan between modernism and postmodernism in

that highly postmodernist form of the list; it has been reproduced in a number of publications, and may be found, e.g., in his *The Postmodern Turn: essays in postmodern theory and culture* (New York: Oxford University Press, 1971), 91–2.

2. Maurice Blanchot, *La Communauté inavouable* (Paris: Minuit, 1983), 26. A footnote indicates that Blanchot is thinking here of both his own earlier work and that of Derrida. A notion of ethics and community is adumbrated here which relates to the work of Blanchot, Derrida, Levinas, Lacoue-Labarthe and Jean-Luc Nancy in his *La Communauté désœuvrée* (Paris: Christian Bourgois, 1986) and *L'Expérience de la liberté* (Paris: Galilée, 1988). For a brief but helpful account of the notion of a heteronomous community, see Clark, *Derrida, Heidegger, Blanchot*, 139–42.

3. Michael Holland, 'Towards a New Literary Idiom. The Fiction and Criticism of Maurice Blanchot from 1941 to 1955' (D.Phil. thesis, Oxford, 1981), 18. This thesis should also be consulted for a detailed exploration of those strategies in respect of the novels and *récits* from *Thomas l'Obscur* to *Celui qui ne m'accompagnait pas*, and particularly *L'Arrêt de mort*. On the *neutre*, the literary, and the theoretical in Blanchot's work, see Holland, 'Le hiatus théorique', *Gramma* 3/4 (1976), 53–70.

4. To my knowledge, Laporte's only allusion to Jabès consists in the epigraph to his study of Derrida, 'Une double stratégie', which is taken from Jabès's *Aely* (Paris: Gallimard, 1972), 105.

5. I have explored the features of Jabès's *Livre des questions* septology to which I refer here more fully in my 'Playing dead: Edmond Jabès's *Livre des questions*'; I would now take a slightly different view of the question of reflexivity in Jabès, treated rather hastily in the closing pages of my article. There is now a great deal of secondary literature on Jabès, although Derrida's studies, 'Edmond Jabès et la question du livre' and 'Ellipse' in *L'Ecriture et la différence*, 99–116 and 429–36, remain unsurpassed, and implicitly shed further light on the parallels between Jabès's work and that of Blanchot and Laporte.

6. On these matters, see e.g. Seán Hand's 'Double Indemnity: the Ends of Citation in Edmond Jabès', *Romance Studies* 12 (1988), 77–85.

7. Hand, 'Double Indemnity', 77, referring to Edmond Jabès, *Yaël* (Paris: Gallimard, 1967).

8. Edmond Jabès, *Le Livre des questions* (Paris: Gallimard, 1963), 9.

9. Jabès, *Yaël*, 49.

10. Jabès, *Le Livre des questions*, 40.

11. Edmond Jabès, *Dans la double dépendance du dit* (Montpellier: Fata Morgana, 1984), 95.

12. 'L'écho du sujet' is collected in Lacoue-Labarthe's *Le Sujet de la philosophie: Typographies I* (Paris: Aubier-Flammarion, 1979), 217–303; the phrase cited and the allusion to *Fugue* occur at 226.

13. 'Lire Roger Laporte', 290.

14. 'Lire Roger Laporte', 299; my emphasis.

15. In making this distinction, I am thinking of the increasingly problematized referentiality of the first phase of Sollers's fiction, up to *Le Parc* (Paris: Seuil, 1961), which already presents some parallels with Laporte's work; then, following *Drame* (Paris: Seuil, 1965), *Nombres* (Paris: Seuil, 1968) and the pivotal *Lois* (Paris: Seuil, 1972), the Joycean 'polylogues' (the term is Kristeva's) may be seen as

constituting a third phase, commencing with *H* (Paris: Seuil, 1973); finally, there is the apparent return to a referential mode marked by *Femmes* (Paris: Gallimard, 1983). For a comprehensive account of Sollers's itinerary as a writer, see Philippe Forest's *Philippe Sollers* (Paris: Seuil, 1992), which contains a detailed analysis of *Drame* and *Nombres* (89–152).

16. Sollers, *Drame*, 21, 65, 82.

17. In Derrida, *La Dissémination*, 319–407. For an account of how, even at this moment of apparently close proximity to Sollers, Derrida may be seen as discreetly taking his distances, see Marian Hobson, 'On the Subject of the Subject: Derrida on Sollers in *La Dissémination*', in *Philosophers' Poets*, ed. David Wood (London and New York: Routledge, 1990), 111–39.

18. 'Bio-graphie' (*QV* 135–44) first appeared in *Critique* 281 (1970), 813–20.

19. Cf. e.g. the collective 'Division d'ensemble' which opens *Tel Quel*, *Théorie d'ensemble* (Paris: Seuil, 1968) (7–10).

20. Cf. Derrida, *De la grammatologie*, 45: 'des identités formelles découpées dans une masse sensible sont déjà des idéalités non purement sensibles'. Once again, Bennington's account is admirably clear on this matter: cf. Bennington and Derrida, *Jacques Derrida*, 30–4.

21. 'Le matérialisme textuel', in Jean Ricardou, *Nouveaux Problèmes du roman* (Paris: Seuil, 1978), 184–6.

22. Derrida, *La Dissémination*, 235.

23. Derrida, *Psyché*, 101.

24. My brief overview does not do justice to the nuances in the conception of textual materialism that emerge in the course of *Tel Quel*'s history or indeed between, say, Ricardou and Sollers, although I would still want to insist that the problematic notion of materiality remains fundamental. Patrick ffrench, *The Time of Theory: a history of 'Tel Quel' (1960–1983)* (Oxford: Clarendon Press, 1995), should be consulted for a meticulously researched account of *Tel Quel*'s theoretical and political positions, though not for entirely reliable statements on the work of Derrida or Blanchot.

25. The notion of communication suggested here is inseparable from the idea of the heteronomous community evoked earlier, and is addressed, for example, throughout Libertson's *Proximity: Levinas, Blanchot, Bataille and Communication*.

26. Derrida, *Parages*, 169, 218.

27. The distinction is Levinas's, most fully elaborated in his *Autrement qu'être ou au-delà de l'essence* (The Hague: Martinus Nijhoff, 1974, 'Livre de Poche', coll. 'Biblio: essais' reprint).

28. This passage from *Lettre à personne* is worth citing in the context of the gift: 'Tant que j'écris, aussi longtemps que j'écris, que je dois écrire, l'épreuve, c'est en même temps la chance: d'abord, à proprement parler, la chance d'écrire (le bonheur de dire), d'écrire un texte qui, une fois écrit, n'exige plus la présence de l'auteur, mais s'offre indéfiniment au lecteur (j'ai été très frappé, très touché du fait que de nombreux lecteurs, fort divers, ont reçu *Moriendo* comme un *don*)' (*LP* 39). The idea of writing as gift is also raised by both parties in the 'Correspondance avec Sylviane Agacinski' (see esp. 78–82).

29. Blanchot, *L'Entretien infini*, 572–3.

30. Derrida, *Donner le temps I: La fausse monnaie* (Paris: Galilée, 1991), 26–7, 59–60, 60.

BIBLIOGRAPHY

The Bibliography is divided into three sections: (1) Works by Laporte;
(2) Studies on Laporte; (3) Other Works.

1. Works by Laporte

i. Books

La Veille (Paris: Gallimard, 1963).
Une Voix de fin silence (Paris: Gallimard, 1966).
Une Voix de fin silence II: Pourquoi? (Paris: Gallimard, 1967).
Fugue (biographie) (Paris: Gallimard, 1970).
Souvenir de Reims (Montpellier: Fata Morgana, 1972).
Fugue: Supplément (biographie) (Paris: Gallimard, 1973).
'Une Migration', suivi de 'Le Partenaire' (Montpellier: Fata Morgana, 1974).
Quinze variations sur un thème biographique (Paris: Flammarion, 1975).
Fugue 3 (biographie) (Paris: Flammarion, 1976).
'Souvenir de Reims' et autres récits (Paris: Hachette, 1979).
Carnets (extraits) (Paris: Hachette, 1979).
Suite (biographie) (Paris: Hachette, 1979).
Gladiator: essai sur Paul Valéry (Montpellier: Fata Morgana, 1980).
Bram Van Velde, ou 'Cette petite chose qui fascine' (Montpellier: Fata Morgana, 1980).
François Martin, l'excès, le manque, photographies de Wilfrid Rouff (Dieulefit: Cheval d'attaque, 1980).
Mozart 1790 (Chennevières-sur-Marne: Portail, 1983).
Moriendo (biographie) (Paris: P.O.L, 1983).
Feuille volante (Paris: Le Collet de Buffle, 1986)
Hölderlin: une douleur éperdue (Seyssel: Comp'Act, 1986).
Une Vie (biographie) (Paris: P.O.L, 1986).
Ecrire la musique (Bordeaux: à Passage, 1986).
Maurice Blanchot, 'l'ancien, l'effroyablement ancien' (Montpellier: Fata Morgana, 1987).
Lectures de Paul Celan (Dijon: Ulysse, Fin de siècle, 1987).
Entre deux mondes (Montpellier: Gris Banal, 1988).

Lettre à personne (Paris: Plon, 1989).
Quelques petits riens (Dijon: Ulysse, Fin de siècle, 1990).
Etudes (Paris: P.O.L, 1990).
Marcel Proust: le narrateur et l'écrivain (Montpellier: Fata Morgana, 1994).
A l'extrême pointe: Bataille et Blanchot (Montpellier: Fata Morgana, 1994).
La Loi de l'alternance (Paris: Fourbis, 1997).

ii. Chapters in books

'Notes sur Giacometti', in *L'Endurance de la pensée*, pour saluer Jean Beaufret (Paris: Plon, 1968), 339–48.
'Une Passion', in Roger Laporte and Bernard Noël, *Deux Lectures de Maurice Blanchot* (Montpellier: Fata Morgana, 1973), 53–155.
'Une double stratégie', in Lucette Finas, Sarah Kofman, Roger Laporte and Jean-Michel Rey, *Ecarts: quatre essais à propos de Jacques Derrida* (Paris: Fayard, 1973), 208–64.
'L'Homme nu', in *Celui qui ne peut se servir des mots*, Hommage à Bram Van Velde (Montpellier: Fata Morgana, 1975), 101–4.
'Désenchantement', in *Misère de la littérature, Première livraison*: ouvrage collectif (Paris: Christian Bourgois, 1978), 75–9.
'Séminaire "littérature": Avis au lecteur' and 'Nulle part séjournant', in *Les Fins de l'homme: à partir du travail de Jacques Derrida*, ed. Philippe Lacoue-Labarthe and Jean-Luc Nancy (Paris: Galilée, 1981), 201–8.
'Maurice Blanchot today', trans. Ian Maclachlan, in *Maurice Blanchot: The Demand of Writing*, ed. Carolyn Bailey Gill (London and New York: Routledge, 1996), 25–33.

iii. Prefaces, forewords, etc.

'Présentation', in Alain Veinstein and Lars Fredrikson, *L'Introduction de la pelle* (Malakoff: Orange Export Ltd., 1975).
'Note du destinataire', in Claude Royet-Journoud, *Lettre de Symi* (Montpellier: Fata Morgana, 1980).
'Postface', in Honoré de Balzac, *Le Chef-d'Œuvre inconnu*, suivi de *La Belle Noiseuse*, un film de Jacques Rivette; présentation de Pascal Bonitzer (Castelnau-le-Lez: Climats, 1990).
'Un enfant sans raison', in Alphonse Daudet, *Le Petit Chose* (Paris: P.O.L, 'La Collection', 1992).

iv. Uncollected articles and other pieces

'"Les 'blancs' assument l'importance"', *Les Lettres françaises* 1429 (1972), 5.
'Bief', *L'Arc* 54, 'Jacques Derrida' (1973), 65–70.

'La genèse d'un roman, ce serait passionnant', *Nouvelles littéraires* 2423 (1974), 10.

'Freud et la question de l'art', *Europe* 539, 'Freud' (1974), 185–9.

'Une peinture lamentable', *Critique* 326 (1974), 666–9.

'La déesse blanche', *Critique* 333 (1975), 217–31.

'Au-delà de l'"Horror vacui"', *Nouvelle Revue de Psychanalyse* 11, 'Figures du vide' (1975), 117–25.

'Un passant considérable', *Archives des lettres modernes* 160, 'Aujourd'hui, Rimbaud', enquête de Roger Munier (1976), 80–1.

'Nuit blanche', *Critique* 358 (1977), 208–18.

'Une œuvre mort-née', *Digraphe* 18/19, 'Roger Laporte' (1979), 17–76.

'Vers "L'absence de livre"', *Revue des Sciences Humaines* 221, 'Narrer: l'art et la manière' (1991), 33–4.

Response to '*Digraphe* enquête: Depuis bientôt un siècle *l'intellectuel* parle et écrit. Mais aujourd'hui? Ni valet ni bouffon, quel rôle pensez-vous jouer?', *Digraphe* 57 (1991), 20–2.

'Heidegger, Beaufret et le politique: témoignage et réflexions sur une longue occultation', *Lendemains* 65 (1992), 72–4.

'De l'égoïsme "sacré"', *Digraphe* 66, '1974–94: Qui est là?' (1993), 45–6.

'Un sourire mozartien', *Ralentir Travaux* 7 (1997), 74–5.

'Présentation', *Revue des Sciences Humaines* 253, 'Maurice Blanchot' (1999), 9–17.

v. Correspondence

'Correspondance avec Sylviane Agacinski', *Digraphe* 57 (1991), 77–94.

vi. Interviews

'Lire Roger Laporte', in Jean Ristat, *Qui sont les contemporains* (Paris: Gallimard, 1975), 281–300 (reprinted from *Les Lettres françaises* 1453 (1972)).

'Entretien entre Mathieu Bénézet, Roger Laporte et Jean Ristat', *Digraphe* 18/19 (1979), 121–55.

'Entretien entre Roger Laporte et Serge Velay (janvier 1980)', *Autour de Roger Laporte* (Nîmes: Cahiers de littérature 'Terriers', 1980), 11–18.

'Roger Laporte au bord du silence' (interview with Jacques Derrida), *Libération* (22 Dec. 1983), 28.

'Entretien avec Roger Laporte, recueilli et annoté par Frédéric-Yves Jeannet', *Digraphe* 57 (1991), 71–6.

2. Studies on Laporte

i. Journals, or parts of journals, devoted to Laporte

'Lectures de Roger Laporte', *Sud* 10 (1973), 68–107 (articles by Clément, Loraux, and Damon, listed below).
Digraphe 18/19, 'Roger Laporte' (1979).
Autour de Roger Laporte, textes et entretien, avec Jean Laude, Claude Minière, Serge Velay et Roger Laporte (Nîmes: Cahiers de littérature 'Terriers', 1980).
Origin 5:2 (1983), 5–28: English translation of *Moriendo* by Cid Corman (followed in 5:3 (1984) by 'Roger Laporte' (52), consisting of two brief remarks by Laporte).
'Dossier Roger Laporte', *Digraphe* 57 (1991), 69–94.

ii. Selected articles

BEAUJOUR, MICHEL, 'Une poétique de l'autoportrait: *Fugue* (1970) de Roger Laporte', in *Miroirs d'encre: rhétorique de l'autoportrait* (Paris: Seuil, 1980), 224–36.
BÉNÉZET, MATHIEU, 'La fonction narrative' and 'Où nous sommes défigurés', in *Le Roman de la langue: des romans, 1960–1975* (Paris: Union Générale d'Editions, collection '10/18', 1977), 39–46 and 261–78.
BENJAMIN, ANDREW, 'The Redemption of Value: Laporte, Writing as *Abkürzung*', in *Art, Mimesis and the Avant-Garde* (London and New York: Routledge, 1991), 197–211 (reprinted from *Paragraph* 12:1 (1989), 23–36).
BLANCHOT, MAURICE, 'Traces' (includes a section on *La Veille*), in *L'Amitié* (Paris: Gallimard 1971), 246–58 (reprinted from *Nouvelle Revue Française* 129 (1963), 472–80).
—— '"Ne te retourne pas"', *Digraphe* 18/19 (1979), 160–3.
—— 'Blanchot ouvre Laporte', *Libération* (6 Mar. 1986), 35.
BOUAZIS, CHARLES, 'Rets', *Critique* 323 (1974), 335–53.
CAHEN, DIDIER, 'Les vies de Roger Laporte', *Critique* 557 (1993), 695–700.
CLÉMENT, CATHERINE, 'Un miroir, c'est-à-dire un piège', in *Miroirs du sujet* (Paris: Union Générale d'Editions, collection '10/18', 1975), 104–61 (reprinted from 'Histoire d'un sourire', *Critique* 276 (1970), 413–37, and 'Le Shamanisme de l'écriture', *Sud* 10 (1973), 68–77).
DAMON, YVONNE, 'L'Ecriture peut-elle s'ériger en biographie?', *Sud* 10 (1973), 89–107.
DERRIDA, JACQUES, 'Ce qui reste à force de musique', *Psyché. Inventions de l'autre* (Paris: Galilée, 1987), 95–103 (reprinted from *Digraphe* 18/19 (1979), 167–74).
DURAND, THIERRY, 'L'écriture ou la vie. Essai sur la biographie', *Etudes françaises* 33:3 (1997), 121–39.

FOUCAULT, MICHEL, 'Guetter le jour qui vient', *Nouvelle Revue Française* 130 (1963), 709–16.

—— 'Le langage de l'espace' (review of *La Veille*, and of works by Butor, Le Clézio, and Ollier), *Critique* 203 (1964), 378–82.

GUGLIELMI, JOSEPH, 'L'Abiographie (note)', in *Llanfair...*, the working notebooks of Anne-Marie Albiach and Claude Royet-Journoud, ed. Peter Hoy, 10 (1972), single sheet.

JALLET, GILLES, 'L'Ecriture de la "Chose"', *Critique* 499 (1988), 1008–20.

JEANNET, FRÉDÉRIC-YVES, 'Roger Laporte à l'épreuve du silence', *Digraphe* 46 (1988), 75–85.

LACOUE-LABARTHE, PHILIPPE, and NANCY, JEAN-LUC (with the participation of Roland Barthes and of Laporte), 'Entretiens sur Roger Laporte', *Digraphe* 18/19 (1979), 175–203.

LEVINAS, EMMANUEL, 'Roger Laporte et la voix de fin silence', *Noms propres* (Montpellier: Fata Morgana, 1976, reprinted in 'Livre de Poche', collection 'Biblio: essais'), 105–9 (reprinted from *Nouvelle Revue Française* 168 (1966), 1085–8).

LORAUX, PATRICE, 'Introduction indirecte', *Sud* 10 (1973), 78–88.

MACLACHLAN, IAN, 'Roger Laporte, Reader of Blanchot', in *Maurice Blanchot: The Demand of Writing*, ed. Carolyn Bailey Gill (London and New York: Routledge, 1996), 21–4.

—— '*Musique-rythme*: Derrida and Roger Laporte', in *The French Connections of Jacques Derrida*, ed. Julian Wolfreys, John Brannigan and Ruth Robbins (Albany: State University of New York Press, 1999), 71–84.

RAMNOUX, CLÉMENCE, '*La Veille*, par Roger Laporte', *Revue de Métaphysique et de Morale* 2 (1964), 232–4.

—— 'Accompagnement pour *Une Voix de fin silence*', *Critique* 235 (1966), 990–5.

RAYNAL, HENRI, 'Roger Laporte ou l'écriture angélique', *Courrier du centre international d'études poétiques* 64 (1968), 3–19.

RAYNAUD, JEAN-MICHEL, 'De la célébration du transi. Poursuites d'un biographe avec l'œuvre de Roger Laporte', *Revue des Sciences Humaines* 224, 'Le Biographique' (1991), 27–41.

SALLENAVE, DANIÈLE, 'Le violoniste exaspérant', *Les Temps Modernes* 268 (1968), 635–40.

SHERZER, DINA, '*Fugue*: The Adventures of Metaphors', in *Representation in Contemporary French Fiction* (Lincoln, Nebraska and London: University of Nebraska Press, 1986), 104–17.

SOJCHER, JACQUES, 'Lettre-Biographie (à Roger Laporte)', in *La Démarche poétique* (Paris: Union Générale d'Editions, collection '10/18', 1976), 287–93.

STURROCK, JOHN, 'The writer as Writer', *Times Literary Supplement* 4357 (1986), 1111.

UNGAR, STEVEN, 'Waiting for Blanchot', *Diacritics* (Summer 1975), 32–6.
VUARNET, JEAN-NOËL, 'La marionnette et ses fils', *Critique* 300 (1972), 430–40.

3. Other Works

ARTAUD, ANTONIN, *'L'Ombilic des Limbes', suivi de 'Le Pèse-nerfs' et autres textes* (Paris: Gallimard, coll. 'Poésie', 1968).
BATAILLE, GEORGES, *La Littérature et le mal* (Paris: Gallimard, 1957, coll. 'Idées' reprint).
—— *L'Erotisme* (Paris: Minuit, 1957).
—— *Œuvres complètes*, vols. v and vii (Paris: Gallimard, 1973 and 1976).
BENNINGTON, GEOFFREY, *Lyotard: Writing the Event* (Manchester: Manchester University Press, 1988).
—— and DERRIDA, JACQUES, *Jacques Derrida* (Paris: Seuil, 1991).
BENVENISTE, EMILE, *Problèmes de linguistique générale*, vol. i (Paris: Gallimard, 1966).
BIDENT, CHRISTOPHE, *Maurice Blanchot: partenaire invisible* (Seyssel: Champ Vallon, 1998).
BLANCHOT, MAURICE, *Faux pas* (Paris: Gallimard, 1943).
—— *L'Arrêt de mort* (Paris: Gallimard, 1948, coll. 'L'Imaginaire' reprint).
—— *La Part du feu* (Paris: Gallimard, 1949).
—— *Thomas l'Obscur (nouvelle version)* (Paris: Gallimard, 1950).
—— *Au Moment voulu* (Paris: Gallimard, 1951).
—— *Celui qui ne m'accompagnait pas* (Paris: Gallimard, 1953).
—— *L'Espace littéraire* (Paris: Gallimard, 1955, coll. 'Idées' reprint).
—— *Le Dernier Homme* (Paris: Gallimard, 1957).
—— *Le Livre à venir* (Paris: Gallimard, 1959, coll. 'Idées' reprint).
—— *L'attente L'oubli* (Paris: Gallimard, 1962).
—— *L'Entretien infini* (Paris: Gallimard, 1969).
—— *Le Pas au-delà* (Paris: Gallimard, 1973).
—— *L'Ecriture du désastre* (Paris: Gallimard, 1980).
—— *La Communauté inavouable* (Paris: Minuit, 1983).
BORGES, JORGE LUIS, *Labyrinths*, ed. Donald Yates and James Irby (Harmondsworth: Penguin, 1981).
BOWIE, MALCOLM, *Freud, Proust and Lacan: Theory as Fiction* (Cambridge: Cambridge University Press, 1987).
—— *Lacan* (London: HarperCollins, 1991).
BRETON, ANDRÉ, *L'Amour fou* (Paris: Gallimard, 1937, coll. 'Folio' reprint).
—— *Manifestes du surréalisme* (Paris: Pauvert, 1962, coll. 'Idées' reprint).
—— *Nadja* (Paris: Gallimard, 1964, coll. 'Folio' reprint).
BULLIVANT, ROGER, *Fugue* (London: Hutchinson University Library, 1971).

—— 'Counter-subject', in *The New Grove Dictionary of Music and Musicians*, ed. Stanley Sadie (London: Macmillan, 1980), iv. 852–4.

—— 'Counterpoint', in *The New Oxford Companion to Music*, ed. Denis Arnold (Oxford: Oxford University Press, 1983), i. 501–6.

CARROLL, DAVID, *Paraesthetics: Foucault, Lyotard, Derrida* (New York and London: Methuen, 1987).

CÉZANNE, PAUL, *Correspondance*, ed. John Rewald (Paris: Grasset, 1978).

CHAR, RENÉ, *Œuvres complètes* (Paris: Gallimard, 'Pléiade', 1983).

CLARK, TIMOTHY, 'Not Motion, but a Mime of it: "Rhythm" in the Textuality of Heidegger's Work', *Paragraph* 9:1 (1987), 69–82.

—— *Derrida, Heidegger, Blanchot: sources of Derrida's notion and practice of literature* (Cambridge: Cambridge University Press, 1992).

CLÉMENT, CATHERINE, *La Syncope: philosophie du ravissement* (Paris: Grasset, 1990).

COLLIN, FRANÇOISE, *Maurice Blanchot et la question de l'écriture* (Paris: Gallimard, 1971).

CONNOR, STEVEN, *Theory and Cultural Value* (Oxford: Blackwell, 1992).

CRITCHLEY, SIMON, *The Ethics of Deconstruction: Derrida and Levinas* (Oxford: Blackwell, 1992).

DÄLLENBACH, LUCIEN, *Le Récit spéculaire: essai sur la mise en abyme* (Paris: Seuil, 1977).

DAVIES, PAUL, 'A Linear Narrative? Blanchot with Heidegger in the work of Levinas', in *Philosophers' Poets*, ed. David Wood (London and New York: Routledge, 1990), 37–69.

DAYAN, PETER, *Mallarmé's 'divine transposition': real and apparent sources of literary value* (Oxford: Clarendon Press, 1986).

DELEUZE, GILLES, *Nietzsche et la philosophie* (Paris: Presses Universitaires de France, 1962).

DE MAN, PAUL, *Allegories of Reading: Figural Language in Rousseau, Nietzsche, Rilke, and Proust* (New Haven and London: Yale University Press, 1979).

DERRIDA, JACQUES, *De la grammatologie* (Paris: Minuit, 1967).

—— *L'Ecriture et la différence* (Paris: Seuil, 1967, coll. 'Points' reprint).

—— *La Voix et le phénomène* (Paris: Presses Universitaires de France, 1967).

—— *La Dissémination* (Paris: Seuil, 1972).

—— *Marges—de la philosophie* (Paris: Minuit, 1972).

—— 'Fors: les mots anglés de Nicolas Abraham et Maria Torok', in Nicolas Abraham and Maria Torok, *Cryptonymie: Le Verbier de l'homme aux loups* (Paris: Aubier-Flammarion, 1976), 7–73.

—— *Eperons: les styles de Nietzsche* (Paris: Flammarion, coll. 'Champs', 1978).

—— *La Carte postale: de Socrate à Freud et au-delà* (Paris: Aubier-Flammarion, 1980).

—— *Parages* (Paris: Galilée, 1986).

—— *Psyché. Inventions de l'autre* (Paris: Galilée, 1987).

—— *Signéponge* (Paris: Seuil, 1988).

—— *Donner le temps I: La fausse monnaie* (Paris: Galilée, 1991).

—— *Passions* (Paris: Galilée, 1993).

DESCOMBES, VINCENT, *Le Même et l'autre: quarante-cinq ans de philosophie française (1933–1978)* (Paris: Minuit, 1979).

FFRENCH, PATRICK, *The Time of Theory: A History of 'Tel Quel' (1960–1983)* (Oxford: Clarendon Press, 1995).

FOREST, PHILIPPE, *Philippe Sollers* (Paris: Seuil, 1992).

FORRESTER, JOHN, *The Seductions of Psychoanalysis: Freud, Lacan and Derrida* (Cambridge: Cambridge University Press, 1990).

FOUCAULT, MICHEL, 'Préface à la transgression', *Critique* 195/196 (1963), 751–69.

—— 'La pensée du dehors', *Critique* 229 (1966), 523–46.

FREUD, SIGMUND, *The Pelican Freud Library*, vols. ix and xi, trans. James Strachey, ed. Angela Richards (Harmondsworth: Penguin, 1979 and 1984).

GENETTE, GÉRARD, *Figures III* (Paris: Seuil, 1972).

—— *Palimpsestes: la littérature au second degré* (Paris: Seuil, 1981).

—— *Seuils* (Paris: Seuil, 1987).

GREEN, ANDRÉ, 'Le double et l'absent', *Critique* 312 (1973), 391–412.

HAND, SEÁN, 'Double Indemnity: the Ends of Citation in Edmond Jabès', *Romance Studies* 12 (1988), 77–85.

—— 'Reading, "Post-modern", Ethics', *Paragraph* 13:3 (1990), 267–84.

HASSAN, IHAB, *The Dismemberment of Orpheus: Toward a Postmodern Literature* (New York: Oxford University Press, 1971).

—— *The Postmodern Turn: essays in postmodern theory and culture* (Ohio: Ohio State University Press, 1987).

HEATH, STEPHEN, *The Nouveau Roman: A Study in the Practice of Writing* (London: Elek, 1972).

HEGEL, G. W. F., *Phenomenology of Spirit*, 'Preface', trans. Walter Kaufmann, in *Hegel: Selections*, ed. M. J. Inwood (New York and London: Macmillan, 1989), 115–51.

HEIDEGGER, MARTIN, *Being and Time*, trans. John McQuarrie and Edward Robinson (Oxford: Blackwell, 1962).

—— *Erläuterungen zu Hölderlins Dichtung*, 3rd edn. (Frankfurt: Klostermann, 1963).

—— *Identity and Difference*, trans. Joan Stambaugh (New York: Harper and Row, 1969).

—— *Poetry, Language, Thought*, ed. and trans. Albert Hofstadter (New York: Harper and Row, 1971).

—— *On the Way to Language*, trans. Peter D. Hertz (New York: Harper and Row, 1971).

—— *On Time and Being*, trans. Joan Stambaugh (New York: Harper and Row, 1972).

—— *Early Greek Thinking*, trans. David Farrell Krell and Frank A. Capuzzi (New York: Harper and Row, 1984).

—— *Pathmarks*, various translators, ed. William McNeill (Cambridge: Cambridge University Press, 1998).

HILL, LESLIE, 'Blanchot and Mallarmé', *MLN* 105 (1990), 889–913.

—— 'Philippe Sollers and *Tel Quel*', in *Beyond the Nouveau Roman: essays on the contemporary French novel*, ed. Michael Tilby (Oxford: Berg, 1990), 100–23.

—— *Blanchot: Extreme Contemporary* (London and New York: Routledge, 1997).

HOBSON, MARIAN, 'Deconstruction, Empiricism, and the Postal Services', *French Studies* 36 (1982), 290–314.

—— 'History Traces', in *Post-structuralism and the Question of History*, ed. Derek Attridge, Geoffrey Bennington and Robert Young (Cambridge: Cambridge University Press, 1987), 101–15.

—— 'On the Subject of the Subject: Derrida on Sollers in *La Dissémination*', in *Philosophers' Poets*, ed. David Wood (London and New York: Routledge, 1990), 111–39.

HOFSTADTER, ALBERT, 'Enownment', *Boundary 2* 4:2 (1976), 357–77.

HÖLDERLIN, FRIEDRICH, *Kleine Stuttgarter Ausgabe*, vols. v and vi (Stuttgart: W. Kohlhammer, 1965).

HOLLAND, MICHAEL, 'Le hiatus théorique', *Gramma* 3/4, 'Lire Blanchot I' (1976), 53–70.

—— 'Towards a New Literary Idiom. The Fiction and Criticism of Maurice Blanchot from 1941 to 1955' (D.Phil. thesis, Oxford, 1981).

JABÈS, EDMOND, *Le Livre des questions* (Paris: Gallimard, 1963).

—— *Yaël* (Paris: Gallimard, 1967).

—— *Aely* (Paris: Gallimard, 1972).

—— *Dans la double dépendance du dit* (Montpellier: Fata Morgana, 1984).

JAMESON, FREDRIC, 'Marx's Purloined Letter', *Ghostly Demarcations: a symposium on Jacques Derrida's 'Specters of Marx'*, ed. Michael Sprinker (London and New York: Verso, 1999), 26–67.

JOHNSON, BARBARA, *The Critical Difference: Essays in the Contemporary Rhetoric of Reading* (Baltimore and London: Johns Hopkins University Press, 1980).

KAHN, CHARLES H., *The Art and Thought of Heraclitus: An Edition of the Fragments with Translation and Commentary* (Cambridge: Cambridge University Press, 1979).

KOFMAN, SARAH, *L'Enfance de l'art: une interprétation de l'esthétique freudienne* (Paris: Payot, 1970).

LACAN, JACQUES, 'Réponse au commentaire de Jean Hippolyte sur la "Verneinung" de Freud', in *Écrits* (Paris: Seuil, 1966), 381–99.
—— *Écrits I* (Paris: Seuil, coll. 'Points', 1970).
—— *Écrits II* (Paris: Seuil, coll. 'Points', 1971).
—— *Le Séminaire, livre XI: Les quatre concepts fondamentaux de la psychanalyse* (Paris: Seuil, 1973, coll. 'Points' reprint).
LACOUE-LABARTHE, PHILIPPE, *Le Sujet de la philosophie: Typographies I* (Paris: Aubier-Flammarion, 1979).
LAND, NICK, *The Thirst for Annihilation: Georges Bataille and Virulent Nihilism* (London and New York: Routledge, 1992).
LAPLANCHE, JEAN, *Vie et mort en psychanalyse* (Paris: Flammarion, coll. 'Champs', 1970).
—— and PONTALIS, JEAN-BAPTISTE, *Vocabulaire de la psychanalyse* (Paris: Presses Universitaires de France, 1967).
LEMAIRE, ANIKA, *Jacques Lacan*, rev. edn., trans. David Macey (London: Routledge and Kegan Paul), 1977.
LEVINAS, EMMANUEL, *En découvrant l'existence avec Husserl et Heidegger*, 2nd edn. (Paris: Vrin, 1976).
—— *Totalité et infini: essai sur l'extériorité* (The Hague: Martinus Nijhoff, 1971; 'Livre de Poche', coll. 'Biblio: essais' reprint).
—— *Autrement qu'être ou au-delà de l'essence* (The Hague: Martinus Nijhoff, 1974; 'Livre de Poche', coll. 'Biblio: essais' reprint).
—— *Sur Maurice Blanchot* (Montpellier: Fata Morgana, 1975).
—— *Éthique et infini: dialogues avec Philippe Nemo* (Paris: Fayard, 1982; 'Livre de Poche', coll. 'Biblio: essais' reprint).
—— *Le Temps et l'autre* (Paris: Presses Universitaires de France, coll. 'Quadrige', 1983).
—— *De l'existence à l'existant*, 2nd edn. (Paris: Vrin, 1986).
LIBERTSON, JOSEPH, *Proximity: Levinas, Blanchot, Bataille, and Communication* (The Hague: Martinus Nijhoff, 1982).
LLEWELYN, JOHN, *Beyond Metaphysics? The Hermeneutic Circle in Contemporary Continental Philosophy* (Atlantic Highlands, NJ: Humanities Press, 1985).
—— *Derrida on the Threshold of Sense* (London: Macmillan, 1986).
—— 'Responsibility with Indecidability', in *Derrida: A Critical Reader*, ed. David Wood (Oxford: Blackwell, 1992), 72–96.
LYOTARD, JEAN-FRANÇOIS, *Discours, figure* (Paris: Klincksieck, 1971).
—— *Le Différend* (Paris: Minuit, 1983).
MACLACHLAN, IAN, 'Playing dead: Edmond Jabès's *Livre des questions*', *Paragraph* 13:1 (1990), 30–43.
MALLARMÉ, STÉPHANE, *Œuvres complètes*, ed. Henri Mondor and G. Jean-Aubry (Paris: Gallimard, 'Pléiade', 1945).
MANN, ALFRED, *The Study of Fugue* (London: Faber and Faber, 1958).

MARTIN, ROBERT L. (ed.), *The Paradox of the Liar* (New Haven and London: Yale University Press, 1970).

—— (ed.), *Recent Essays on Truth and the Liar Paradox* (Oxford: Oxford University Press, 1984).

MEHLMAN, JEFFREY, 'Orphée scripteur: Blanchot, Rilke, Derrida', *Poétique* 20 (1974), 458–82.

NANCY, JEAN-LUC, 'Les raisons d'écrire', in *Misère de la littérature, Première livraison*, ouvrage collectif (Paris: Christian Bourgois, 1978), 81–96.

—— *La Communauté désœuvrée* (Paris: Christian Bourgois, 1986).

—— *L'Expérience de la liberté* (Paris: Galilée, 1988).

NIETZSCHE, FRIEDRICH, *Basic Writings of Nietzsche*, ed. and trans. Walter Kaufmann (New York: Random House, 1966).

—— *Untimely Meditations*, trans. R. J. Hollingdale (Cambridge: Cambridge Universty Press, 1983).

OLSCHNER, LEONARD, 'Fugal Provocation in Paul Celan's "Todesfuge" and "Engführung"', *German Life and Letters* 43:1 (1989), 79–89.

PONGE, FRANCIS, *'Le Parti pris des choses', précédé de 'Douze petits écrits' et suivi de 'Proêmes'* (Paris: Gallimard, coll. 'Poésie', 1968).

—— *La Fabrique du pré* (Geneva: Skira, 1971).

RAMNOUX, CLÉMENCE, *Héraclite ou l'homme entre les choses et les mots*, 2nd edn. (Paris: 'Les Belles Lettres', 1968).

RAPAPORT, HERMAN, *Heidegger and Derrida: Reflections on Time and Language* (Lincoln, Nebraska and London: University of Nebraska Press, 1989).

RICARDOU, JEAN, *Problèmes du nouveau roman* (Paris: Seuil, 1967).

—— *Nouveaux Problèmes du roman* (Paris: Seuil, 1978).

RICHARDSON, WILLIAM J., *Heidegger: Through Phenomenology to Thought*, 2nd edn. (The Hague: Martinus Nijhoff, 1967).

ROYLE, NICHOLAS, *Telepathy and Literature: Essays on the Reading Mind* (Oxford: Blackwell, 1991).

RUBBRA, EDMUND, *Counterpoint: A Survey* (London: Hutchinson University Library, 1960).

SHERZER, DINA, 'Postmodernism and feminisms', in *Postmodernism and Contemporary Fiction*, ed. Edmund J. Smyth (London: Batsford, 1991), 156–68.

SILVERMAN, HUGH J., 'Derrida, Heidegger, and the Time of the Line', in *Continental Philosophy II: Derrida and Deconstruction*, ed. Hugh J. Silverman (London and New York: Routledge, 1989), 154–68.

SMITH, ROBERT, *Derrida and Autobiography* (Cambridge: Cambridge University Press, 1995).

SOLLERS, PHILIPPE, *Le Parc* (Paris: Seuil, 1961, coll. 'Points' reprint).

—— *Drame* (Paris: Seuil, 1965, coll. 'L'Imaginaire' reprint).

—— *Nombres* (Paris: Seuil, 1968).

—— *Logiques* (Paris: Seuil, 1968).
—— *Lois* (Paris: Seuil, 1972).
—— *H* (Paris: Seuil, 1973).
—— *Femmes* (Paris: Gallimard, 1983, coll. 'Folio' reprint).
STEINER, GEORGE, *Antigones* (Oxford: Clarendon Press, 1984).
STRAVINSKY, IGOR, *Poetics of Music in the Form of Six Lessons*, bilingual edn. (Cambridge, Mass.: Harvard University Press, 1970).
Tel Quel, Théorie d'ensemble (Paris: Seuil, 1968).
VALÉRY, PAUL, *Monsieur Teste* (Paris: Gallimard, 1946, coll. 'L'Imaginaire' reprint).
—— *Cahiers I*, ed. Judith Robinson (Paris: Gallimard, 'Pléiade', 1973).
WILDEN, ANTHONY, *The Language of the Self: Lacan's 'The Function of Language in Psychoanalysis'*, trans. with notes and commentary by Wilden (Baltimore and London: Johns Hopkins University Press, 1968).
WOOD, DAVID, *Philosophy at the Limit* (London: Unwin Hyman, 1990).

INDEX